SOMATIC C

Films can hold personal psychological meanings that are often at odds with their narratives. Examining the intersections between mental health and the cinema, *Somatic Cinema* represents the cutting edge of film theory, evaluating the significance of this phenomenon both in therapy and in the everyday world.

Luke Hockley draws on the insights of phenomenological and Jungian film theory and applies them alongside more established psychoanalytic approaches. The result is to combine the idea of affective bodily experience with unconscious processes as a means to explore a new ontology of the cinema. The emphasis is therefore shifted from pure intellectual insight to greater inclusion of personally constructed meanings and experiences. Several key concepts are developed and explored throughout the book. These include:

- the idea of the 'third image', occupying the intersubjective space between viewer and screen, and therapist and client;
- the concept of the cinematic frame (as opposed to the film frame), the container of the psychological relationship between viewer and screen;
- the use of the cinematic experience to encapsulate the somatic expression of unconscious effects that develop while a film is viewed and which are central to the creation of personal psychological meanings.

With a focus on examining why we develop a personal relationship with films, *Somatic Cinema* is ideal for academics and students of film studies, media studies and analytical psychology.

Luke Hockley is Professor of Media Analysis at the Research Institute for Media, Art and Design (RIMAD) at the University of Bedfordshire. He also works as an integrative psychotherapist in private practice in London and Bedfordshire. He co-edited *Jung and Film II: The Return* and *House: The Wounded Healer on Television.*

SOMATIC CINEMA

The relationship between body and screen – a Jungian perspective

Luke Hockley

Routledge
Taylor & Francis Group
LONDON AND NEW YORK

First published 2014
by Routledge
2 Park Square, Milton Park, Abingdon, Oxon OX14 4RN

and by Routledge
711 Third Avenue, New York, NY 10017

Routledge is an imprint of the Taylor & Francis Group, an informa business

British Library Cataloguing in Publication Data
A catalogue record for this book is available from the British Library

Library of Congress Cataloging in Publication Data
Hockley, Luke.
Somatic cinema : the relationship between body and screen : a Jungian perspective / Luke Hockley.
pages cm.
Includes bibliographical references.
1. Motion pictures–Psychological aspects. 2. Motion picture audiences–Psychological aspects. 3. Psychoanalysis and motion pictures. 4. Jungian psychology. I. Title.
PN1995.H5865 2013
791.4301'9–dc23 2013018316

ISBN: 978-0-415-66922-1 (hbk)
ISBN: 978-0-415-66923-8 (pbk)
ISBN: 978-1-315-88014-3 (ebk)

Typeset in Times
by Wearset Ltd, Boldon, Tyne and Wear

MIX
Paper from responsible sources
FSC® C013056

Printed and bound in Great Britain by
TJ International Ltd, Padstow, Cornwall

TO ALL WHO LOVE THE MOVIES, AND THE NARRATIVE OF SELF-DISCOVERY

CONTENTS

ACKNOWLEDGEMENTS

The preparation of this book relied on too many people to mention. That said, a special thanks should go to everyone who with generosity of spirit kindly gave their permission for their stories to appear in this book. In particular, I thank the students of the C. G. Jung Institute in Zurich, and also those at the International School of Analytical Psychology (ISAP), also in Zurich. Likewise, the students on the MSc in the Psychodynamics of Human Development at Birkbeck College, University of London, have provided a great testing ground for many of the ideas contained in the following pages.

A particular and very special heartfelt thank you goes to my wife Mary who painstakingly read each chapter, and whose insights and comments helped to refine and clarify my thoughts. The book needed her care and attention and I am forever grateful to her.

Numerous individuals have helped with specific chapters. But particular thanks are due to Greg Singh and Nadi Fadina who have added to the life and soul of this work in ways that could not have been anticipated, but which were much needed and very welcome.

There are many at Routledge who should be thanked, and I apologize for not naming all of you personally. But a special mention is due to Kate Hawes for believing in this book and for taking the plunge in publishing it. I am also most grateful for the care to attention and detail that Rosamund Howe, as the copy-editor of *Somatic Cinema* has brought to the book. Thanks also go to Hilary Faulkner who, as an indexer, is one of the unsung heroes of scholarship.

Finally, I owe a debt of gratitude to the Research Institute for Media, Art and Design (RIMAD) and the University of Bedfordshire. Both have been generous and gracious in their support of this research.

INTRODUCTION

Somatic Cinema sets out to explore the relationship between audience and films. More specifically, it examines how the body of the viewer and the cinema screen itself are interrelated sites of meaning. In doing so, it challenges the ubiquity of the Lacanian-inflected psychoanalytic model of film theory, along with its suggestions of decentred subjects, fragmented bodies and an inherently fragile concept of self. In its place, *Somatic Cinema* uses the language and approach of clients in psychotherapy who talk about films. It will combine these clinical examples with insights derived from Jungian psychotherapy. Specifically, the therapist–client dyad will be used as a paradigmatic relationship and metaphor through which to get a deeper understanding of the relationship that viewers have with the cinema. This will be used to show how meaning both in therapy and in the cinema is not just an intellectual undertaking but is also felt and embodied. In other words, we will come to see how the psychological meaning of films involves a somatic experience.

Using the clinical metaphor takes us into the thorny area of inscribed and negotiated meanings, personal and collective hermeneutics and just how, and where, meaning resides in the cinematic experience. The attempt to locate and reconceptualize the location of cinematic meaning is a development of the 'third image', which my research has been addressing. The third image is akin to the intersubjective space in therapy between client and therapist. It refers to the unlooked-for, unaddressed, unseen, unbeckoned and unexpected personal responses that clients, and viewers, can have to films. Sometimes in these experiences of the third image the narrative meaning of a film is lost, or at least heavily inflected, and in its place individuals come to find a personal meaning. It appears that something new comes into being that is not on the screen or in the mind of the viewer but in the psyche-laden space that exists between the two. That is the space that I refer to as the third image. The perspective offered by the third image also suggests a somewhat different ontology of the cinematic to the one proposed in the Lacanian model; it has the additional effect of causing us to reconsider if this fresh understanding of how films communicate emotion might also alter our sense of being-in-the-world.

Of course the shift from the individual in therapy to the personal interpretation of films is quite a jump, and the problems of transposing a theoretical paradigm from the object of its study to another are well known. Perhaps the most notorious, and thankfully now historical, example was the use of Darwinian theories of evolution to form sociological judgements and political policy in an approach that is referred to as Social Darwinism. This theory was invoked by fascism, used to support eugenics and variously co-opted to apparently legitimize a variety of other repugnant ideologies. This serves to remind us that we need caution and care when theories intended for one purpose are used for another. Yet with that caveat firmly in mind, it is nonetheless interesting to reflect on the distinctive way that clients in therapy talk about films, and to see if this might tell us something new and fresh about how films convey and make meanings that are psychological and emotional.

In focusing on the individual interpretation and experience of films, I realize that I lay myself open to charges of empiricism. While I can understand that line of argument, any such charges would be somewhat misplaced. *Somatic Cinema* argues for an interpretative space that allows for, and finds value in, the personal meanings we have when watching films and our subsequent reflection of those experiences. That does not suggest that others must subscribe to any subjective view of a given film. In fact, I will argue that each of us has a unique relationship with a film that cannot be replicated by anyone else – it is ours, and ours alone. Cultural theory, including film theory, has found little room for such an individual perspective. The grand theories of structuralism, semiotics and post-modernism which dominated European cultural criticism in the latter half of the twentieth century and into the third millennium have played a valuable role in providing a means through which to articulate the ways in which cultural artefacts are culturally encoded. However, the dominance of these approaches has left little room for the subjective and the personal. Somewhere under the weight of these theories the individual has been crushed and the arguments they develop resist most attempts at personal meanings. Even the action of 'reading against the grain' of the film's narrative did not give voice to the individual and instead created a new collective space, albeit one that existed in opposition to the dominant ideology. Personally and culturally we were cut adrift in a sea of semiotic chains of meaning that could never be coherently connected, and the infinite regressions of the signifying practices which post-modernism elucidated meant the image remained unknowable. It is only relatively recently that these questions of the personal and the subjective have undergone a revaluation in mainstream film studies, in particular with the resurgence of the notion of cinephilia (cf. Singh, 2011). This is particularly apt given the state of technological innovation through which home cinema and fan practices have been given a new lease of life. The historical antecedents of this are obvious, but it is perhaps no small accident that these ideas have undergone a renaissance in the age of digital cinema.

Historically, psychoanalytic film theory too was influenced by these grand cultural theories and for those reasons it emphasized the structural aspects of Freudian and post-Freudian thinking and not its more clinical elements. In particular the work of Jacques Lacan was, and indeed is, of importance. His theories gave media theorists a pre-made way of tying together structural concerns with the formal semiotics of language in a psychoanalytic model that was predicated on the psychological life of the individual. It seemed that this would finally allow for a theory that would adequately account for the subjectivity of the self, which was something that previous and more abstract and ideologically inflected theories had failed to do. However, again the theoretical position that emerged became somewhat totalizing and once more there was little space within the Lacanian variant of psychoanalytic film theory for individuals to articulate a position for themselves. This is because the way film theory (particularly in the UK) interpreted Lacan, language itself was seen as prescribing the role of the individual – it is only in and through language that the individual can articulate him or herself. But the catch is that language does not allow for such articulation and therefore the only outcome is a state of fragmentation and struggle that is propelled by the doomed and illusory quest for wholeness and meaning.

In *Somatic Cinema* I head in the opposite direction. While not arguing that films are coherent texts with unified and fixed meanings, I do propose that it is through the individual relationships we have with films that they become personally meaningful to us. Central to this are two key aspects. First is the experience of ourselves in relationship with film. The second is that this relationship is encapsulated by what Jung refers to as the psychological 'image'. It is not so much that such images exist outside the semantic realm: it is more that the image makes its meaning known through the presence of affect. The conscious articulation of the image is the point at which the experiences of the psychological image can be transformed into language. As we will see in a moment, and at repeated points through this book, such psychological images need not be visual, and can be felt, intuited or more generally somatized.

Which films and where?

Somatic Cinema is an attempt to explore the lived reality of the cinematic experience. And to do so it takes what to some might seem a curious and certainly unusual approach. As someone who is both psychotherapist and a professor of Media Analysis, I have been struck by the ways that my clients talk about films in therapy and how very different this is to the way that psychoanalytic film theory understands films and how my students at the university write about films. Of course, academic discourse is not the same as therapeutic discourse. However, there are points of overlap, intersection, difference and dissonance, and it is these that I seek to address.

Throughout, the book will move between film theory and Jungian theory, and we will find ourselves in and out of both the cinema and the consulting room. Underpinning this movement is a consideration of the ways in which clients' real engagement, dialogue and lived experience with film arrive in the therapy room ready to contribute to their individual processes and the ways in which these living dynamics can in turn contribute to our understanding of the psychological power of the cinema. In the process, we explore how inscribed meanings in films and our personal responses to films can move us in unexpected ways.

Most of the examples that I give are concerned with mainstream Hollywood narrative film, though several of the films that I write about come from outside that tradition. This does give the book a partial quality. There is no mention of documentary film. While international cinemas do make an appearance, the references are confined to Europe and Eastern Europe. Fine art filmmaking is mentioned only via those writers who are interested in phenomenology and artistic practice. On the one hand, this might seem a rather strange state of affairs. After all, it is films by directors such as Ingmar Bergman, Federico Fellini, Yasujiro Ozu and numerous others which set out explicitly to explore psychological themes, and they often do so with an aesthetic sensibility that produces compelling films. But the reality is that in therapy clients do not normally talk about such films; instead they want to understand the feelings they were having when watching the latest movies at the multiplex or on television. This is not a matter of class or education, as clients from all walks of life routinely talk about 'Hollywood' films but rarely, if ever, do transnational cinemas or 'art' cinema make an appearance. At different points in this book I will explore why this might be the case. For the moment I want to notice that there does not seem to be much of a connection between the intellectual and aesthetic quality of a film and its psychological impact. This is an observation that I will return to because one of the ideas which underpins this book is that the important psychological aspects of the cinematic that I will be discussing are not on the screen, or at least not exclusively so.

Throughout the book I refer to the cinematic experience. It is interesting that in an age when home cinema is not unusual the cinema has continued to thrive and is indeed enjoying something of a renaissance. When I refer to the cinematic experience I generally have in mind seeing a film in a cinema auditorium, as this tends to provide the optimal conditions in which to 'experience' a film. However, large-screen televisions and high-quality sound go some way to replicating those conditions at home. That said, I will explore in some detail (mainly in Chapter 2) the other important differences between the cinema and the home environment. For example, at home typically we have control over when we watch a film, we can start and stop it at will, there's no entry charge, and then there are the range of distractions that fill everyday life, including the limiting factor of broadband speeds and buffering when watching on line. Cinema does not allow us that degree of control or flexibility. Finally, and importantly, a television screen does not fill the field of vision in the same way the cinema screen does, and the image in the cinema is of a much higher resolution and quality than even a very good domestic television. All these factors mean that the cinematic experience at home is somewhat different to the cinema, and consequently the way it functions psychologically is different too. I do not think this difference is a radical one and instead it is more as though the psychological experience of watching a film in the cinema, on television, or via a mobile device (such as a computer or mobile phone) exists on a continuum.

However we see a film, the film itself will have been made with a view to being watched; accordingly, the visual structure of any film positions its viewers in particular ways. Sometimes using point-of-view shots places viewers inside the film, at other times they are positioned outside the narrative as observers. The assumption of viewers and their positioning has been something of a focus for text-based criticism, where it is assumed that the implied existence of the viewer is significant in coming to a view about the meaning of a film. However, there is another possibility which is that some viewers sometimes develop meanings that are not implied or directly suggested by the audio-visual structure of the film. Partly for that reason I normally use the term 'viewer' in *Somatic Cinema*, as it corresponds more closely to the phenomenology of the cinematic experience; a key point of this book is that while there is certainly spectacle in the cinema viewers do not just 'spectate', they participate. So sometimes I use the term 'spectator', particularly when considering psychoanalytic themes as here the term invokes the particular legacy of that theoretical discourse, and also of the scopic regime. When I am writing about the personal psychological relationship we have with cinema I tend to write about viewers.

The downside to that term is that it continues the tradition in film studies of privileging the visual and scopic over the other aspects of the cinematic. That said, the focus of this book is explicitly on the way that meaning is made in the cinematic experience, and not just as a consequence of the visual and aural realms of cinema. I concentrate on the psyche in order to get eventually into the ontology of the cinematic viewing. I hope the main argument will serve to counterbalance the bias of the terminology. Here the way in which Jung understands the concept of 'image' is particularly helpful. For Jung, a psychological image is not necessarily visual. Instead he uses the term to encapsulate a field of understanding which contains the psychological meaning of a given moment. This involves the interplay of the unconscious with consciousness through the mediating presence of the body and it creates an embodied awareness that feels, thinks, and intuits the psychological meaning. It is this experience of meaning that takes us into a psychological zone of being, an idea which Geoff Dyer echoes in the following quotation:

> The best directors all invert Coriolanus's claim that there is a world elsewhere. No, the world beyond the screen is just a continuation of the world we are seeing. To either side and behind there is more of the same. We are not even in a cinema; we are in a world. Or, rather, there is nothing but cinema; there is only the Zone.
>
> (Dyer, 2012: 196)

Current debates

Recently several books have sought to bring the body back into film theory (Elsaesser and Hagener, 2010; Sobchack, 1992; Barker, 2009). This development is welcome as it recognizes the phenomenological reality that when viewing films we regularly respond with feeling, in the body – as if it could be located anywhere else. The location of meaning is also the subject of Introna and Ilharco's (2006) 'On the Meaning of Screens: Towards a Phenomenological Account of Screenness'. That the meaning of films is at least partly felt is a somewhat obvious point but significantly it is one that historically film theory has tended to overlook.

However, what none of these authors account for, at least in any depth, is the presence of the unconscious. Not, more specifically, do they give a Jungian understanding of the unconscious. Of course psychoanalytic film theory has sought to bring the body into film theory, but here the body is not something that can be relied upon as stable and predictable as it is imbued with an unconscious that is full of drives and instincts. Such theories emphasize the fragmentary nature of the body, both on screen and in terms of the 'subject' as the viewer. The tendency to assume the 'subject' is fractured is part of the legacy that has been left by Lacanian film theory and its subject is decentred, fragile in construction and lacking in identity and agency. As such, it 'mirrors' the fleeting, fragmentary surface of film itself. Film and subject are yoked together, albeit in a somewhat unstable, if inevitable, manner. Typically, this is seen in somewhat structural and formal terms.

Academic film theorists have found this complex state of affairs appealing and it is easy to see why. The idea that the construction of films might, in some way, turn out to replicate the construction of the unconscious clearly has an academic appeal. It is elegant, complicated and cannot be proved, and that makes it ideal intellectual territory. The problem is that despite the allure, this theory does not seem to capture (or embody) the reality of what it is like, phenomenologically, to engage in the act of viewing a film and experience the immersive qualities that are part of the cinematic experience. We simply do not see or typically experience ourselves as being decentred, disempowered or deconstructed by films. Of course, this illusion of wholeness might be because the film has seduced us and, in so doing, rendered our sense of self mute – a line of attack which Marxist-inflected psychoanalysis exploits.

Jungian theory provides an alternative and no less satisfying way through which to reconceptualize these and related issues. With its focus on the image and the inner life of the psyche, it opens up new avenues through which to explore the interiority of meaning in the cinema. The fundamental insight of Jungian psychology is that the individual is both personal and collective – just like the cinema where meaning is partly inscribed in the film and partly negotiated on an individual basis. Jungian theory too is concerned with transference and countertransference and, while clinical in origin, these ideas can, nonetheless, be usefully co-opted to help in gaining an understanding of the viewer–screen relationship. The somatic location of meaning in clinical work between client and therapist is also a heavily theorized subject. Again, this body of knowledge can usefully be deployed to help explore another relationship, namely the one that exists between the viewer and the cinema screen.

In summary, *Somatic Cinema* makes a case for the shift from considering 'viewer, screen' and instead asserts the primacy of the 'viewer–screen' paradigmatic relationship as the key way through which to better understand the cinematic experience.[1] This raises the question of where meaning resides in the cinematic experience. My answer is the third image, which is a theoretical concept based on clinical insights and which looks at meaning making in the intersubjective space between viewer and screen. It offers a new ontology of viewing-in-the-cinema and how this might relate to being-in-the-world.

Overview of the contents

The first chapter, 'The consciously constructed film', explores the way that filmmakers, scriptwriters and producers sometimes deliberately set out to make psychological films. The general argument of this chapter is that this type of conscious intention interferes with how the unconscious works. Consequently, films that set out to be psychological may end up being emotionally flat and lifeless. Of course even when approached with the intention of producing a psychological film, making films is a creative process and one in which unconscious mechanisms are at work. Nonetheless, it is the seemingly non-psychological film that can turn out to have the most psychological value (a point that was originally made by Jung about novels). This insight puts unconscious processes in both production and interpretation at the centre of this book's inquiry.

Chapter 2, 'Being in the cinema', examines what it is like to experience a film, not just to watch it, the difference being that experience suggests that awareness is brought to the whole process, as the act of being in the cinema is perceived via the totality of the senses. The suggestion is that culturally constructed and commercial images, as in films, can have a personal psychological quality. This becomes clear when we realize that the boundary between inner psychological imagery and images in the outer world is somewhat permeable. (Questions about the dream-like qualities of some films and the psychological mechanism of projection will be explored in Chapters 6 and 7.) The chapter will also explore the idea that film exists as a type of transitional object and that cinema can be understood as a transitional phenomenon.

Chapter 3, 'Reflections of the body', looks at the ways in which film theory has historically addressed the question of bodies on screen and the viewer's relationship with them in terms of Lacanian psychoanalytic theory. One of the advantages of a Lacanian approach is that it incorporates the body within its theoretical structure. However, the drawback is that the 'Lacanian body' is imaginal, reflected, and is seen as an expression of the decentred and fragmented nature of the psyche. In this view of the cinematic, viewers lack agency as they struggle to hold the fragmented self, as objectified on the screen, into a coherent whole. Within these constraints coherence is unattainable. Drawing on a Jungian understanding of transference and countertransference, this chapter suggests a different model in which screen and viewer are seen in relationship, just as client and therapist are in relationship. From this alternative perspective, meaning is regarded as partly conscious and cognitive, and also partly unconscious and embodied.

Chapter 4, 'Being mindful of the image', introduces the idea of mindfulness as a practice of bringing one's attention to bear on the present moment, so that a heightened sense of awareness is achieved. Mindfulness is now part of the therapeutic repertoire of cognitive behavioural therapy (MBCT) and is used by some integrative psychotherapists and also in existential psychotherapy. Philosophically, its roots lie in meditative practice and also in phenomenology. The act of bringing awareness in a focused way into the present moment is not unlike the process of viewing a film where a complex but singular source of light and sound demands the full attention of viewers. Perhaps the very act of viewing a film and of establishing a felt relationship with the screen in which viewers bring their bodily awareness to the process can be psychologically beneficial.

Chapter 5 'Seeing the image', examines what appears to be a rather obvious point about the to-be-looked-at-ness of cinema. It suggests that this very ubiquity disguises some important points. First is that while a two-dimensional image, films are full of depth cues, inviting the viewer to look into the screen, and not 'at' it. The action of watching is that of seeing a narrative unfold on a two-dimensional screen, but the act of gazing (of viewing) draws the viewer into the depths of the image and into its interior landscape (cf. McGuinn, 2005). Thus, the look bridges the gap between viewer and screen, and through its diegetic construction the film encourages this elision. It is my contention that what also happens in bridging the gap between screen and viewer is that the inner psychological images of viewers are brought to the surface. This goes some way to explaining the rather dream-like nature of some films. The cinema is the medium of projection par excellence, and this can be seen when clients talk about films in therapy, where the strong emotional responses they have to films are often clear. Interestingly, such reactions generally have little to do with the narrative meaning of the film. Instead clients invest films with personal meanings, and can prefer these to the inscribed collective meanings intended by filmmakers. Examples of this from work with clients include *Mamma Mia!* (2008) and *Happy-Go-Lucky* (2008).

In Chapter 6, 'Being touched by the image', we explore how the film theorist Vivian Sobchack (1992) has noted the ocular-centric focus of much film theory. Experiencing films or, as we might also put it, being in relationship with a film, is a full-body experience. At one level the audience can have a tactile response to films and, as Sobchack makes clear, the senses do not work in isolation. Further, the filmic diegesis makes it possible for the look to pave the way for other sensory and meaning-making responses in the body's relationship with the screen. Sobchack uses the work of Merleau-Ponty to explore the interconnection of the senses and the way that cinematic experiences and life experiences can reinforce each other. However, no account is taken of the unconscious in her debate, and consequently a key means through which to understand the phenomenology of the cinematic experience is missed. The chapter takes the undoubted strengths of her phenomenological approach and combines them with the idea that the unconscious maintains a psychological agency in creating and finding meaning in the cinema. Again, taking examples from the consulting room, it becomes possible to see how the unconscious can inflect and even structure a viewer's relationship with the screen and the meanings that are derived from it.

Chapter 7, 'Feeling the image', is the culmination of this psychological enquiry into the cinema. It focuses on the therapeutic dyad and how meaning is constructed between client and therapist. There are several key notions here. One is the existence of an intersubjective field which is constellated between the two parties and in which meaning is created at an unconscious and bodily level. As a paradigm for the viewer–screen relationship, this suggests that, far from meaning residing on the screen or in the mind of the viewer, it in fact exists in a space somewhere between the two – this I call the 'third image' and it is characterized by an apperceptive response to films in which collective inscribed meanings are overwhelmed by unexpected, unanticipated personal and emotional responses.

The suggestion is that to greater and lesser extents this third image is always present. At times it is palpable, and it is on these occasions that a personal relationship with a film is formed which can be quite at odds with the film's narrative. This is one explanation of why a film can enthrall one person and bore another, as psychologically and phenomenologically these two people have not seen the same film. It is also why someone can become obsessed with a film, quite literally in love with it, while everyone else is mystified about its appeal. These are examples of the apperceptive response to films in which personal meanings are created which can be at odds with a consensual view of what the film is about. I call this 'losing the plot'. Of course, in losing the plot we gain insight into ourselves.

Conclusion

Hugo Munsterberg's account of the cinematic experience *The Film: A Psychological Study* (1916) is an early work of film theory that is often overlooked by film scholars and has not received much attention from clinicians writing about the cinema either. Yet this short book lays out the foundations for much of our speculations here. For example, Munsterberg notes, 'The characteristic features of many an attitude and feeling which cannot be expressed without words today will then be aroused in the mind of the spectator through the subtle art of cinema' (Munsterberg, 1916: 56). *Somatic Cinema* is an investigation into the subtle art of cinema, the subtleties of the psyche and the subtle nature of the body that experiences the two. Throughout his book Munsterberg explores the ways in which film, or as he terms it 'the photoplay', manages to combine in its expression the inner world of the mind and the physical world we live in. For him, the photoplay is based on fundamental emotions which are 'common to all and which are understood by everybody' (ibid., 94). The compression of time into cinematic time 'heightens the feeling of vitality in the spectator. He feels as if he were passing though life with a sharper accent which stirs his personal energies' (ibid., 94). These ideas will inform our exploration of the way in which clients talk about films in psychotherapy and also the ontology of the viewing experience in the cinema. In particular the following observation seems prescient:

> The photoplay shows us a significant conflict of human actions in moving pictures which, freed from the physical form of space, time and causality, are adjusted to the free play of our mental experiences and which reach complete isolation from the practical world through the perfect unity of plot and pictorial appearance.
>
> (ibid., 82)

Being-in-the-cinema does not offer an escape from the real world. Rather, it provides a means by which to descend into one's own inner world. The cinema provides a gateway through which to enter into the interiority of our being, to bypass the defences of consciousness and to gain valuable insights into the core of our psychological being.

1

THE CONSCIOUSLY CONSTRUCTED FILM

This chapter explores the way that some filmmakers, scriptwriters and producers deliberately set out to make psychological films, such as *Titanic* (Dir. Cameron, 1997), *The Fountain* (Dir. Aronofsky, 2007) and *Star Wars: Episode IV – A New Hope* (Dir. Lucas, 1977). It examines how this type of 'knowing' conscious intent can interfere with the way in which the unconscious works. The contention is that films that aim to be psychological often end up being flat and lifeless, and, contrary to expectations, turn out to be the least psychological films of all. Of course even when filmmakers set out or want to make psychologically affective films, their production processes are creative ones in which unconscious mechanisms remain at work. Nonetheless, it is seemingly the non-psychological film that turns out to have the most psychological value. Subsequent chapters will show how films such as *Mamma Mia!* (Dir. Lloyd, 2008) and *Happy-Go-Lucky* (Dir. Leigh, 2008) came to be important for clients in long-term psychotherapy. The importance of unconscious processes as they influence both production and interpretation is at the centre of this book. Of course, commercial film production companies generally set out to make films that will be financially successful, and not films that are psychologically beneficial. Yet, as illustrated by the previous examples, what appears to happen is that we invest seemingly non-psychological films with personal psychological meanings. Normally these meanings are quite at odds with the narrative meaning of the film itself and, rather than coming just from the film, they are instead a result of the intermingling of personal unconscious concerns with the narratives of films from commercial mainstream cinema. Curiously, films which set out to evoke psychological responses and which are knowingly structured around psychological themes can fail in the very mission they set out to achieve.

Why some deliberately psychological films don't work

It is not an uncommon experience to have high hopes for a film before we watch it. Typically we might have seen other films by the same director, or it might be that we are interested in the actors, or perhaps we have read good reviews of the film. Yet after watching the film we are left feeling empty, disillusioned and unfulfilled. We wonder how it is possible for films like this to get made and what those so-called experts who review films could have been thinking of. We tell ourselves that clearly we have seen a different film ... Those 'objective' measures of a film's appeal are poor predictors of how we will react to it psychologically. The reason for this is that such external indicators of quality cannot take into account our subjectivity nor can they anticipate the role our personal unconscious concerns will play in making meaning. However poor they are, these external influences remain a core part of film's narrative image, as indicated by film theorists such as John Ellis (1982) and Stephen Heath (1981). The relationship in contemporary cinema between viewer and viewed is of increasing importance, not just in fan cultures where it is the subject of considerable theoretical attention (Jenkins, 1992) but also in film blogs, where sites like Rotten Tomatoes (www.rottentomatoes.com) are leading a more intense discussion of films than those provided by any television or radio film review programme. Such 'auxiliary texts' feed back in an iterative manner into the meanings that are created in the interactions between viewers, texts and institutions and in so doing they form part of the cycle of viewer expectations.

This difference between expectation and experience is termed 'cognitive dissonance'. The dissonance arises as a result of the difference between expectation and reality: we were promised a wonderful time at the cinema but the reality was dismal. No matter what the situation, the wider the gap between our expectation and our actual experience, the larger our disappointment, and this also holds true for films. The concept of cognitive dissonance is certainly helpful in understanding what might have happened in the above example. However, perhaps other factors are at work too. This book explores how it is that viewers can have such divergent and even opposing emotional reactions to the same film. In so doing, it will suggest that this seemingly simple problem will actually help to develop a new paradigm through which to understand the relationship that viewers have with the cinema screen.

This chapter focuses on the 'psychologically informed' film. The type of film I have in mind here is one that knowingly attempts to deal with psychological themes. These are films where the filmmakers set out to embed psychological devices into the narrative and the visual structures of films. In doing so filmmakers move images, thoughts, ideas and processes that are the mechanisms and material of the unconscious into consciousness. Why is this a problem? After all, much of the work of therapy is about making people more aware, or more conscious, of what is happening in their lives. Without doubt, consciousness and rational thought have a clear and central role to play in psychological insight. Why then am I focusing on a similar process in the cinema and what is it that is so problematic about filmmakers setting out to engage the unconscious? Sometimes it is not problematic at all. In his later films Alfred Hitchcock knowingly used the manipulation and subversion of audience expectation through exploring the psyche as both a narrative theme and a meta-form of cinematic storytelling. Why then does the same not apply to other filmmakers who attempt something similar? To answer these questions it is necessary to use some Jungian concepts and these will, while not exactly answering the question, at least point us in the right direction. However, in showing why these Jungian ideas are useful I am going to make an argument that at first might appear contradictory.

Jungian psychology regards the conscious part of ourselves as shifting and, as it does so, increasing in awareness. While Jung stresses that the way we understand our relation to the world is largely conscious, at the same time he argues that there are parts of the psyche which are unconscious and which he insists we need to pay attention to. One of the clearest ways these unconscious elements manifest themselves is in dreams. Unconscious elements also appear in irrational acts, unpredictable emotions and creative outpourings and, I would add, in the cinema. It is my contention that in this latter setting an awareness of these unconscious processes will help us both to reframe what is on the screen and also to understand why viewers react emotionally and psychologically as they view films. Jung observes that it is a struggle for consciousness to understand the unconscious. Yet the struggle is essential, as consciousness needs to become increasingly aware of the part of the person which remains a mystery, unknown and hidden. Put another way, Jung suggests that it is a life-long challenge for us, for the ego, to hold the unconscious and conscious parts of ourselves together and to accept that the unconscious can never be fully understood. Here is the tension: consciousness is essential, but it is not enough, as part of ourselves always remains unconscious.

Jung was not alone in making this observation. Indeed, the idea that there are aspects to our unconscious lives that we will never know in full is also central to much of Freud's writing. Yet one of the elements that distinguishes Jung's analytical psychology from Freud's psychoanalysis is the extent to which it considers it desirable to become aware of the contents of the unconscious. From both the Jungian and Freudian perspectives, the unconscious needs to be made conscious, as this is the main means by which psychological complexes can be detected and eventually dissolved. However, for Freud the majority of the unconscious needs to be constrained or, as he puts it, repressed. This is because it contains sexual material that is related to the impossibility of the Oedipal situation. By contrast, Jung tends to put his focus on releasing the unconscious, as for him the unconscious has a role that is both teleological and homeostatic. Here then are the two differing orientations – Freud who emphasizes the significance of childhood sexuality and the need for repression and Jung who regards the unconscious as something which gradually unfolds into consciousness over the course of life. This is rather to caricature and over-simplify the differences. But the general point holds: namely that the unconscious has a somewhat different role in Freudian and Jungian theory and this directly influences how consciousness relates to and understands the unconscious.

Given the positive role that Jung ascribes to consciousness in human development, where then is the problem with filmmakers taking unconscious material and rendering it on the cinema screen? Jung was certain that when we have to deal with the psychological difficulties of life, consciousness alone was never enough. He also thought that consciousness had a tendency to interfere with the work of the unconscious. This is seen every day in the consulting room of psychotherapists when they hear their clients struggling to change their old patterns of behaviour and at the same time see them desperately resisting change. Indeed, it would not be unreasonable to suggest that this is one of the core dynamics of therapy. However, Jung went further. He claimed that ideally we should simply let the unconscious do its work; that what we need is to let the archetypal structures of the unconscious, and their propensity to form images, simply happen. When this occurs the images that appear relate directly and purposefully to an individual's life situation. As Jung (1952: para. 608) puts it, 'The unconscious mind of man sees correctly even when conscious reason is blind and impotent.' In the following quotation Jung develops this idea.[1] In doing so he stresses the primacy of the unconscious and the need to hold together in a productive and creative tension the conscious and unconscious parts of ourselves:

> The unconscious is an autonomous psychic entity; any efforts to drill it are only apparently successful, and moreover are harmful to consciousness. It is and remains beyond the reach of subjective arbitrary control, a realm where nature and her secrets can be neither improved upon nor perverted, where we can listen but may not meddle.
>
> (Jung, 1953/68: para. 51)

This idea was developed by James Hillman (1979) and is at the centre of his theories about how to work with dreams. In his writings on praxis, he explores the significance of holding images in our imagination and in so doing letting the dream do its work, without the intervention of consciousness. One of the implications of this is that if images are to work psychologically then it is important that we do not force them into the rational and intellectually active parts of ourselves. This is one of the many problems with interpretation, as evidenced in some Jungian film scholarship but also in more general film analysis. Instead, we need to engage with films at the level of affect, and in so doing to allow their images to resonate with the themes of our lives. Of course the conscious part of the psyche is often resistant to this idea. Observing that we have an unconscious aspect to ourselves is not without its frightening qualities and there is the very understandable concern that if we let go of consciousness we will lose our way in the world. We fantasize that we might even find the unconscious overwhelming.

The tension between the desire to know the unconscious aspects of ourselves and the fear of knowing those same aspects means that if we are going to understand the psychological meaning of an image, be it in a dream or in a film, the intellect is going to be important. From its earliest days, film theory has been struck by the likeness or analogy between film and dream (cf. Bordwell, 1997). In the 1970s Christian Metz developed the idea that in some way films mirrored intrapsychic processes and the cinema screen could be considered a type of 'dream screen'. These ideas have been developed by numerous theorists (Heath, 1981; Lebeau, 1995; and many others). It is also striking that Steven Spielberg, Jeffrey Katzenburg and Dave Geffin called their film studio Dreamworks. But the intellect alone will not be enough. What I am suggesting here is the development of an approach to understanding the psychological qualities of the cinematic experience which is not just intellectual but is also somatic. Such an approach incorporates our full being, conscious and unconscious, mind and body, as a means by which to understand how our emotional reactions to films become encoded in us and in our psychological responses.

This is not to suggest that the intellect is without a role in understanding films. Far from it, as it must surely be the case that without the assistance and insights offered by the intellect any film would be incomprehensible. The intellect is needed for an understanding of film literacy and of the basic conventions and tropes of film style and constructed meaning. Nor do I want to devalue the work of academic film criticism, on which we are going to draw heavily. Rather, the general point is that if we are to understand the psychological reactions that we have to films we need to use more than just our intellect. The second and specific point is that one way to do this is to explore what happens when film-makers consciously attempt to embed in films unconscious mythological material in an attempt to engage with and manipulate the unconscious of the viewers. Analysing such films provides a useful way of highlighting the limitations of a purely rational, conscious and intellectual approach to understanding how films work psychologically.

Of course all films engage in emotion manipulation. But I want to suggest that there is a significant difference between wanting the viewers of a film to feel something at a certain point and embedding archetypal material in the hope that it will speak to some universal and mythic part of the psyche. To expand on this theme a little more I am going to offer three examples. The first comes from an unlikely source and is the Walt Disney film *Dumbo* (Dir. Armstrong *et al.* 1941). Perhaps *Dumbo* is not the first film that springs to mind when we think about psychologically meaningful films. But there are aspects of the film that continue to move viewers today and do so by deploying well-established filmic devices. The scene I want to consider is where some rowdy children poke fun at the size of the baby elephant Dumbo's ears. His mother (Mrs Jumbo) unleashes her temper as she rears on her back legs and trumpets loudly, her eyes turning red with rage. Later in the film she is imprisoned in a circus carriage that carries the sign 'Mad Elephant'. The baby Dumbo is taken to see his mother by his friend Timothy Mouse, the music swells as the trunk of Mrs Dumbo makes its way through the bars of her cage, gradually finding her son, and a tear of recognition roles down her cheek. There's not a dry eye in the house. This is sentimental schmaltz at its peak, which is surely what the animators had hoped for. There is also something powerful in seeing a mother reunited with her son after she has been incarcerated; her only crime was having tried to protect her child. It remains moving even though we know that we are only watching cartoon elephants. Something in the mother–child bond remains touching. Remember, this is a film made primarily for children but when we watch it as adults we can sense that here is a portrayal of the psychological attachment between parent and child and we recognize the power of the mother–child bond.

In a moment we will compare the psychological qualities of *Dumbo* to the more knowing approach of *The Fountain* (Dir. Aronofsky, 2006) and *Titanic* (Dir. Cameron, 1997), both of which in their different ways attempt to deploy unconscious archetypal material. What I am suggesting is that a film like *Dumbo* succeeds in maintaining its affective charge because it deals with emotions that are relatively close to consciousness. Films such as *Titanic* and *The Fountain* are much less successful in this regard because they try to render in the light of consciousness what is essentially an unconscious process. That said, it will also become evident that the process is actually more complicated than this suggests. But for the moment I want to foreground the distinction between those films that deal with emotions that are relatively easy to access, and those that knowingly set out to deploy the archetypal aspects of the unconscious.

I accept that I am making a personal subjective judgement about films that work emotionally: it is in part a reflection of my own tastes and indeed of my psychology. That said, my views about these films are also informed by having shown them, or extracts from them, to numerous groups and discussed people's responses. In doing so I was attempting to find out why films that it seemed would work psychologically left me cold. If you find yourself in strong, powerful and emotional disagreement with me then you might want to jump to the final chapter in this book where I get to the nub of the personal psychological relationship that individuals have with films, both in the cinema and in therapy. However, I am not the first to suggest that the relative psychological neutrality of a film, novel or play might actually turn out to offer fertile ground for psychological material. Jung did not write much about literature, or film, or art, but he did sometimes attempt to reflect psychologically on them. On one such occasion he comments:

> In general, it is the non-psychological novel that offers the richest opportunities for psychological elucidation. Here the author, having no intentions of this sort, does not show his characters in a psychological light and thus leaves room for analysis and interpretation, or even invites it by his unprejudiced mode of presentation.... An exciting narrative that is apparently quite devoid of psychological intentions is just what interests the psychologist most of all. Such a tale is constructed against a background of unspoken psychological assumptions, and the more unconscious the author is of them, the more this background reveals itself in unalloyed purity to the discerning eye. In the psychological novel, on the other hand, the author himself makes the attempt to raise the raw material of his work into the sphere of psychological

> discussion, but instead of illuminating it he merely succeeds in obscuring the psychic background. It is from novels of this sort that the layman gets his 'psychology': whereas novels of the first kind require the psychologist to give them deeper meaning.
>
> (Jung, 1930/50: para. 137)

A quite common way to talk about films is as the creation of their directors. Along with film stars, directors are household names while editors, camera operators, special effects technicians and the other members of the production crew are much less familiar to film viewers, although one or two composers of film music have become well known. However, it is primarily directors who carry with them the pervading myth of authorial intentionality and vision. Film studies has been somewhat critical of this notion, seeking to see meaning as more complex and distributed than the 'auteur theory' suggests (cf. Caughie, 1981). In particular, recent theoretical work on fan culture has shown how the meaning of films exists outside the confines of the authorial text, as fans appropriate films for their own purposes. From this perspective it is not quite so surprising that our psychological responses might run counter to the intentions of a film's director.

The interference of consciousness with creative processes

In psychotherapy, it is known that when something that is unconscious is made conscious much of its affective power is removed. It therefore appears that when we are unduly anxious about something an unconscious process takes over and, quite unwittingly, we make sure, to the very best of our ability, that whatever is worrying us is kept hidden from our everyday lives. For example, someone might hold the erroneous belief that other people constantly judge him or her. This idea so distressing that it seems the only option is to hide it away in the unconscious: to acknowledge it would, the person believes, be intolerable. After all, who could bear the thought of being constantly judged by everyone, even a stranger in the street? Interestingly, these judgements are always negative in character – I have yet to encounter a client who is troubled or intrigued by the prospect of strangers mistakenly having positive thoughts about them. Even though we do not set out to bury these thoughts we still do exactly that and it requires a great deal of psychological energy to keep them hidden. Of course, as well as these mistaken beliefs there are also those events in life that are truly traumatic. These too can get repressed and again there can be considerable merit in exploring them with the rational part of the mind, particularly if they appear in dreams or in other creative forms. (The psychological mechanisms around trauma are rather too complicated to go into here in what in any event is not principally a clinical book. For a full exploration see Kalsched, 1996.)

Freud recognized that we could only be partially successful in our on-going efforts to hide unwanted thoughts and ideas from our conscious selves. He showed how the unconscious evades these attempts at repression and how the true meaning will always out: sometimes as a parapraxis (Freudian slip) and also in dreams. In the latter case the meaning presents itself in a disguised and transformed manner with symbols that come to take the place of our unconscious wishes, fears and anxieties. For Freud, such fantasy wish fulfilment is held in place by the superego. This is because this material that is largely sexual and Oedipal in nature cannot be expressed in its naked form in a manner that is socially and culturally acceptable. For Freud it is inevitable that our unconscious sexual thoughts will make themselves known despite our best attempts to keep them in their place.

Jung takes a rather different approach: although he too suggests that we unknowingly give expression to the unconscious, he regards this in a rather more positive manner than Freud. Jung realized that what he conceived of as 'communications' from the unconscious were in fact part of an innate system through which the psyche was attempting to maintain itself in a state of good health. While everyone who leads a fulfilling and psychologically aware life is engaged in this activity he gave artists a particular status. It is worth keeping in mind that Jung's conception of art was a rather conservative one. He tended to write about specific individuals whom he regarded as in some way psychologically interesting such as Picasso and James Joyce and who he believed were attuned to what was happening in society. His general cultural value system was that of the radical conservative: conservative because he tended towards the romantic in his view of art and radical because he took a solidly psychological view of the value of such creative endeavours. That said, there is no reason why, in principle at least, the same creative and psychological processes cannot also apply to more collective activities such as making a film or staging a play, opera, ballet and so forth. What Jung particularly valued was the manner in which the creative process could take an age-old archetypal idea and translate it into something that was socially and culturally meaningful. To this extent we can see that he is suggesting that cultural processes, and the process of cultural production, mirror the intrapsychic process of dreaming.[2] The work of artistic production is a more conscious replica of dreaming. This is not to suggest that films are dreams, any more than any other media are. Rather, Jung is making the structural claim that similar psychological processes are at work whenever the unconscious is given the opportunity to express itself creatively. He puts it the following way:

> The creative process, so far as we are able to follow it at all, consists in the unconscious activation of an archetypal image, and in elaborating and shaping this image into the finished work. By giving it shape, the artist translates it into the language of the present, and so makes it possible for us to find our way back to the deepest springs of life. Therein lies the social significance of art: it is constantly at work educating the spirit of the age, conjuring up the forms in which the age is most lacking.
>
> (Jung, 1922/31: para. 130)

This collective process is still mirrored in the individual psyche even of someone who might not regard him or herself as particularly creative. While such people might not have any particular artistic claims they nonetheless find in their everyday lives a creative solution to their worries and concerns. In a clinical setting the release of affect this provides is necessary, as it means that the client finds the emotional grip of something they did not understand has been weakened. For example, they might find that there is less inclination to be irrationally worried, unduly afraid, constantly anxious and so forth. This type of release can also happen in the cinema. Without expecting it, we can find ourselves reacting strongly to a film, feeling powerful and unlooked-for emotions. It is almost as though we suddenly see ourselves on the screen and we imagine that we are exposed and vulnerable and the sole object of other people's attention. What I am going to argue is that the likelihood of such an experience is stronger with films that are non-psychological in intention as, importantly, such films are not consciously inscribed with psychological meanings.

Intentionally rendering something that was conscious unconscious is a useful and appropriate psychotherapeutic tool. However, at times it can have an undesirable effect in the cinema and this happens when filmmakers intentionally set out to tap into material that is unconscious and archetypal. I imagine their aim is to mine a deep and fundamental seam of primitive and universal psychological material (of which more in a moment). However, far from communicating with the film's viewers at a basic and mythic level, what happens is that the filmmakers bring the archetypal material into consciousness and in doing so they lose its affective qualities: what works well in therapy has the opposite effect in the cinema.

One of the reasons for this is that in therapy the decision to work in a particular way is made by the therapist, generally in discussion with the client, or a specific way of working is suggested as a direct result of the material that the client is presenting. The therapeutic work that is undertaken is specific, focused and directly relevant to the life of that person. By contrast, the cinema sets out to be general in its appeal. Filmmakers start from the premise that part of their role is to inscribe meaning into films, and filmmakers want their viewers to react in ways that are broadly predictable. However, as we will see as this book progresses, people also find highly personal meanings in films which appear at times to border on the idiosyncratic. Far from reacting to the cues and prompts that are so carefully planned as part of the film's production process, sometimes people find a personal or unique meaning in a film. I think of these meanings as coming from an individual's negotiation with the film text and at times the meaning they have and the attendant emotional responses can be quite at odds with what the filmmakers expected. Significantly, I am suggesting that this is more likely to happen in non-psychological films. I write this because this is the type of film that my clients talk about in therapy. Despite many of my clients being well educated, not a single one has mentioned a film that is explicitly psychological. Directors such as Hitchcock, Nicholas Roeg, Bernardo Bertolucci and Bergman remain unmentioned while pieces of popular entertainment such as *Mamma Mia!* (Dir. Lloyd, 2008) and the Harry Potter film series make more regular appearances. It might well be the ubiquity of these films – their ready availability and television showings and their heavily promotion with marketing saturation strategies – that explains their popularity in therapy. However, I am reminded of the director Robert Bresson's musing that 'Hollow idea of "art" cinema, of "art films." Art films, the ones most devoid of it' (1975: 118) which suggests rather knowingly that it is those films without any such intentions that engage the psychological aspects of life most artfully.

Of course this division between the psychological and non-psychological film is not clear cut. A film such as *Eat, Pray, Love* (Dir. Murphy, 2010) that is in part psychological, part romance and part travelogue seemed to strike a chord with some clients. But in such cases, what clients wanted to talk about was not necessarily their personal emotions that had been awakened by the film, but rather a sense of self-recognition in what is a true-to-life story. They seemed to identify something that is happening here and now, and which also has a universal quality – they were beginning to formulate their personal myth. What seems to define a psychological film, then, is that its meaning is sufficiently fluid for individuals to find space for their own understanding as such a film allow for the activation of unconscious material. Again, the parallel with dreaming is instructive as the psychological significance of a dream does not stem from its aesthetic quality or the clarity of its meaning. Instead, what is important is the way such dreams are open to interpretation. For those who prefer a more technical turn of phrase, it would be possible to say that it is those texts and images that tend towards the psychologically polysemic which allow for the possibility of personal psychological meanings. In contrast, those texts where the meaning is relatively anchored to closely prescribed ideas are less available for individual negotiation. That is one of the reasons why films with inscribed psychological themes often do not work as psychological films, as the possibility of a personal psychological relationship with the film has been restricted and perhaps even closed down.

The writer's journey and the work of Christopher Vogler

There is quite a growth in books that offer advice to writers on how to ensure that their scripts will eventually become psychologically effective films. Perhaps the most influential writer is Christopher Vogler. His book *The Writer's Journey* (1997/99) demonstrates how mythic structures can be replicated in film narratives. In particular he uses the monomyth of the hero that Joseph Campbell (1949) identified as a means through which to provide story and plot devices that, he contends, will result in psychologically compelling films. Campbell identified seventeen stages in the monomyth, though Vogler pares these down into a twelve-stage structural model, which he combines with eight major archetypal figures. His latest book *Memo from the Story Department* (Vogler and

McKenna, 2011) has chapters that reprise his ideas about Campbell and Jung but he extends them. One of the chapters uses the work of the Russian formalist Vladimir Propp, while others explore the writing of Aristotle's follower Theophrastus. In both cases he combines these approaches with a variety of other practical tools for writers such as 'reciprocal action', the 'want list' and 'polar opposites' (2011: xii). *Memo from the Story Department* engages readers in thinking about the themes of their lives and the themes of their favourite films, while at the same time noting the similarity between the 'wants' of readers' lives and the desires of characters in films.

Vogler is clear that the purpose of these techniques is to release psychological energy – partly in the writer but also, presumably, in the work itself (1992: xiii). Vogler himself is modest about the impact of his work, noting only on his blog:

> It's hard to tell how much influence 'The Writer's Journey' and my thinking have had on current cinema. I work on a lot of projects behind the scenes but rarely get a screen credit and usually can't talk about what I've done because my contracts forbid it. It's difficult to guess how much the book may be shaping modern storytelling.
>
> (http://chrisvogler.wordpress.com/, 8 December 2011)

Despite his reticence, Vogler has been, and continues to be, a significant influence on the American film industry. The website for the Raindance festival lists a number of films that Vogler is credited with directly influencing including *The Lion King* (Dir. Allers and Minkoff, 1994), *Fight Club* (Dir. Fincher, 1999) and *The Thin Red Line* (Dir. Malick, 1998).[3] Further, Vogler also acknowledges his direct influence on the work of Darren Aronofsky and indeed we will look at *The Fountain* (2006), which Aronofsky directed, a little later in this chapter.

Films that should be psychologically effective but fail

Perhaps the best way to see how Vogler works is to look in detail at one of the lengthy film analyses that he presents in *The Writer's Journey*. Vogler sets the stage by locating *Titanic* (1997) not in its filmic context but in its mythological setting. What is of interest to Vogler is not where the film sits within the work of its director James Cameron, nor the innovations in special effects technologies with virtual cameras and actors. Instead Vogler focuses on the mythological. His use of mythology and also, as we will see, of psychology, is eclectic. For him, *Titanic*, the film and the disaster itself, can best be understood in mythological terms. What is curious about the way he does this is that any sense of real emotional connection either with the film or with the terrible loss of human life that resulted from the sinking of the actual *Titanic* is downplayed as the mythological takes centre stage. As he puts it, 'The Titanic disaster became part of Western popular culture, a subject of abiding fascination like the Pyramids, UFOs, or Arthurian romance' (1992: 241). With this introduction he sows the seeds of his forthcoming analysis. At this point it is worth noting how these different mythological ideas are juxtaposed. If we pause for reflection it is actually quite clear that Arthurian romance, pyramids and UFOs come from quite different mythological discourses (the TV series and film *Stargate* notwithstanding). But with his broad sweep and involving rhetoric Vogler carries us along. I suspect that Vogler might contend that his mythology of eclecticism reflects a fundamental concern for Campbell's monomyth of the hero's return. However, this leaves open the question of whether Campbell's view is as all embracing as Vogler implies. It also flattens the distinction between sign and symbol into a postmodern bricolage where all images are given a relatively even weight, regardless of their psychological qualities.

While much of the analysis of the film looks at the structural components of filmmaking and not the psychology of the characters, Vogler does not ignore the industrial aspects of the film business. Far from it, he actually devotes a fair amount of time to reflecting on the implications for the industry in his analysis. Vogler starts his chapter about *Titanic* by deftly noticing the difference between the expectations of the film and its eventual financial success. As he observes, at the time of its production *Titanic* was one of the most expensive films in the history of cinema. As he quite rightly points out, stacked against its success were the costs of production, a tragic conclusion, and a story of which everyone knew the ending. It is also a long film, at a running time of 193 minutes. Vogler could also have cited the pioneering use of digital effects, including one of the first uses of virtual actors and a hugely ambitious digital model of the ship itself. As we know now, the film turned out to be successful: it remained at the top of the US box office for sixteen weeks; won eleven Oscars; and had a soundtrack that soared to the top of the charts. The Internet Movie Database lists the film's worldwide gross takings at $2,185,372,302 (9 June 2012). A tribute to its enduring success is that a 3D version of the film was released early in 2012. Set against this background, my contention is that while *Titanic* is without doubt a highly successful film, it is a poor psychological film. What makes this particularly curious is that the film is structured around Jungian themes and ideas. As the director of the film James Cameron wrote,

> The script for 'Titanic' is earnest and straightforward, wearing its heart on its sleeve. It intentionally incorporates universals of human experience and emotion that are timeless – and familiar because they reflect our basic emotional fabric. By dealing in archetypes, the film touches people in all cultures and of all ages.
>
> (Letter to the *Los Angeles Times*, 28 March 1998, cited in Vogler, 1999: 243)

Given these intentions, it would be reasonable to expect the film to be emotionally powerful, moving and able to communicate in a direct and psychologically meaningful way with its viewers. Doubtless there are those who are moved in just that way by the film. I have to confess that it leaves me cold and, as will become clear in a moment, I am not alone in this response. I found myself wondering why it was that this film, which by objective standards I should like, I really did not. I say 'should like' because the film was calculated to appeal to precisely those aspects of life I value: relationships, myth and Jungian psychology! I was also well disposed towards Cameron, having enjoyed many of his earlier films. I think that the answer to my puzzle can be found in Vogler. Not that Vogler was intending to explain why I was left unmoved by the film; he was actually attempting to demonstrate the opposite: why *Titanic* is mythically and psychologically effective. His analysis shows with great clarity how the structure of the film can be understood in terms of Joseph Campbell's monomyth of the hero's adventure.

> Part of that synergy is the use of motifs and archetypes of the Hero's Journey, such as tests, crossings, ordeals, suspense, death, rebirth, rescues, escapes, chases, sacred marriages etc. These devices give the audience reference points in the long story and contribute to making it a coherent design, directed to maximum cathartic effect. In the tradition of the Hero's Journey, *Titanic* explores death but makes the case for the full embrace of life. Ultimately the success of the film is a mystery – a secret compact between the audience and the story. Like the men in the mini-sub we can shine some light on this mystery, but in the end we must simply withdraw and wonder.
>
> (Vogler, 1999: 265–6)

In *The Writer's Journey*, Vogler presents a detailed structural analysis of *Titanic* that shows how the film is built around the monomyth of the hero's return, as described by Joseph Campbell in *The Hero with a Thousand Faces* (1949). He does this with a considerable degree of success. Vogler takes his reader through the inner workings of the narrative of the film and the narrative arc of each of the key characters. In turn he convincingly demonstrates how each is called to adventure and crosses thresholds, how ordeals are overcome and the culmination of the return is reached. Vogler supplements this by illustrating how characters have an inner dilemma and an outer dilemma. For example, he comments:

> Rose's INNER PROBLEM will be to break away from her ORDINARY WORLD, to re-align herself with the freedom and ability to fly that Jack embodies. Her OUTER PROBLEM will be sheer survival so she can implement what she's learned in a long, happy life.
>
> (Vogler, 1999: 248; capitalization as original)

Making his exegesis still more convincing he introduces the idea of archetypes noting that Rose is a 'damsel in distress', a 'hero' and a 'victim' (ibid., 259, 246). He carries out a similar detailed analysis for most of the other characters.

Nor does Vogler ignore what are the weakest parts of the film, namely the character of Cal Hockley and the quality of the scriptwriting (ibid., 252–3).

It is interesting that people are polarized in their responses to *Titanic*. James Cameron's letter was written in response to the film critic Kenneth Turan's lambasting of the film that he decried as 'almost making you weep in frustration'. (http://articles.latimes.com/1997/dec/19/entertainment/ca-39, (accessed 16 November 2011). That is one of the kinder things he writes about the film: he opines that *Titanic* has characters that 'are clichés of such purity they ought to be exhibited in film schools as examples of how not to write for the screen'. Turan is far from alone. Indeed a quick search of the Internet will turn up numerous websites and Facebook pages explaining why their authors hate *Titanic*.

But I want to suggest a couple of other problems, of which the main one is psychological. I mentioned earlier that it is often the case that when the unconscious is made conscious it loses its affect. The suggestion is that the same happens in filmmaking. I have already suggested that deliberately constructing characters and their motivations around mythological imperatives is likely to lend them a flat and hollow quality, which is of course the opposite of what is intended. Perhaps the same also holds true of the use of symbolic imagery in films. When unconscious material is used in a calculating and conscious manner it is unable to speak with the voice of the unconscious. A good example of this is the symbol of the Heart of the Ocean. In the film this is the necklace that Rose (Kate Winslet) is supposed to have left behind on the *Titanic* in a safe that was in her cabin. A salvage team is looking for the jewellery when instead they uncover a miraculously undamaged nude drawing of Rose as a young woman wearing the pendant. The film ends with Rose returning the Heart of the Ocean to the sea. The necklace stands for love, lost hopes, youth and the sadness of a life that was never lived. Vogler points this out and more in his mythological amplification (1999: 245). What strikes me about the Heart of the Ocean is that it as though the symbol comes straight from the pages of a Jungian book of dreams although in fact it is nothing like the typical dream or dream images that people want to talk about in therapy. Generally speaking, dream images are talked about because they somehow, and in a manner which is not always immediately apparent, strike the dreamer as important and they are nearly always connected to the dreamer's immediate personal situation. The 'big' dream that has a universal or collective quality is a rare occurrence. What the Heart of the Ocean lacks is numinosity, it lacks affect and it does not speak as a symbol – the use of it as a conscious narrative device means it has become a sign, a rich and interesting sign but that is all. Put another way, the Heart of the Ocean is stereotypical rather than archetypal. It is immediately recognizable as a symbol whose collective power has been emptied through a rather obvious appropriation of a metaphorical device.[4]

So what is it about the film that made it the highest-grossing film in history (that is, until Cameron overtook that record with another mythological blockbuster of his, *Avatar*? If I am suggesting this is a poor psychological film then what other reasons are there for its financial success? The answer is plenty. It is a very well-crafted film. The special effects are outstanding, particularly the way in which the camera soars into the sky: this is innovative and magical and does give the film a fantastic quality that is well suited to the nickname of the *Titanic* – the Ship of Dreams. Undoubtedly the soundtrack, which did well in the charts, drew people to the film, as did its two key actors Kate Winslet and Leonardo Di Caprio. The love story is touching and effective and the way that the film is framed as a flashback of the memories of Rose in old age is compelling. All this is carried not by the psychology of the characters or the mythic structure of the plot. Rather, I am suggesting that the film succeeds despite such conscious interventions. A key part of this is the effective way that the film was marketed: a well-orchestrated media hype ensured that the 'secrets' of the computer-generated imagery were known about long before its opening weekend. It was almost impossible not to know about *Titanic* in 1997.

We can find another example of this type of psychological literalization in the film *The Fountain* (Dir. Aronofsky, 2006). This is a visually impressive piece of filmmaking that is quite beautiful and at times transcendental to watch. There are three interconnected stories in the film in which the same actors (Rachel Weisz and Hugh Jackman) play the central characters. In the first of these narrative threads the Conquistador Tomàs is commissioned by Queen Isabella to travel to Guatemala in search of the biblical tree of life. In the second Tommy is a neuroscientist working on a cure for his wife Izzi's brain tumour that he eventually finds in a piece of bark taken from a Guatemalan tree. In the final strand Tom travels in a space ship that takes the form of a large bubble containing what appears to be the dying tree of life. Over the course of the film Tomàs dies when he drinks the sap of the tree, Izzi dies just before the cure for her cancer is found and finally Tom dies while talking to an apparition of Izzi, at which point the space ship and its contents explode. Throughout the film certain words and phrases recur in each of the narrative strands, a golden ring appears in each story, as does the tree of life. What each character seems to deal with is the acceptance of death as an integral part of life. Certainly Izzi and Tom approach their deaths with a certain peaceful attitude of mind.

When the film premiered at the Venice Film Festival several critics booed, although at the screening to the general public the following day it was received much more favourably. The film only earned back just over half of its production costs, and as such was not regarded as a success by the film studio. Critical reception of the film was varied but generally its eclectic and excessive mix of Mayan, Tao, Christian and New Age imagery and metaphor was not well regarded.

What remains after numerous repeated viewings of this film is just how emotionally uninvolved I find myself with any of the characters. There are numerous reasons for this lack of empathy. One is that the narrative of the film is complicated and I find myself rather intellectually engaged in trying to work out what is going on at any one time. Sometimes Tommy has a shaven head like Tom, and then in the same scene Tommy's unkempt hair and beard return. At one level this rather underlines the interconnectedness of the various narrative strands. However, it also has the effect of making me feel somewhat emotionally distant. The same goes for the different rings which are in each of the narratives. Even at the death of Izzi, where one might normally expect to feel some sense of loss, at least on behalf of Tommy, the absence of affect is distinctly noticeable. Nor could I say that what I felt was that sense of serenity with which Izzi prepares herself for her death. Instead, I was just not involved with the characters.

The same observation holds good for the visual dimension of the film. The effects are wonderful and glorious to look at but they too are uninvolving. Aesthetically, I was left cold. Normally a film that is as spectacular to look at as *The Fountain* gives some satisfaction from the visual elements, whether at the level of scopophilic engagement, spectacle or some sublimated libidinal pleasure in the aesthetic engagement of looking. But here the effects are overblown and crudely rendered. In particular, the ending of the film in which flowers erupt from the body of Tomàs to bury him alive seems, quite frankly, ill judged.

You will probably have guessed from my preceding comments that the symbolic structure of the film was somewhat planned. Here I want to make a distinction between the normal planning that is essential in the production of any film and the degree to which symbolic material is deliberately planted into the narrative of the film. I accept to some extent that most films have some sort of symbolic encoding. What seems curious about the symbols in *The Fountain* is that their meanings are somewhat prescribed. The viewer faces what amounts to a conceptual challenge when watching this film. The task is to piece together the different narratives in their correct order and find the interconnections. The symbols in the film are designed to help in that process and provide a type of intellectual key with which to unlock the puzzle of exactly what is going on.

The documentary directed by Niko Tavernise that accompanies the DVD of the film is most helpful in spelling out the extent to which these symbolic motifs were planned. For example, the corridors in the film are supposed to be interpreted as birth canals – thus the themes of birth, and its opposite death are not only depicted in the film but implied too. Over the course of the film the lighting shifts from darkness to light. In the opening sequences characters' faces are obscured by shadow, windows are dark and overall the lighting tends towards the low key. By the end of the film this has changed to high-key low-contrast lighting symbolizing the bright end of life and the peaceful transition to death.

In the interviews on the DVD Hugh Jackman talks about his understanding of the film:

> Everything in the movie seems to be going from dark to light, from feeling of closed … to expansion. And by surrendering all our ideas of how we should do things … there is actually an expansion and a feeling of letting go that happens at the end of the movie.
>
> (Hugh Jackman, DVD interview)

This is not fanciful construction on their part as the film is quite clearly structured around such themes, as we have seen from previous comments. Yet again, it seems that at the centre of this is a somewhat structural understanding of myth, and the intention of filmmakers to exploit the capacity of cinema for mythmaking. Hugh Jackman comments:

> Funnily enough I had been reading Joseph Campbell and I felt that it [the script] was like a myth, a modern day myth.... Yeh, this is what life is about. I think I really connected with the fear of death and actually fully dealing with death before you can live.
>
> (Hugh Jackman, DVD interview)

It is not my intention here to privilege the views of the actors, or the DVD producer or the director. Rather I offer these comments to support the suggestion that in films that set out to create new universal myths one of the elements they have to contend with is the way that conscious mythmaking can diminish affect. To reprise a quote from Jung used at the start of this chapter, 'In general, it is the non-psychological novel that offers the richest opportunities for psychological elucidation' (Jung, 1930/50: para. 137).

The *Star Wars* saga – why therapists groan and male audiences remain enthralled

When the topic of Jung and film is raised it is not unusual for George Lucas's *Star Wars* films to be discussed. When this happens it is often men who engage with the conversation, rather than women.[5] There seems to be something particularly male about this version of the hero myth in which the central characters are either men (Han Solo, Ben Obi-Wan Kenobi) or caricatures of maleness (C3PO, R2-D2). It is well known that in writing the script for the 1977 film Lucas was influenced by the work of Joseph Campbell and in particular the book that, as we have already seen, provides the cornerstone for Vogler: *The Hero with a Thousand Faces.* Of course we know that Campbell in turn was highly informed about the work of Jung, although he did not regard himself as a Jungian but rather identified himself as a scholar of comparative religion. Perhaps unsurprisingly, there have been several books that explicitly explore the Jungian dimension to the *Star Wars* films. Typically they concentrate on the last three films in the series, *Star Wars: Episode IV – A New Hope* (1977), *Star Wars: Episode V – The Empire Strikes Back* (1980) and *Star Wars: Episode VI – The Return of the Jedi* (1983). Iaccino (1998) places his attention on the father archetype in the films. He carefully tracks the function of this archetype and indeed the actual psychological relationship that Luke Skywalker has with his biological father Darth Vader.

A different view is offered in the book *The Journey of Luke Skywalker* (2001) where the Jungian analyst Steven Galipeau chooses to stick closely to the narrative detail of the films as he charts their psychological aspects. Galipeau raises the interesting question of why the force is still with us. His answer is that the film takes a spiritual theme and presents it as a technological one, and in so doing finds an appropriate myth for our age. Alongside this he observes that there is enough psychology in the film to keep viewers engaged. Another commentator, Stephen Simon, derives the title of his book, namely, *The Force is with You* (2002), from the films' main ideas (the force). He echoes the point made by Galipeau and finds a special significance in the fact that the first of the films was released in 1977, in a decade which he identifies as one of writing about spiritual journeys. He notes that *Illusions* (Back, 1977), *Zen and the Art of Motorcycle Maintenance* (Pirsia, 1974), and *The Education of Oversoul Seven* (Roberts, 1973) were all published during the 1970s. With its focus on the mystical power of the force, Simon argues that *Star Wars* belongs to this genre of spiritual, some might say New Age, books and films. Certainly the character Ben Obi-Wan Kenobi, who tells Luke that 'the energy that binds us, that guides us, that is everywhere at once', has something of the quality of a guru. Those with a Jungian background will immediately be struck by the similarity between this language and the way that Jung writes about libido. Jung's view of libido is different to Freud's who regards this psychological energy as predominantly sexual in nature. Jung argues that while libido does have a sexual component it is better understood as psychological life-energy in general. He writes:

> By libido I mean *psychic energy*. Psychic energy is the *intensity* of a psychic process, its *psychological value*. This does not imply an assignment of value, whether moral, aesthetic, or intellectual; the psychological value is already implicit in its *determining* power, which expresses itself in definite psychic effects.
>
> (Jung, 1921: para. 777; original italics)

Are these, then, the reasons why the film *Star Wars IV: A New Hope* has such an appeal? Perhaps it goes some way to providing us with a partial answer, as the film seems to find a metaphorical way of representing something similar to Jung's conception of psychic energy. But this does not provide us with a full answer and clearly it also contradicts my previous point about conscious intent. This is a problem that we will return to throughout the book but for the moment we need to note that even if a film does portray psychological material, as we have already seen, this is no guarantor of success. *Titanic* and *The Fountain* both sought to portray universal archetypal images and ideas but in so doing diminished rather than augmented the affective, libidinal energy. Second, the power of the Force in *Star Wars* is only very roughly similar to the Jungian understanding of libido, which Jung is at pains to make clear is not a force but rather an energy which has an observable and emotional effect. As such, the film is not attempting a literal rendering of a psychological principle. It is helpful to locate Jung's conception of libido outside the realms of personal psychological energy and to see it in collective or cultural terms too. Jung often suggests that the individual and society need to be seen in relationship with each other. While it is certainly the case that the individual provides the paradigm for Jung through which to understand larger cultural phenomena it is also the case that cultural phenomena influence the individual. The relationship then is a reciprocal one, even if it is also asymmetric:

> When Nature is left to herself, energy is transformed along the line of its natural 'gradient'. In this way natural phenomena are produced, but not 'work'. So also man when left to himself lives as a natural phenomenon, and, in the proper meaning of the word, produces no work. It is culture that provides the machine whereby the natural gradient is exploited for the performance of work. That man should ever have invented this machine must be due to something rooted deep in his nature, indeed in the nature of the living organism as such.
>
> (Jung, 1928/31: para. 80)

Later in the same essay Jung observes, 'The psychological mechanism that transforms energy is the symbol. I mean by this a real symbol and not a sign' (ibid., para. 88). I want to suggest that where these films succeed is that they create a new myth through which to understand something fundamental about human psychology. I suspect that it is no accident that the more recent prequels in the *Star Wars* series have generally not been as well received as the first three. *Star Wars: A New Hope* appealed to a generation in a way that later characters such as Jar Jar Binks who appears in *The Phantom Menace* does not. One of the many criticisms made of this character is that he was created in order to appeal to children and to maximize the merchandising potential of the film.[6] Indeed, the point has been made that this trend started with the appearance of the Ewoks in *Return of the Jedi*. Another criticism staunchly denied by Lucas is that Jar Jar Binks is a racist character.[7] Whether he is racist or not, it would certainly seem to be reasonable to notice that as the *Star Wars* series has unfolded it has increasingly started to trade in stereotype rather than archetype, as exemplified Jar Jar Binks.

To put this in more psychological language we might say that when the narrative of a film is overly influenced by off-screen marketing some of the libidinal energy of the film becomes dissipated. This tends to result in the production of signs, not symbols. This is not to argue that paratexts such as trailers, merchandise, movie ephemera always lack affect. Far from it, as sometimes they can actually amplify the affect of the original film: for example, movie theme parks can add an additional dimension to the experience of watching the original film which is suffused with creative, libidinal and imaginative energy. Also, we are going to see later in this book the ways that individuals find and keep affect alive in films, even when the collective affective impact of the film is diminished, but they do so by finding personal meanings in films and not by sharing collective affective responses.

This chapter has focused on films that set out to create the conditions for psychological engagement and interest. The key point has been that in and of itself psychological intention is not enough. Indeed, it is possible that in the attempt to produce psychologically rich and engaging material overly conscious structuring of the film strips away some of the affect that typically characterizes images which arise from the unconscious. Of course the situation is not quite so clear cut as this suggests, as it seems that sometimes filmmakers hit on the balance between the desire to produce a film with mythic and psychological power and the need for a compelling cinematic experience. This happens when a new myth is created rather than when an old myth is retold. Put another way, psychologically effective films that have a collective appeal seem to find a means through which to express something that is fundamental in the psyche. It is significant that this is not just an intellectual insight, as it appears to inflect the creative process in an overly conscious and rational direction. Rather, what happens in psychologically affective films is that the libidinal energies become channelled into the creative process of filmmaking and in thereby the film becomes an expression of unconscious cultural processes and concerns. There is a sense that some filmmakers are able to take on the work of the unconscious, as their films become ways for cultures to dream.

In the next chapter the emphasis moves from the film to the cinematic experience itself. It suggests that in coming to a psychological view of what happens in the cinema it is helpful to reconceptualize the process of watching a film and see it not as an audio-visual activity but as a psycho-somatic process in which experience and meaning are not confined to what we see and hear.

2

BEING IN THE CINEMA

This chapter examines what it is like to experience a film, not just to watch it. The term 'experience' is in some ways problematic as it might be misunderstood to suggest that there is one experience, or that one's personal experience takes precedence over the facts of a given situation. In this context I am using the term to encapsulate the idea of 'being' and in particular being-in-the-cinema. More specifically, experience refers to the report of what happens when we watch a film. This is not just an account of the film but of the sensory experience and the interplay between conscious and unconscious responses. The difference between watching a film and experiencing a film is that to experience suggests that an awareness is brought to the whole of the cinematic process, as the act of being-in-the cinema is related via all the senses. In therapy, this type of sensory awareness is often focused on the body (more of which in Chapter 4) in relation to environment and in particular nature (cf. Abram, 1996). However, in this chapter the body as a site of meaning is seen as part of how meanings are found and constructed in the films we watch, and how these are embodied in our personal cinematic experiences. The suggestion is that culturally constructed and commercial images, as in films, can also have personal psychological qualities.

The importance of our personal psychology in creating meaning becomes clear when we realize that the boundary between inner psychological imagery and images in the outer world is somewhat permeable. This is a central idea for psychotherapy and it is also one which film theory has sought to address, albeit from a psychoanalytical and Lacanian perspective. The iterative and reflexive qualities of the cinema screen and how they form part of the cinematic will feature in Chapters 6 and 7 where we will examine the dream-like qualities of some films, and the psychological mechanism of projection. To enable an exploration of the cinematic experience, the chapter will start by considering some of the phenomenology of the cinema. It will then explore the etymology of the noun 'screen' and the verb 'to screen' and in particular the idea that cinema is something that both reveals and conceals aspects of ourselves. As a screen, the cinema is both site of protection and source of insight. This observation is related to the previous idea that the boundary between the inner and outer world is more diffuse than is often recognized. This chapter will then consider how the cinematic experience can be understood as something transitional. In doing so it will examine how cinema can be conceptualized as both liminal and akin to Winnicott's (1953) formulation of the transitional object. Throughout, the focus will be on in-between and indeterminate spaces, and how the body of the viewer responds to the experience of being in the cinema. This chapter interweaves depth psychological theory with phenomenological exploration as a means to approach the space between screen and viewer, as it is this space which contains the affective aspects of the cinematic experience.

The phenomenology of the cinematic experience

In his book *The Power of the Movies: How Screen and Mind Interact* (2005), Colin McGuinn makes the observation that in some respects cinematic and religious experiences are similar. For him, the image on the screen is reminiscent of the ephemeral bodies of spiritual beings, an observation that might well also call to mind the phantasmagorical antecedents of cinema. Likewise, he notes how the forward-facing arrangement of Christian churches with a central point of focus is echoed in the design of cinema auditoria. While he confines his comments to Christianity, he could have looked at similar spatial ideas in other religious settings, both ancient and modern:

> If spiritual bodies, analogous to angels, confront us on the screen, then is watching a movie anything like a religious experience? A darkened, gloomy interior; a wall blazing with light; tales of good and evil; reigning gods; a trance like state; music; an audience – what am I talking about, a church or a movie theatre?
>
> (McGuinn, 2005: 78)

Therapy too is not without its spiritual dimension (the term 'psychotherapy' means literally care of the soul[1]). Thus, the therapy room becomes a container for the process of psychotherapy and in so doing it takes on something of the *temenos*. Jungian psychology uses the term *temenos*, which is the classical Greek word for a sacred space, to describe the arena of psychological change that surrounds a psychological complex. For Jung, complexes are at the core of change and embody the affective process in which unconscious material both palatable and less so can enter our conscious lives. Perhaps too the way in which cinema can awaken the unconscious psychological aspects of our lives means that it too is more than tinged with the *temenos*. In both the cinema and in therapy to experience the *temenos* is to experience the processes of inner change and how it is facilitated through the sense of 'being' in a place which is both part of everyday life and also somewhat different to it.

As McGuinn pointed out, the seating arrangements in the cinema and in Christian churches have elements in common. So too in therapy, there is a single forward-facing point of interest: for the therapist it is the client, and for the client, the therapist. Cinema, therapy and many religious ceremonies involve the act of focusing on a single object or source, and this is also a technique that is at the heart of many meditative practices. The action of looking into something for meaning is not restricted to spiritual practices and it permeates our everyday lives.[2] For McGuinn, looking is a hermeneutic activity and he suggests that to look is not just to see, rather it is to look for meaning and in so doing to gain insight.

> the very act of looking through one thing to see another gives us pleasure, as if our eyes were performing a magical feat – traversing one domain of reality to reach another. Often such looking is accompanied by visual curiosity – we are looking *for* something, something of interest or moment. We look into the sky or a person's eyes in order to discern something there that interests us – a star, a self.
>
> (ibid., 5)

This chimes with an observation made by Jung who suggested that we look at and into things (both literally and metaphorically) because the unconscious part of ourselves recognizes itself in what it sees. More specifically, we create images that contain unconscious meanings. This does not mean solely internal psychological images, such as in dreams or fantasies, as Jung also observed these cultural meanings in myths, fairytales and more curiously in ancient alchemical writings. These are cultural images that are made in an act of cultural psychological production. But they can also have a meaning that is unique, or we might say more directly relevant for an individual, as Jung comments:

> In fact, the whole of mythology could be taken as a sort of projection of the collective unconscious. We can see this most clearly if we look at the heavenly constellations, whose originally chaotic forms were organized through the projection of images. This explains the influence of the stars as asserted by astrologers. These influences are nothing but unconscious, introspective perceptions of the activity of the collective unconscious. Just as the constellations were projected into the heavens, similar figures were projected into legends and fairytales or upon historical persons. We can therefore study the collective unconscious in two ways, either in mythology or in the analysis of the individual.
>
> (Jung, 1928/31: para. 325)

The suggestion is that cinema and psychotherapy have more in common than might be immediately apparent as both revolve around personal unconscious concerns and collective narratives. We have already seen how both psychotherapy and the cinema evoke a sense of *temenos* that acts as a container for our psychological anxieties. We have also seen how both psychotherapy and cinema screenings need special places – places that are reserved for a specific purpose which gives the experience a semi-sacred or magical quality. Even when therapy takes place in a therapist's home, as far as the client is concerned for that hour the room becomes somewhere that he or she can fully enter into the confidentiality of the therapeutic relationship. Therapy rooms are generally reasonably neutral, private and quiet, and promote a sense that this space is different to other spaces that we use on a day-to-day basis. Indeed clients often talk about returning to the 'real world', as though the door to the therapy room acts as a portal to another world, rather like the doors of the wardrobe in the Narnia novels of C. S. Lewis.[3] Likewise, cinemas are generally bespoke buildings that are designed to enable the transition, or crossover, from everyday life into another world that is different. Historically the exotic picture palaces of the 1940s, in the UK at least, drew on a mixture of motifs derived from art deco and classical Egyptian imagery. Modernist design combined with papyric columns, ancient Egyptian symbols and figures, and in so doing offered a sense of how the modern and the ancient could be intertwined. The now restored Louxor in Paris is a rich example of this type of architectural mélange.[4] Even contemporary multiplex cinemas, which tend to be more minimalist in design, are regularly bedecked with tiny ceiling lights that imitate the stars and constellations of the night sky. In this way, the architecture and interior design of cinemas help us to realize that we are moving into a transitional space that has only one foot in the waking world, with the other in the world of myth, dream and mystery.

There are other parallels. Both cinema and therapy happen at set times which are outside the control of the client or customer. As consumers, we have to fit in with a schedule that has been designed by someone else. Interestingly, both cinema and therapy have a single visual focus – in the cinema it is of course the screen. These days in therapy face-to-face contact between client and therapist tends to be preferred over the classical Freudian couch. Finally, therapy and cinema both have to be paid for, but what you purchase is not an object – there is nothing concrete or physical to take away from either. The purchase of a commodity is not what is significant and instead what matters is the meaningful ritual of transaction which gives rise to an experience. The fact that this experience lacks materiality is one of the reasons why it needs to be felt so powerfully and why it can contain and express powerful emotions.[5] By these comparisons I do not mean to suggest that therapy and the cinema are the same; of course they are not. Yet it is interesting that there are strong similarities that suggest there is something intrinsically psychological, perhaps even psychotherapeutic, about the cinematic experience.

Watching a film – *séance*

Perhaps in concentrating on the type of detail that I am presenting about the cinematic experience I might be accused of not seeing the wood for the trees, or the film for the frames. Yet when we burrow down into the activities which provide the context for going to the cinema, we can see that far from being trivial they reveal how small actions and details encapsulate many aspects of the larger experience – a type of synecdoche. With that thought in mind I am going to shift to one of the basic and necessary elements of the cinematic, and yet it is one that is rarely thought about, namely the cinema screen. Here we will consider how 'screen' as noun and 'screen' as verb are both central to a psychological understanding of the cinematic experience.

The noun 'screen' has a complicated and fascinating etymology. In their overview of the development of film theory Elsaesser and Hagener (2010) provide a fascinating tour around the history and various meanings of the noun, 'screen'. In doing so they explore in a phenomenological manner what happens when cinema is conceptualized as a frame (they undertake a similar task for cinema as door, eye, ear, skin and so forth). Their contention is that the etymological origins of the word help us to understanding the implications of what it is that cinema frames and how it is framed:

> The word 'screen' developed in the early fourteenth century from the old Germanic term 'scrim' which opens up a rich semantic field. A 'scrim' acts like a shield and protects us from enemies or adverse influences (such as the heat from a fire or the weather), thus allowing us to get closer. Yet again, a screen also denotes an arrangement that hides something or someone by dividing a space (e.g. by putting up a paravent). In this sense, the screen can mean the exact opposite of displaying something, making something visible or bringing something closer, but refers instead to keeping a safe distance.
>
> (Elsaesser and Hagener, 2010: 38)

Rather than thinking in terms of either a physical protection or a device to allow closeness, we, instead, 'reframe' (to use a psychological term): we can see how the cinema screen facilitates psychological insight while at the same time it provides protection from the proximity to the unconscious which it paradoxically enables. To borrow an image from alchemy, cinema acts as a container for psychological change; it both causes a reaction and contains that reaction. In this sense, cinema is a psychological catalyst: while it remains unchanged the reagent (viewer) is altered. Another way of thinking about this is to see cinema as an *enantiodromaic* medium. Jung used the term *enantiodromia*, which he borrowed from Heraclitus, to suggest that opposites, far from pulling in different directions, in fact turn out to run into each other. When seen in this light it is apparent that the cinema is both a place of psychological encounter yet equally it provides a safe space for this encounter to happen. It appears, then, that the cinema screen is not a neutral reflective surface but that instead it plays an active role in the creation of the cinematic experience. Elsaesser and Hagener develop this line of enquiry:

> A further meaning of screen as a protective filter or coating is that of a curtain restraining sunlight and thus protecting light-sensitive persons

> or objects. This attribute is also linked to visibility and light, but in contrast to the screen in the cinema auditorium it does so in a negative sense ... The proverbial 'silver screen' was used in the projection of Lanterna Magica-images, one of the predecessors of the cinema as popular entertainment, while the projection technology of the phantasmagoria introduced the term 'smoke screen', because the images were not projected on a material carrier, but reflected-refracted on smoke or fog: the air itself was made intransparent, so that light and shadow no longer passed through it, but made it appear 'material' and physical, perceived as a division or obstacle.
>
> (ibid., 38)

The *Shorter Oxford English Dictionary* (sixth edition) lists a number of other meanings which are no less redolent with psychological value: a decorated partition of wood that separates the nave from the chancel or choir; a sight screen – used in cricket to give the bowler and batsmen a clear line of sight of the ball; a measure used to avoid attack; an arrangement of parallel wires to reduce loss of power to the earth; in printing a pattern of crossed lines behind which is a sensitive surface – and there are numerous others. In every case screening involves either hiding something or its opposite, revealing something or, at the very least, it involves the act of bringing something into sharper relief.

Of course, there are other meanings too and we can see these if we shift from the noun to the verb: 'to screen' means to check for disease, to select by weeding out, and of course it also means to conceal. What I am suggesting is that the word 'screen' is the site of rich cultural meanings in which the body is the hermeneutic locus. Bodies are: protected though a sun-screen, for example; screened for disease and for treatment; screened from physical danger. Of course, screening is not always positive, screening can also be used as a form of discrimination; bodies are used to mark or foreground racial and anatomical differences; screening may be used to restrict access and the rights of specific groups, on sexual, racial and socioeconomic grounds. All this seems some way from the rather more prosaic and utilitarian sense of the projection screen and yet these are nonetheless its cultural overtones.

A further amplification comes from one of the French words for the screening of a film: a *séance* and this points directly to the legacy of the phantasmagoria, mentioned by Elsaesser and Hagener. The phantasmagoria is one of the precursors of the modern-day cinema. Invented in France in the late eighteenth century, phantasmagoria spread through Europe during the nineteenth century. The entertainment took place in medium-sized rooms and used a modified 'magic lantern' to project ghosts, skeletons and other supernatural images. As phantasmagoria used multiple mobile projectors, the images could be made to change in size and shape as they moved around the room. Intriguingly, the Marxist cultural critic Walter Benjamin (2002), in reflecting on his experience of the Parisian arcades, commented on the phantasmagorical qualities of commodities in capitalist culture. And so we find ourselves now back in the commoditized multiplex. I realize that I am not proceeding logically here as I jump from phantasmagoria to arcades to modern-day cinemas. What I am attempting to do is to let ideas and themes associate with each other as a means to explore hidden psychological connections, a process which in Jungian theory is termed 'amplification'. In this case I want to suggest that the commercial qualities of cinema are not necessarily at odds with its other more psychological aspects. Indeed, it is the very sense and idea of commodity that provides the entry point into the *enantiodromaic* world of the other. The modern-day equivalent of placing a coin in the mouth of the deceased in order to be carried across the river Styx and into the underworld is the cost of admission to the cinema. As such, it is partly a ritualistic act, and one that gives us access to the transformative experience of the underworld.

If the function of the screen is to act as a container, then we might usefully consider what it is that is being contained. As psychotherapists know, psychological change is often characterized by the release of affect and Jung makes this point repeatedly. Change that occurs in the consulting room can have a lasting effect. Likewise, any affect that is released as part of the cinematic experience does not simply fade away at the end of the film. Of course, we take our memory of the film with us as we leave the cinema. But I also want to suggest that the cinematic experience leaves a bodily encoding of its affective impact. By bodily encoding, I mean the response our body makes to the affect that the film has released and it is this that leaves us with an emotional imprint of the experience. Sometimes clients report leaving a cinema exhilarated, or tired. They might find they notice a backache or upset stomach. Or they might be in a bad mood with their companions or perhaps they are overly talkative. Watching *Avatar* (2009) for the first time, I was left with a headache that took several days to clear. (From my comments in the previous chapter about another of director James Cameron's films, *Titanic*, you might guess why the film gave me such a pain, although at the time I was quite unaware of what was happening to me.) Of course a 'negative' response does not mean that an experience should be avoided or that it is not psychologically beneficial. In therapy and as part of the cinematic experience such responses might be a positive sign of a change or shift in awareness.

We know that when a complex is active it is characterized by a strong affect and that the affect can take on a physical quality. This is another way to say that psychological complexes can make themselves felt physically in the body. Jung puts this in a straightforward manner: 'A wrong functioning of the psyche can do much to injure the body, just as conversely a bodily illness can affect the psyche; for psyche and body are not separate entities, but one and the same life.' (Jung, 1917/26/43: para. 194).[6] The body, then, responds to life's situations and watching films is no exception. Indeed I would argue that cinema as a medium is closer to the unconscious than many other media, for reasons that we will explore later in this chapter. Let me approach this topic from another direction.

One way to circumvent the desires of the conscious part of ourselves in its attempt to keep the unconscious hidden is to talk about our experience. This is the essence of psychotherapy – that by talking about our lives with another and attending to the feelings that arise we can learn more about our unconscious and live more fulfilling lives. What happens in therapy is the creation of a new narrative of a person's life. Sometimes this involves something that is felt and embodied in the relationship. This is what Jung refers to as a psychological image. Like therapy, the cinema has the capacity to activate the image-making capacity of the psyche and in so doing it creates an image that encapsulates the reality of an individual's psychological situation. This 'image' may be a concrete one which can be captured or even sometimes seen, but more often it is a metaphorical image, a sense, a thought or feeling that has arisen as a result of watching a film even if it does not appear to be directly related to its narrative. This is somewhat like the way music can conjure up images in our mind which in turn evoke powerful emotions.

Perhaps at an intuitive level this is one of the reasons we enjoy or need to have a discussion of a film after we have seen it. When we have such a discussion we are not just reflecting on a shared experience, we are creating a narrative by which to understand what has happened to us in the cinema. This is similar to the way we tell people about our dreams, not realizing that in doing so we are providing the listener with access to our unconscious selves. So, too, when we talk about the meaning that a film has for us (as opposed to the narrative meaning of a film) we bring out into the open something which we would normally keep private. We might therefore think of the process of discussing a film as a social custom that facilitates the exploration of personal psychological concerns. It is also a means by which to keep the experience fresh and alive for longer. Again, this seems somewhat analogous to the process of dreaming. Even if while we are dreaming the experience is vivid and seemingly real, when we wake the dream can evaporate and it can become extremely difficult to remember even the key points, or the most general sense of what has happened. Sometimes we are left with a mere impression that we had an important dream. So, too, talking about a film both prolongs the experience and ensures it is kept close to consciousness for as long as possible. Thus the post-film discussion provides a forum for personal exploration that is contained in a socially acceptable convention (cf. Singh, 2014).

One of the curious aspects to these discussions is the extent to which our views of films differ – sometimes quite radically – from those of other people who have seen the same film. This particularly applies to all those movies to which we have a strong connection or affinity. It can seem puzzling to us that a film we found deeply moving and powerful is for someone else boring and dull. This is not necessarily because we are more attentive or perceptive as film-goers than the people we are with – although that is of course a possibility. But I have had these types of experiences in groups of film academics where everyone has strikingly divergent views about a film. This is an important point: when we evaluate a film in terms of our emotional reaction to it we find a key to what is happening psychologically for us. For Jung, feeling was an evaluative function and evaluation itself draws on critical judgement, gut senses, taste and sensibility, and physical contexts such as mood, state of health and 'frame of mind', not merely emotions. When we say this film was boring and dull or, by contrast, powerful or insightful it provides a strong indication that something personal in our individual psyche has been awakened by it. This is the affect mentioned above which is associated with a psychological complex and which indicates the potential for psychological transformation.

It follows that one way of coming to understand what a film might have meant psychologically for us is to be attentive not just to the thoughts that enter our mind but also to what our bodies are telling us. We do this partly by being aware of the feelings in our body but also by discussing the film with other people, which is another way in which we can bypass the defences which can prevent us from gaining access to the psychological material which the film has stirred up in us. Cinema can awaken personal psychological complexes and this happens more readily and frequently than might be supposed. The emotional response we have to what we see on the screen is not just due to the inscribed or collective meaning of the film. That said, responding to films in the manner that was intended by the filmmakers is probably what most of us usually do. However, we also react to films in a highly personal manner and in doing so we find not collective and shared meanings in them but highly personal and individual meanings. To this extent, we can say that phenomenologically we all see different films, and that each time we watch a film, a different film is seen – each screening of a film constitutes a unique cinematic experience which helps us to understand the importance of repeat viewings of a film and the significance that is behind the retelling of a film.

Viewers are in relationship with the screen and negotiate meanings

Cinema audiences have a relationship with films in which meanings are not just transmitted from the screen to the viewer. Rather, individuals negotiate meanings with films. Sometimes this happens consciously when, for example, we work hard at interpreting a film, at being sensitive to its cinematic and aesthetic qualities and at becoming attuned to its use of metaphor, symbol and the subtleties of its narrative. However, this negotiation of meaning can also take place at an unconscious level. In such cases a personal complex is activated, and our cultural and aesthetic sensibilities are overwhelmed by the strength of the affect. When this happens the meaning and values that are found and placed in a film can be a mystery to others. Just as dreams do not have to be a work of art and yet are psychologically effective, so, too, our emotional and psychological responses are not in any way an indicator of the aesthetic worth of a film. We can find powerful meanings in the most unlikely of places. Indeed, it is possible that a beautifully crafted film might not be as psychologically powerful as something more rough and ready. For example, while I can appreciate the cleverness and beauty of Sokurov's *Russian Ark* (2002), psychologically it leaves me cold.

While we have collective and shared responses to films I want to suggest that our personal responses to films are no less important in influencing the meanings that we find. Of course, it is important not to lose sight of the collective, social and institutional dimensions of filmmaking. However, the type of meaning that I am concerned with derives from the personal responses we have to films and the ways in which these may be at odds with more collective views.

Jung regularly moved between the individual and the collective. Indeed, this is both a strength and some would say a weakness in his writing. As Susan Rowland (2005) has so adroitly shown, Jung's work can best be understood in literary rather than scientific terms. This approach reveals in Jung's prose what, at times, can seem like an almost poetic quality and perhaps this is one of the reasons why he can often seem difficult to understand. Jung tries not to proceed on an either/or basis, he tries not to separate psychological life into formulas or processes. Instead he attempts to see it imaginatively and creatively, at which point it becomes more akin to a metaphor or image. His own struggle to escape the literal and live the poetic comes through repeatedly as he puts forward contrasting and sometimes contradictory points of view. First he adopts one position and then the opposing one. For example, Jung will argue when it comes to interpreting a dream that meanings are not fixed, that only the patient can validate the meaning and that the analyst fails if he is tempted to force his understanding of a dream on a client. Then he will write that in dreams the sea is an image of the unconscious, as are forests, and that the labyrinth is an image of the life maturation process which is also termed individuation. So, too, when it comes to the personal and collective we have in Jung's thinking a separation of the personal and the collective and also a bringing together of the individual and shared aspects of the psyche.

Jung suggested that the unconscious had two components, the personal and the collective unconscious. This is how Jung presents matters when he is trying to advance an argument or theory. The personal unconscious is the result of an inherited genetic predisposition which is combined with experiences of life from conception through to death. By contrast, the collective unconscious is a fundamental aspect which underpins this and which regulates the growth and development of the individual. As just noted above, Jung asserts that this aspect of the unconscious can only really be understood by seeing parallel images in mythology, to which we can add the cinema and other arts. The manifestation of this unconscious collective imagery is termed by Jung a complex. This is not to be confused with the manner in which psychoanalysis uses the term, although they share certain qualities. Rather, the complex for Jung is an affect-laden image in which individuals find that they are in the grip of something that appears to be outside their control, and yet which feels intensely personal.

Recently there has been growth of interest in extending the idea of the personal complex to formulate a theory of the cultural complex. Most of the authors writing in this field have in mind the idea of a cultural complex as a means by which to understand how large numbers of people can suddenly find themselves swept along and caught up in collective processes. Intense collective emotions seemingly possess or take over an individual and without much recourse to rational thought they find themselves moved to action. Sometimes, this action can be destructive, violent, racist, anti-Semitic or xenophobic. At other times a mood of collective grief can sweep the country; in the UK the death of Princess Diana in 1997 was the source of a shared and unexpected period of mourning and a sense of loss which continues today, accompanied as it is with an abundance of conspiracy theories around the details of her death. Singer and Kimbles comment:

> cultural complexes are based on repetitive, historical group experiences which have taken root in the cultural unconscious of the group. At any ripe time, these slumbering cultural complexes can be activated in the cultural unconscious and take hold of the collective psyche of individual members of the group. The inner sociology of the cultural complexes can seize the imagination, the behavior and the emotions of the collective psyche and unleash tremendously irrational forces in the name of their 'logic'.
>
> (Singer and Kimbles, 2004: 7)

While Singer and Kimbles are concerned with the social behaviour of groups it is interesting to wonder if one of the reasons why a film may unexpectedly find popularity is because it gives expression to some latent unconscious fantasy. One of the themes that runs through *Somatic Cinema* is that the separation between collective and individual meanings is not as clear cut as Jung would suggest, and that film theory has yet to account adequately for the ways in which individuals negotiate, create or find personal meanings in the collective narrative of films. Instead, for a number of years, film studies has emphasized that films and indeed film movements need to be set in social, political and industrial contexts if they are to be fully understood. For example, the *films noirs* of 1940s American cinema with their alienated and psychologically distressed characters were made during and immediately after the Second World War. Italian neo-realism emerged at a similar period, but here the concern is with the everyday lives of working-class Italians. Of course, this is to simplify the analysis but it seems clear that films express cultural developments.

My suggestion is that while this approach has considerable benefits, it focuses on the collective view at the expense of the individual. So, while wanting to maintain the benefits of seeing cinema as in part determined by social and political forces I also want to suggest that it exists in what can be thought of as a liminal cultural space. We have begun to see how cinema buildings exist as both commercial buildings and ventures and how they also provide a point of entry into the interiority of the self that everyday life cannot readily afford. So too the films on screen both represent aspects of society that we know about and represent unconscious psychological concerns which are both collective and individual. Here, then, are a set of ways in which cinema occupies a liminal space. It is the shore between the ocean of the collective and the land of the individual; it sits between the commercial imperative of business and the illumination of inner life; it encapsulates what we know about ourselves and our culture and also what we have yet to comprehend about our social life and our individual psyches.

A parallel to the idea of liminality can be found in the idea of the transitional object. Winnicott, who coined this term, presented it most clearly in his 1953 paper 'Transitional Objects and Transitional Phenomena: A Study of the First Not-me Possession'. As Winnicott was writing from a psychoanalytical perspective it is important to note that underpinning the idea of the transitional object is the assumption that it is, in part, a substitute for the mother's breast and hence is invested with sublimated sexual energy (a point that is explored further below). More descriptively Winnicott observed:

> There is a wide variation to be found in a sequence of events which starts with the newborn infant's fist-in-mouth activities, and that leads eventually on to an attachment to a teddy, a doll or soft toy, or a hard toy. It is clear that something is important here other than oral excitement and satisfaction, although this may be the basis of everything else.... I have introduced the terms 'transitional object' and 'transitional phenomena' for designation of the intermediate area of experience, between the thumb and the teddy bear, between the oral eroticism and true object relationship, between primary creative activity and projection of what has already been introjection between primary unawareness of indebtedness and the acknowledgment of indebtedness.
>
> (Winnicott, 1951: 89)

Significantly, Winnicott, in writing about the realm of subjective experience, goes beyond the straightforward idea of an object invested with psychological quality and stresses the importance of experiencing an intermediate area which he suggests exists between inner fantasy and outer reality – or, to use his terminology, between oral erotic engagement and actual relationships with objects. He observes that our sense of self-identity is built up from more than personal relationships and that, in and of themselves, our childhood experiences do not constitute a sufficient base upon which to build our adult characters. For Winnicott, subjective experience of both inner and outer realities is important in determining the formation of our psychological identities. He suggests 'Keeping inner and outer reality separate yet inter-related' (ibid., 90) and in so doing preserving what he terms the 'substance of illusion'. It is not entirely clear what he intends this phrase to mean but it seems to refer to the area between the subjective and that which is objectively perceived and is concerned with accepting and holding together differences and similarities. The experience of such contradictions (derived as they are from oral excitation for Winnicott) in the transitional state is as something to be enjoyed even when the experience is internally deployed as a defence against anxiety, even depressive anxiety.

Echoes of this idea are found in Roland Barthes's reflections on the nature of the experience of going to the cinema. For example, in 'En sortant du cinema' (1975) he alludes to the distinction between the act of cinema going (as transitional phenomenon) and the film itself (as transitional object). In so doing, he situates the viewer in a space that fetishizes the nature of the experience itself. Here again we have the difference between goods and services, and the product and the experience. This difference is reminiscent of the gap that exists between commercial filmmaking and the self-insight that occurs when watching a film.

> in allowing oneself to be fascinated two times: by the image and by what surrounds it, as if I had two bodies at the same time: a narcissistic body which looks, lost in the close mirror, and a perverse body, ready to fetishise, not the image, but precisely that which exceeds it: the grain of the sound, the theatre [cinema] itself, the darkness, the obscure mass of other bodies, the rays of light, the entrance, the exit: in brief, to distance myself, 'unstick', I complicate a 'relation' by a 'situation'.[7]
>
> (Barthes, 1975: 106–7)

Barthes's notion of becoming 'unstuck' evokes the opposite of the Lacanian suture (of the unconscious) which in the case of watching a film bridges the divide between the viewer and the screen and represents the 'stitching' of ourselves into the film's narrative. Thus, pleasure for Barthes comes not just from the image as object but also from the experience of the phenomenon. Again, an echo of this idea can be found in Winnicott's suggestion that both the transitional object and the transitional state are derived from the child's experience of the mother's breast. The pleasure that comes from the use of transitional objects during the transitional state is a form of what in Lacanian terminology might be termed *jouissance*. This is the state of bliss, which in extreme, recalls sexual orgasm and the pleasure and pain of sexual climax. It embodies the attempt to overcome a lack of the 'real' and its substitution by the 'symbolic' order. Barthes (1973) refers to this as 'the pleasure of the text', an idea that is derived from Freud's theories in his article 'Beyond the Pleasure Principle' (1922) which notes how such pleasure can be sublimated into other activities coming close to death and marking the desire to return to the preorganic state preceding life.

Perhaps the quality of the cinematic experience evokes these sensations too. If so, this would position the viewer as a conflicted individual who is both drawn to the realism of the illusion of the on-screen fiction while at the same time acknowledging its lack of reality. If the film is regarded as a transitional object, then the transitional phenomenon, or experience, manifests itself in the transgressive and voyeuristic act of watching. This in turn evokes notions of the primal scene which comes to invade the act of looking itself. Seen from this perspective, the image is like the transitional object with its antecedence in the breast, and it brings pleasure to the act of recognizing how 'individual' and 'other' can be separated as the lack of the real serves to propel the viewer into the realms of the imaginary and symbolic.

It is worth pointing out that when Winnicott writes about 'objects' he is not using the term in a Kleinian sense, as he notes:

> The transitional object is *not an internal object* (which is a mental concept) – it is a possession. Yet it is not (for the infant) an external object either.... The transitional object may therefore stand for 'external' breast, but *indirectly*, through standing for an 'internal' breast.
>
> (Winnicott, 1953: 94)

Hence, the transitional object has something of a symbolic quality which indeed is essential if it is to contain the ambiguity that is felt in coming to an understanding of the contradictory nature of self and other, or reality and illusion and inner and outer worlds. The idea that transitional objects, and their associated symbolic qualities, last beyond childhood is clearly something that Winnicott was alert to. In his list of defining characteristics of the relationship one has with the transitional objects he clearly notes how this experience is fundamental and pervasive. (It should be noted that the other six characteristics have less relevance to the cinematic situation.)

> Its fate is to be gradually allowed to be decathected, so that in the course of years it becomes not so much forgotten as relegated to limbo. ... It loses meaning, and this is because the transitional phenomena have become diffused, have become spread out over the whole intermediate territory between 'inner psychic reality' and 'the external world as perceived by two persons in common', that is to say, over the whole cultural field.
>
> (ibid., 91)

Winnicott's use of the term 'cultural field' is open to several interpretations. One involves restricting the meaning of 'cultural' to the immediate experience of the family. The strength of this is that it serves to ensure that environmental factors are allowed for in understanding the function of any given transitional object. However, it is quite legitimate to go further because in linking the transitional object to the pleasure principle Winnicott positions the object outside the realm of primary identification. Consequently, meaning for the child is created as a result of the need to be fed by the mother and the necessity of forming an independent identity. This need to come to a symbolic understanding of the world is clearly continued in adulthood. As Winnicott notes:

> to speak in terms of man's cultural life, which is the adult equivalent of the transitional phenomena of infancy and early childhood, and in which area communication is made without reference to the object's state of being either subjectively or objectively perceived. It is my opinion that the psycho-analyst has no other language in which to refer to cultural phenomena. He can talk about the mental mechanisms of the artist but not about the experience of communication in art and religion unless he is willing to peddle in the intermediate area whose ancestor is the infant's transitional object.
>
> (Winnicott, 1965: 184)

It is open to question whether Winnicott is right in his view that the only language available for the psychoanalyst to understand cultural phenomena is associated with the transitional object. After all, starting from Freud and continuing to the present day there is a long-standing tradition of using a range of psychoanalytic terminology as a means by which to understand the functions of culture. However, he is surely right to note that a psychoanalytic understanding of culture will be particular, partial even. It is interesting that cultural commentators, whether from the social sciences, humanities or psychoanalysis itself, have not bought to the fore the notion of the transitional object, though it has not gone completely unmentioned either (cf. Allen, 1977: 139; Kuhn, 2013). Yet it would seem that in the case of film theory they might usefully have done so, as it provides some underpinning for the assertion that intentionality and authorship are less important for interpretation than the co-creational relationship between viewer and viewed.[8]

The cinema can blur where I end and the other starts

One way of formulating the cinematic experience is as a means to provide a psychological opportunity to explore what is me and what is not me. This can involve the fantasy that what is experienced has nothing to do with me at all. When this happens it is often imagined as other and as belonging just to the world of the film and the characters on screen. This is what lies behind the everyday idea of escaping into a movie or indeed a book, though actually the meaning of such escape is less clear cut. The ambiguity becomes obvious when we conceive of cinema films as transitional objects. If film is a transitional object then film-going is a transitional cultural phenomenon. Here our foreknowledge of genre, star, actor bring a degree of intertextuality to the transitional phenomenon, meaning that we come 'expecting' something. So too the detail of the setting, the timing of the film, all prepare us for the transition to an inner psychological space in which we know that what we are going to experience is not completely predictable.

As such the distinction between transitional object and transitional phenomenon is not absolute and the two intermingle. This is rather like the 'squiggle game' that Winnicott played with his young patients in which he would start by drawing something which the child would be encouraged to develop in which two lines come together to form something new and meaningful. So, too, what seems to happen is that in the act of recognizing what is me and what is not me on the screen a new psychological image comes into being. Winnicott talks about the transitional object – the object which is invested with affect and which is used to test out the boundaries of the self. Thus the object becomes the recipient of unconscious projections and fantasies which in turn are used as a means through which to define the self – the unknown helps us to understand ourselves. Of course in the cinema there isn't an object per se which can be invested with this libidinal affect. Instead there is an image on screen and we think of this as something 'transitional' – a transitional image, if you will. In many ways the cinematic experience seems close to Winnicott's transition object/image/phenomenon, particularly when he notes that it is 'not part of the infant's body yet … not fully recognised as belonging to external reality' (Winnicott, 1951: 89). If we extend this to the cinema we can see that at times there is a temporary confusion between reality and illusion that is embodied in involuntary motor responses such as sharp intakes of breath or sudden movements of hands or legs. These, along with the experience of emotions, belong to the intermediary space that exists between inner and outer realities. The experience both binds us into the film and separates us from it.

While not addressing this issue from precisely the same perspective, the film theorist Christian Metz nonetheless adopts a cognate perspective. In *Psychoanalysis and Cinema* (1982), Metz began to track the similarities and differences between the condition of watching films and the dream state. This may seem like quite a jump from Winnicott's concerns but, as noted above, transitional objects like dreams are secondary processes. In some ways dreams function as a bridge between the conscious and the unconscious or, put another way, between what is known and what is unknown; or, as Winnicott might have put it, as transitional phenomena located between objective and subjective realities – between reality and fantasy. But the curious part is that because we relate to this transitional image as something both shared and highly personal we take it out of its narrative setting and instead invest it with personal affect. In so doing, we take a collective image and make it our own. The idea of blurring the boundary between the collective and the individual is of course core to Jung's understanding of the psyche. In personal analysis the analysand becomes aware of both his or her own complexes and their archetypal, transpersonal or collective aspects. Thus a negative mother complex, for example, will be built up from both actual personal experiences of being mothered and also the archetypal, collective aspect of the negative mythic devouring mother, as in both *Alien* (1979) and *Aliens* (1986).

So what we experience in the cinema is composed of: what is me and what is not me; what is real and what is illusory; what is personal and what is collective; what is historical and what is mythic; what the narrative of the film means and what meanings I negotiate with the film on a personal basis. No matter how the cinematic experience is defined, and whatever taxonomy is created, the key point remains that psychological exploration and change are intrinsic to the cinematic experience, as the tension has to be held between personal and collective concerns. The way this happens is through the encounter of an individual with collective fantasy material, and the effect of this is both temporary and difficult to grasp. Such change is encapsulated in the individual relationship a viewer has with a film, and, at risk of labouring the point, this only partly arises from the narrative of the film and is in no small part influenced by the subjectivity of an individual's unconscious. The process is analogous to the manner in which individual analysis can allow for an encounter with the collective as a means for the individual to become more fully the person he or she is.

It is worth noting that this sense of negotiation with the film in the attempt to hold the tension between the collective inscribed meaning of the film and a more personally derived meaning is rather different, and importantly so, to the traditional psychoanalytic and Lacanian accounts of the cinematic experience. These will be explored in more detail in the next chapter but for the moment it is enough to note the twofold view of what happens while we are watching a film. First, the viewer becomes aware that what they are seeing on the screen is a collection of body parts which have been metaphorically dissected by the camera and which need to be reconstituted into whole people. The viewer is able to perform this task as they see on the screen a mirror of their own internal sense of self which is equally fragmented. Just as the child who sees themselves reflected in a mirror believes that what they see is their own idealized self, so too the viewer attempts to reconstruct the characters on screen into an idealized form of themselves. Of course such a reconstruction can only be temporary as the film moves onward, cut follows cut, so no sooner is the image rebuilt than it fragments again. Thus the mechanisms of cinema turn out to reproduce the internal mechanisms of the psyche. This idea will make a reappearance in the next chapter in relation to Kleinian ideas and object relations as a way to reformulate the Lacanian view of the unstable self.

A central part of the process is the narcissistic fantasy of the idealized self, which is momentarily constituted through the act of looking. Just as Narcissus recognized his own beauty when he saw his face reflected in a lake, so too the child fantasizes about the idealized ego as seen reflected in the mirror. According to Lacanian theory, this is how the viewer is positioned or constructed in and through the cinematic process. The address of the camera posits the existence of a viewer and it momentarily seems possible for the fragmented image on screen to be reassembled. In the process the idealized ego is reconstituted and can again be introjected.

In the above account the term that is used to show how the fragmented and inherently unstable sense of self is held together, albeit precariously, is suture. (This idea will be explored more fully in the next chapter.) The idea that the individual is stitched into the text of the film makes for a powerful and intellectually appealing image. It seems likely that something of the sort does indeed happen, sometimes and with some films. However, there are several problems with this idea. First, it assumes that the grammar of cinema is somewhat fixed, as this is what underpins the similarity of the cinematic apparatus and the structures of the unconscious. This is something of an issue as it is quite clear that the lexicon of cinema is in a process of constant change. Second, the assumption that the self is in a state of constant disruption and likely to fragment seems to have more basis in academic appeal than emotional reality. The sense of fragmentation is not something that is experienced either intellectually or emotionally in the cinema – indeed, if anything, the opposite is true, that momentarily we experience connection, recognition of myself in others, emotional release and so forth. This is not to suggest that the psyche is not fragmented but rather that cinema seems to help us contain that fragmentation. Further such fragments are not equivalent to the Lacanian pieces of the fragmented self, rather they are the tensions that exist between me and my personal complexes and shared cultural complexes. What cinema can help us do is to bring these unconscious aspects of ourselves and the culture closer to consciousness. It thereby lets us contain the inevitable and irresolvable tensions.

A counter-argument would propose that it is not helpful, or necessary, to regard films as either stable or unstable, at least in terms of how meaning is created and how viewers identify with the film and so become sutured, both in terms of their intrapsychic state and their relationship with the film's narrative. Rather, films can better be thought of as relatively open psychological signifying systems which at times we need to see as closed, while at other times we reconstruct the narrative in accord with our own psychological needs. A good indication that this is happening is when we have a very strong affective relationship with a particular film, filmmaker or body of films. In all cases, what we are attempting psychologically is to hold the transitional qualities of the cinematic experience as both collective and individual; as both closed in meaning and available for individual meanings; as both an intertextual entity and existing in the here and now.

Being disturbed by the cinema

It is not an everyday occurrence for clients to want to talk about films in their personal therapy but it does happen more frequently than might be expected. Psychotherapy clients are often in a state of considerable emotional distress and are looking for some way through life's difficulties and it is perhaps surprising that they find some solace in the cinema. Yet it seems that at times the recognition that others have gone through either similar or even worse problems can provide a profound level of reassurance for clients as they come to realize that they are not as alone or isolated as they had believed. R. D. Laing writes about such an experience in *The Divided Self* (1959) where he recounts how a schizophrenic patient suddenly presented herself in a quite transformed manner. She attributed this to having watched the film *La Strada* (1954). Crucially, she identified with the sufferings of the film's central female character Gelsomina (Giulietta Masina) and yet she was also clear that in many important respects she was not like her at all. But what really struck her was how Gelsomina in the face of considerable difficulties did not cut herself off from life, irrespective of how awful it was. This type of existential concern is also central to the work of therapy in which clients explore how they want to be in the world and the extent to which life's experiences have pulled them away from their authentic selves. Laing comments:

> From the 'objective', clinical psychiatric point of view, one would say that there was an arrest in the process of progressive schizophrenic deterioration probably on an organic basis. From the existential point of view one could say that she had stopped trying to murder herself. She saw that her life had become a systematic attempt to destroy her own identity and to become nobody.
>
> (Laing, 1965: 156)

It would be a mistake to infer from the above that clients have a uniformly positive association or relationship with the cinema screen. Like everything that is psychologically affective, it can have a positive or a negative charge. Indeed, when such an affective response is encountered it is not always clear which is which, as negative events can lead to personal insight and apparently positive experience can be a defence, and mask some underlying anxiety. It follows from this that of course clients can also be disturbed by what they encounter on the cinema screen, as can everyday viewers who are not in therapy. However, in this instance I am thinking of a particular client who had an affair, the spouse had discovered it and whether the marriage would continue was uncertain. As a couple they enjoyed going to the cinema but just at this difficult time in their relationship it seemed that every film they went to see featured marital infidelity. My client commented on the deep shame of seeing something that was supposedly private there on the huge cinema screen being made only too public. The rest of the film and its narrative paled into insignificance alongside these intense and disturbing feelings. On the one hand, the film was clearly a reminder about what had recently happened in the marriage. But there is another sense in which the identification with the characters on screen was so strong that my client momentarily believed that the film was about her life. This is a type of powerful delusion in which our waking reality is momentarily suspended and it is more than a little reminiscent of the dream. Here I want to emphasize how in both states the rational part of the mind, or psyche, is temporarily suspended and the delusion becomes psychologically real. Again it is possible to see how cinema occupies a liminal space. It is here, between reality and delusion, that we have a space which we can variously term mythopoetic, affective or full of *temenos*, and it is this space which comes into being as a result of the unconscious encounter of an individual psyche with a collective fiction. A film by itself is just that and it only becomes meaningful when watched. At such times it seems as though the rational part of the mind becomes suspended and what we know to be a fiction becomes a sort of psychological documentary. It is as though someone has taken what we believed to be personal, private and unique to ourselves and projected it on the cinema screen. At its most acute, this experience gives rise to feelings of paranoia and persecution as though the filmmakers have been spying on us. Rather than finding a source of inspiration in the cinema, as Laing's patient did, or finding a sense of a shared normality, what my client felt was a deep sense of shame: the appalling feeling that despite her best efforts to keep what was happening private, she had quite against her will been exposed in public.

I am emphasizing the way that personal psychological meanings are intrinsic to the cinematic experience and that to locate meaning solely in the text is an error. The unconscious too has a crucial role in meaning making and this is not a rational or intellectual process. Here I am deliberately blurring the distinction between two different types of activity. The first takes the form of an intellectual enquiry into the meaning of a film. The second is concerned with what the film means to me, which is a psychological enquiry. I want to suggest that in the cinema we are always engaged in both but not equally and indeed that the balance between one and the other will vary. But as is probably clear by now, I am also suggesting that we have yet to recognize fully the role that the psychology of the individual plays in finding and creating meaning in the cinema.

3

REFLECTIONS OF THE BODY

Traditionally psychoanalytic film theory has addressed the question of the viewer's relationship with on-screen images through the lens of Lacanian theory. One of the many advantages of the Lacanian psychoanalytic approach is that it incorporates ideas about the human body as a central part of its theoretical structure. However, the drawback is that the body in Lacanian theory is also imaginal and reflected. Consequently it becomes an expression of the decentred and fragmented nature of the psyche. Another issue is that in this Lacanian view of the cinematic, viewers lack agency as they struggle to hold their fragmented selves, as objectified on the screen, into a coherent sense of themselves. Indeed this desire for coherence is one that from the Lacanian perspective will always fail. By drawing on a Jungian understanding of transference and countertransference, this chapter offers a different model in which screen and viewer are seen not as fragments, but in instead in relationship with one another.

At its core Jungian psychology is psychosomatic as it regards psyche and body as united. Yet despite this interconnectedness, the role of the body in Jungian writing remains relatively under-theorized. This is not to say it has been ignored, as the work of Samuels (1989), Romanyshyn (2007), Maguire (2004), Ramos (2004) and others demonstrates. Notwithstanding these valuable contributions, the extent of theoretical attention to this area still does not fully reflect the centrality of the concept in Jung's writing. Chapter 6 explores how the work of phenomenologically orientated film theory can help in developing a different psychological perspective. As a precursor to those ideas, this chapter looks at the relationship between psychological structures and the body, and the relevance of this in critiquing Lacanian film theory. It will demonstrate how a Jungian understanding of clinical processes can be used to develop a Jungian theory of the cinematic and in so doing provide an alternative perspective to the Lacanian view of the fragmented self.

Archetype as somatic concept

Jung suggests that there is a common set of psychological structures that influence the psychological growth and development of human beings. These same structures also serve to keep the mind and body in balance with each other. They are in constant use because life's experiences tip us first one way and then the next, with the result that a state of balance is not achievable. Jung does not suggest a single model of how we should respond to these oscillations. Rather, he suggests that it is important for individuals to live their lives in the way that is right for them. Here again we have the familiar tension in Jungian psychology between the role of individuals becoming fully who they are and not being just what life has turned them into, and the need to accept we are in relationship not just with those closest to us but with culture and society as a whole.

The basic patterns of psychological growth are termed by Jung 'archetypes' and include persona, shadow and the contrasexual archetypes of *anima* and *animus*. The technical use of the term 'archetype' needs to be distinguished from the way it is used in everyday language, where it tends to mean either the most typical form of something (the archetypal building of art deco is...) or it is used as a synonym for stereotype. In Jungian psychology 'archetype' refers to something rather different. Jung's ideas about what constituted an archetype changed over time and he variously described them as primordial images, nodes and patterns. By the end of his life he thought of archetypes as an inherent disposition to behave in a certain way. While this disposition might be relatively fixed and shared, the form it takes (what Jung terms the archetype's image) changes as a result of cultural factors and personal circumstances.

> The archetypal representations (images and ideas) mediated to us by the unconscious should not be confused with the archetype as such. They are very varied structures which all point back to one essentially 'irrepresentable' basic form. The latter is characterized by certain formal elements and certain fundamental meanings, although these can be grasped only approximately. The archetype as such is a psychoid factor that belongs, as it were, to the invisible, ultra-violet end of the psychic spectrum. It does not appear, in itself, to be capable of reaching consciousness.
>
> (Jung, 1928/31: para. 417)

The model put forward by Jung allows for the influence of both personal and cultural factors in the psychological development of individuals. It is also worth noting that Jung referred to this as the archetypal hypothesis. To this I would also add that it is usefully thought of as a metaphor. Rather than regarding archetypes as fixed, formal and concrete structures, it is more helpful to say it is 'as though' we have a 'shadow', 'animus' and so forth. Some classical Jungian analysts might disagree with this view, preferring instead to literalize the figures suggested by archetypal theory. However, it is those aspects of Jungian thinking which emphasize how psychological images are metaphorical, symbolic, affect-laden, drawn from dreams and other creative acts such as painting and literature that are most helpful when thinking about the cinematic experience. I am not alluding to a post-modern view here (for an account of that, see Hauke's *Jung and the Postmodern: the Interpretation of Realities*, 2000). Instead I want to invoke a psychotherapeutic discourse and co-opt it to see how it can be used to help us understand the ways in which mediated images communicate. It will also be useful in exploring the role that personal psychology plays in finding and negotiating meanings in such imagery.

This process of finding a personal meaning in the world is one way to describe Jung's idea of individuation. Starting at birth, if not before, the child seeks to establish a relationship with the world in which the inherited tendencies composed from collective and individual genetic material (which Jung conceived of as archetypal patterns) express themselves in a variety of ways. Jung observed what appears to be an innate need in us to understand the world in terms of images that are partly individual and partly collective. This is the role of the fantasy-image. In the following quotation Jung steers away from regarding the image as something literal and instead he shows how the fantasy-image serves a hermeneutic purpose and not a biological one.

> It is in my view a great mistake to suppose that the psyche of a new-born child is a *tabula rasa* in the sense that there is absolutely nothing in it. In so far as the child is born with a differentiated brain that is pre-determined by heredity and therefore individualized, it meets sensory stimuli coming from outside not with *any* aptitudes, but with *specific* ones, and this necessarily results in a particular, individual choice and pattern of apperception.... They are the archetypes, which direct all fantasy activity into its appointed paths and in this way produce, in the fantasy-images of children's dreams as well as in the delusions of schizophrenia, astonishing mythological parallels such as can also be found, though in lesser degree, in the dreams of normal persons and neurotics.
>
> (Jung, 1936/54: para. 136; original italics)

Developmental model versus the development of the psyche

It will be apparent that the idea that there is a life-long process of psychological growth and awareness is a core formulation in Jungian psychology. However, there is a distinction between what is often referred to as the 'developmental approach' and the development of the psyche. Despite their similarity in language, these two terms refer to rather different ideas. The situation is further complicated as some branches of Jungian therapy are rooted in the developmental model while others are more concerned with the development of the psyche. While I am presenting these as opposites, I do so for the sake of clarity and it will become clear that in fact each point of view subscribes to aspects of the other. What distinguishes them is more a question of emphasis, but it is one in which the emphasis is significant.

The developmental model regards the behaviour and psychological outlook of adults as largely determined by their experience as babies and children. By understanding the development of what are complicated patterns of behaviour and the acquisition of beliefs about the world, it becomes possible to explore whether these beliefs are indeed accurate. If they turn out to be inaccurate, which is often the case, therapy helps to explore how they have accrued as specific responses to life's difficulties. According to this theory, what happens in therapy is that the client regresses to an infantile or child-like state and treats the therapist as some troubling and difficult person from the past, typically a mother or father. The father or mother complex is thereby activated, and this is contained by therapy and eventually 'worked through' and resolved. Such therapy is by design somewhat anxiety-provoking as long-standing and uncomfortable relationships are relived in the consulting room. Here the work of Melanie Klein and the British School of Object Relations has been influential.

Of particular importance is Klein's identification of the paranoid schizoid and depressive positions, which are regarded as a normal part of child development. In the paranoid schizoid stage which takes place between the ages of three and six months (though some adults continue in this mode) the baby regards the mother not as a whole entity but as a collection of body parts. These body parts are variously nourishing (good) or destructive (bad) as in particular the mother's breast alternatively offers oral contentment and threatens to overfeed and suffocate. The baby defends against the ambiguity by splitting the breast (hence schizoid) into two objects – good breast and bad breast. The depressive position occurs when the baby realizes that the mother is in fact not an object but a whole person and is left with feelings of guilt and anxiety around their previous behaviour which aimed to destroy the attacking breast and cherish the nourishing breast.

Some film theorists have been taken by this idea and perceived in the cinema the replaying of these internal mechanisms. In particular they have stressed the importance of negativity in their theories of spectatorship and subjectivity (Gordon, 2013). As mentioned in the previous chapter, from this point of view the dissections of the body on screen into a series of shots, each framing various body parts, becomes both a source of libidinal pleasure and also a site of excesses that threatens to overwhelm the viewer. Perhaps this idea can also be extended to film genres. Here viewers form a particular like or dislike of certain types of films. For one person, horror films might be pleasurable while for someone else they are terrifying. Equally, it might be that one person might love musicals, while others find them boring and insipid. Of course, these are simplistic generalizations, but they serve to highlight that our psychological preferences are not based just on rational criteria such as director, actors and actresses, trailers, reviews and so forth. Instead they come from the psychological relationship we have with films.

Many schools of psychotherapy, including Freudian, Jungian and Adlerian, agree that experiences early on in life have an effect on our adult lives. However, not all would agree that the best way to go about resolving or understanding this is to re-experience traumatic events from childhood. An alternative approach can be found in the other type of 'developmental' psychology in which the psyche is regarded as something that unfolds, or 'develops', over time. Here the idea of development refers not to something that is left over, or which is 'stuck' from infancy, but to the potential of the psyche to grow into greater awareness. Academics have been less attracted to this idea, stemming as it does from a humanistic understanding of the unconscious rather than a structural one with all the possibilities this offers to develop a deconstructive point of view. Nonetheless, from this humanistic and developmental point of view the attraction of the cinema becomes somewhat easier to understand as it is not necessary to invoke the complexities of the psychoanalytical position, redolent as it is with the mirror stage, sublimated libido, the scopic regime and the tendency towards deconstruction. Instead, we can acknowledge that at times all these aspects get played out and they might contribute to the enduring appeal of the cinematic experience. But it is also the case that in the cinema viewers find something which is more psychologically appealing and beneficial than psychoanalytic film theory allows for.

The Jungian point of view puts the image centre stage. In doing so, Jung is not just writing about actual concrete images, though he certainly does write about art, plays and so forth. What he explores is the idea of image as something closer to a metaphor – something that is felt or experienced, and which contains an important psychological meaning. The image is much more than representation. For Jung, image is a psychosomatic concept and this is rather different to the psychoanalytic use of the term and in particular to how Lacanian theory has been applied to films. As Lacanian ideas form the dominant mode of psychoanalytic film theory in the academy we will now look at these in some detail before moving on to develop a more Jungian and phenomenologically orientated view of the cinematic experience as a means to foreground the meaning of felt experience.

Problems and limitations of the mirror phase for film theory

The previous chapter introduced the Lacanian idea of the mirror phase and mentioned its relevance to film theory. Here we will explore this concept in more detail. The reason for doing so is that the idea has been highly significant in psychoanalytically informed film theory and it is the dominant psychoanalytic mode and makes an appearance wherever psychoanalysis and cinema is taught.

Ecrits was first published in French in 1966 and subsequently translated into English in 1977 where it came to exert quite an influence on English film education. In it Lacan elaborates the idea of the mirror stage that he had started working on some thirteen years earlier. In the essay 'The Mirror Stage as Formative of the Function of the I as Revealed in Psychoanalytic Experience' he suggests that the mirror stage manifests when the baby is about six months old.

Prior to learning to walk or acquiring language, the baby learns to recognize him or herself reflected in a mirror. The significance of this for Lacan is first associated with the primacy of the event; second, the baby quickly learns that the image is empty: it is not another body at all but a reflection. However, this specular image, as Lacan terms it, is seen not as an accurate reflection but as an idealized form of the baby's body. As well as being idealized, the image is a distortion in which the size of the body can be changed and which also reverses the sides of the body. The effect is that the reflection is both idealized and distorted in its form, and is simultaneously a source of attraction and of alienation.

From this position Lacan theorizes that the human condition has a type of organic insufficiency which the reflected image in part rectifies. The mirror stage then establishes a relationship between the body (or organism, as Lacan puts it) and its reality. To recap, the body is made of fragmented body parts, which the baby attempts to bring into a whole. The attempt at coherence is based on the misrecognition (*méconnaissance*) of a seemingly idealized self-image. It therefore follows that, for the subject both as a baby and into adult life, any sense of unity and wholeness or coherence in being is temporary and illusionary, although this does not prevent us from searching for such a unity. The mirror stage exemplifies how we fail to understand that our psychological condition and our way of existing in the world does not stem from ourselves, but rather is reliant on others and on the symbolic systems of culture, and of language in particular.

In these ideas the media theorists of the 1970s found much that was both intellectually and politically appealing. In London, the Society for Education of Film and Television (SEFT) and its journal *Screen* were partly educational projects. The organization and its journal were also explicitly political and adopted a left-wing position in which media education concerning the processes, structures, audiences and representations contained within moving images was used as a deconstructive act. By deconstructing mediated images they aimed to reveal the ideological foundations of cultural representation. Psychoanalysis in its Lacanian variant not only provided a new tool for the work of SEFT but also possessed a certain elegance in which the psychological mechanisms of the mirror phase were replicated in the cinematic apparatus itself.

Suture and projection

Central to the process of the misrecognition of self in the cinema is the way in which the individual becomes stitched, or 'sutured', into the on-screen world of the film diegesis. In the act of suture a certain similarity is presumed between the projection of the film and the act of psychological projection by the individual, so that an internal psychological process is replicated or 'mirrored' in the external mechanisms of cinema. From this perspective, the techniques of how a story is told on screen, such as the way shots are framed and edited, how music relates to images, and so forth, suggest something like a grammar of film which as viewers we learn to interpret. If the gap between the on-screen world and the viewer in the auditorium is to be bridged we need to read this grammar without thinking about it. If we notice the narrative techniques such as the way the image is lit and framed, or how the camera moves from one edit to the next, then the unconscious mechanism of identification and projection is disrupted and the illusion of the reflection is destroyed. The parallel here with the mirror phase is self-evident. Just as the baby prior to its acquisition of language and the development of coherent motor skills entered into a defining relationship with its reflected images, so too when we watch a film we find ourselves identifying and entering into a relationship with the fictional world on the screen.

In watching a film we experience both pleasure and displeasure. The pleasure comes from the momentary recognition of the possibility of a unified and whole self. Of course, shot follows shot, and so any sense of coherence is quickly destroyed before the prospect of coherence is once again offered before once again being disrupted. Historically feminist psychoanalytic film theory developed this argument to suggest that narrative films from Hollywood, and in particular those of the heyday of the studio system, were predicated on an implied male audience. They posited that these films embodied the repressive structure of looking itself, and that this 'look' was fixed in its masculine orientation. In the way the camera dissected the bodies of women for enjoyment, the look gave the viewer a sadomasochistic pleasure and power. The most well-known and influential article on this topic is 'Visual Pleasure and Narrative Cinema' (Mulvey, 1975). As John Berger also pointed out, the historical antecedents of this visual control of women's bodies go back to antiquity (Berger, 1972). We can also add popular entertainments such as the Mutoscope (popularly known as 'What the Butler Saw' – which shows a woman undressing) that originated at the same time as cinema in the late nineteenth century and were also predicated on the eroticization of the heteronormative male look. Thus, the look, and the scopic regime, were shown by SEFT to be part of the cultural oppression of women and they consequently argued that cinema contributed to the furtherance of repressive patriarchal structures, with the coherence and fragmentation that cinema offers being a male fantasy of dominance, control and perverted pleasure.

What this offered was a striking demonstration of how coherence and fragmentation can sit side by side and in so doing contribute to perpetuation of ideological systems, and that was something which SEFT was keen to explore. Yet it also raises numerous problems, not least of which is the issue of female positioning and pleasure in the cinema and this is not easy to solve from this theoretical position. In practice it seems somewhat easier to recognize that there is something bisexual, or contrasexual, in the look of cinema, which can assume at any one time both male and female positions. Without wishing to occlude the specifics of gender identification and positioning, perhaps another starting point might be to assume that the sources of pleasure for both sexes are broadly similar. The cinema, which indeed exists clearly in the scopic realm, offers what appears to be a voyeuristic pleasure in the prurient and transgressive act of watching the lives of others, albeit that these lives are fiction.

I want to suggest that we can preserve some of the appeal of Lacanian theory in which internal psychic structures can be mirrored by the cinematic. I also agree that part of what we find projected on the screen is our own interiority, albeit in a somewhat reworked or altered form. However, where I differ from the Lacanian view is that what we find in the *cinema* (note, not the film) is not a fragmented ego but rather a projection of the innate capacity of the psyche to perceive archetypal patterns as images. Agreed, the formal structures of cinema facilitate this process but there is, it turns out, no need to implant archetypes on screen (cf. Vogler, 1992/99) because the internal psychological mechanisms of viewers will do this by themselves. Certainly there will be times when this will involve the experience of collective shared meanings, which might stem from the intentional use of archetypal images. At other times the activation of personal material (a personal complex) will mean that individual and unique meanings are found in films. Here I am making a distinction between archetypal images that have been deliberately put in a film and the activation of personal complexes, which might have a collective quality, by the cinematic process. For example, a negative mother complex has collective aspects, but what a film does is facilitate the expression of an individual mother complex. This has some ramifications for the gendered quality of the gaze. If meaning resides more in the act of looking than as an act of inscription in the film, it follows that there is a sense in which the cinematic look is contrasexual, which is to say it might facilitate the projection and identification of the unconscious and contrasexual aspects of the psyche.

How do psychological complexes manifest bodily?

One of the insights of psychotherapy concerns the ways in which body and psyche work together as a psychosomatic whole. To put this another way, we could say that the body expresses anxieties, stress and worries of which we are only partly aware. Indeed, it would be reasonable to extend this claim and to note that disruptions to the body's normal 'healthy' state are often indexical of underlying psychological complexes. In one sense there is nothing controversial or remarkable about this claim. Many of us know that our bodies tell us when we are under stress. We might not sleep well or have acid reflux problems; odd sensations such as numbness or headaches appear when we have anxiety-provoking situations to deal with. However, I want to take this a step further and suggest that this is not just a question of phenomenological observation, in which it becomes possible to notice how stomach pains coincide with, say, a particularly difficult time. Instead, I am suggesting that there are psychological mechanisms that tie together the unconscious and the physical response of our bodies. First, a caveat: I am not suggesting here that all illness has a psychological component or that all illness should be thought of psychologically. In working with clients who are exhibiting what I suspect may be psychosomatic symptoms I always get them to check for an underlying medical condition first. However, it is commonplace for clients to come back and report that while the consultant found something wrong, it certainly should not be causing this much pain. Alternatively, they might have been given a clean bill of health but they are still getting dizzy spells and such like. It seems that the reassurance of medical professionals does little to dispel the deep-rooted beliefs and anxieties which clients can find themselves gripped by and which can have disturbing physical manifestations.

The reasons for this are as yet uncertain but it appears that there is a greater degree of connectedness between the brain and the expression of emotions in our bodies than has previously been recognized. Margaret Wilkinson (2006) and Ginette Paris (2007) have written about this from a Jungian perspective. In particular the discovery of mirror neurons supports the view that our understanding of the world is mediated to us through the experience of our senses and the presence of affective and emotional states. This has some interesting implications for our understanding of the cinematic experience as it suggests that films have the capacity to activate these mirror neurons in a similar way to our experiences of actual people. Elsaesser and Hagener draw attention to this and in particular the opportunity it affords to develop a theory of the cinematic that is able to contain many of the existing dichotomies between realist theories and those with a more structural emphasis.

> What has attracted special attention was the discovery in the mid 1990s of so-called 'mirror neurons'.... For the body of the spectator this theory implies a total wiring between the senses and the processing of information by the brain: body–brain correlation, motor-sensory control, seeing and doing (when considered from the perspective of brain activity) become one and the same ... we have yet to see what kind of overall theory of the cinema and the film experience these new theories will deliver around mirror and face. Perhaps the old polarity between phenomenological-realist and discursive-constructivist theories can be overcome and replaced with a more comprehensive one.
>
> (Elsaesser and Hagener, 2010: 77–9)

For our purposes it is not necessary to pursue this argument in depth. However, what remains is the general principle that we need to understand the mind–body system holistically. The confirmations of neuroscience are significant in that they locate the neurological and physiological basis of the mechanisms which psychotherapy has been using for over a century. It is important to remember that Jung's archetypal hypothesis at its core postulates a psychosomatic unity. The basic idea is that just as there are biological mechanisms which regulate our body, so too there are psychological mechanisms or, as Jung tends to put it, 'structures'. This is not the place to go into the detail of how Jung's ideas on this point changed over time, and they have been well tracked and explored by others, not least by Andrew Samuels (1985), who offers a clinically orientated perspective, and Sonu Shamdasani (2003), who adopts a more historical point of view. My argument here is that to understand the psychological aspects of the cinematic experience we need to develop a holistic and somatic approach, which is why the following two points are particularly important. First, Jung emphasized the importance of the interconnectedness of mind and body in a manner that suggests that bodily symptoms indicate the existence of psychological complexes. Second, Jung noticed how these mechanisms, which he termed 'archetypes', aim to keep the psyche in a reasonably balanced and well-adapted state. The exact nature of this state varies from person to person, and one of the insights of the Jungian therapeutic method lies in its attempt to help clients become who they are in the face of the normative behaviours and expectations of families, friends and society. This is what Jung called the 'individuation process' and it entails living life as the person you are while at the same time accepting that we are always in a relationship with others and our culture at large. He puts it as follows:

> this process [individuation] follows the natural course of life – a life in which the individual becomes what he always was. Because man has consciousness, a development of this kind does not run very smoothly; often it is varied and disturbed, because consciousness deviates again and again from its archetypal, instinctual foundation and finds itself in opposition to it. There then arises the need for a synthesis of the two positions. This amounts to psychotherapy…
>
> (Jung, 1935/54: para. 84)

It follows that one of the tasks of psychotherapy is work with a person as a whole (mind and body) and entering into a dialogic process. Significantly, Jung emphasizes that this cannot be just a rational process but requires a real 'coming to terms' with one's unconscious (ibid., para. 85). When the mind–body system gets disrupted the result can be physical manifestations. Anne Maguire is among a group of Jungian analysts who have written about the somatic manifestations of unconscious contents. In *Skin Disease: A Message from the Soul* (2004) she writes from her joint perspective as an analyst and a Fellow of the Royal College of Physicians to explore how our skin can manifest deep psychological disturbances in the form of eczema, psoriasis, alopecia and other dermatological symptoms. You might have concluded from this that the psyche is not an entirely benign force, and indeed that *is* Jung's position. However, he was also clear that our best course of action is to pay attention to the unconscious and in so doing 'hold' or 'contain' the contradictions that are inherent to life in a manner that is productive rather than destructive.

At this point you might well be wondering how this relates to the cinematic experience. The answer can be found in the observation that the presence of archetypes is characterized by intense, unlooked-for affect in which we suddenly find ourselves behaving in an emotional manner that our rational minds cannot seem to explain. My suggestion is that this type of bodily affective response to films is a key part of the cinematic experience. Just as therapy offers the opportunity to reflect on aspects of our lives that we find troubling or puzzling, so too the intense affective responses we have to films provide an opportunity to reflect on the connections between what is happening on the screen and what is happening in our lives. This type of affect is also central to the meanings that we find in films; it characterizes the unconscious relationship we have with films and shows the role our own complexes have in the meanings we find in the cinematic experience.

In order to explore this more fully we need to introduce another piece of 'therapy thinking' that in this case comes from the clinical writing around the processes of transference and countertransference that take place in therapy. Using these ideas, I am going to suggest that the way therapists conceive of meaning making in therapy can be applied to the cinema and that in very broad terms we can regard the client–therapist dyad as something of an analogue of the viewer–screen relationship.

Does therapy thinking around transference and countertransference help to understand the psychological relationship viewers have with films?

The therapeutic dyad is one of the central elements of psychodynamic psychotherapy. Much has been written about how it effects and facilitates psychological change. The focus of that writing is concerned with how emotion is constellated, embodied and then used to inform the work of therapy. I am going to suggest that this piece of psychotherapy thinking can be used to inform the relationship that viewers have with the screen and that it is one way to understand the psychology of the cinematic experience. As we have seen, psychoanalytic theories of the cinema tend to emphasize the structural relationships between psychological processes and cinematic structures, both in terms of the construction of a film and in how this allows viewers to identify with or to engage with it. Instead, I want to foreground an insight from the practice of psychotherapy: psychological meaning is something that is co-created between client and therapist and these meanings are not fixed or universal. Rather, they are transitory, shifting, sometimes hard to grasp and deeply felt: often they are embodied. If we apply this to the cinema then the site of psychological meaning shifts away from the film towards the individual and the personal relationship we have with films.

In contemporary psychotherapy the central importance of the therapeutic dyad is well established. Indeed some research shows that the quality of this relationship is more important than the type of psychotherapy that is being practised, or even the experience of the therapist (cf. Cooper, 2008). However, the relationship has not always been regarded as quite so important. Indeed, today there persists in certain quarters, which are normally medically orientated, the belief that therapy is something which a therapist does to a patient. From this point of view there are assessments, diagnoses, manuals of treatment and so forth. Probably the best known of these orientations is cognitive behavioural therapy (CBT). In reality CBT is a broad church and in its more sophisticated and developed aspects allows for the change of complex and deeply held systems of personal belief and behaviours. This is termed schema change and in principle at least is as involved and relationship-based as other forms of psychotherapy. It aims to change core processes and correct mistaken ways of understanding the world, and, in so doing, to restructure the scheme by which we organize the world and our role in it. However, much CBT does not adopt this approach. Instead, some CBT consists of techniques which are taught to practitioners, and which are subsequently passed on to patients. Let me reiterate that this type of therapy has its role, uses and can be effective for clients, but it is not psychotherapy as there is no 'psyche' in the processes. Indeed the same point of view pervades much contemporary psychiatry, where the treatment is likely to be drug-based. These comments should not be taken to suggest that procedures such as CBT have no role whatsoever in maintaining psychological health; rather, I am suggesting that they are not in and of themselves psychotherapeutic.

Interestingly one of the recent developments in cognitive behavioural therapy has been the emergence of mindfulness (mindful cognitive behavioural therapy MCBT). I give this particular example as it indicates clearly how just 'doing' something to a patient is not enough. It suggests that the therapeutic relationship, and the way the body encodes psychological messages, have a central role to play in therapy. What I want to stress is a view which most schools of psychotherapy hold to: namely, that the therapeutic relationship is the kernel of psychological insight, and it is this which holds and propels the work of psychotherapy. You will infer from this that I am going to suggest that a focus on the model of the therapeutic dyad can helpfully be transplanted from the consulting room to the world at large. In doing so, the intention is to help us understand more generally how meanings are created and, in particular, to show how the therapeutic dyad provides the basis upon which a psychological understanding of the cinematic experience can be predicated.

Centrality of the relationship as 'healing'

Jung was certainly aware of the importance of the relationship between psychotherapist and patient, and its determining role on the therapy. To put it extremely simply, Freud tended to regard the analyst as something of an informed expert, a consultant if you like, to whom patients went in order to be cured of their symptoms. The analyst was privy to expert information regarding how the symptoms could be understood, how dreams could be interpreted and the meaning behind parapraxis, the now famous 'Freudian slip'. That said, he acknowledged that the unconscious of the analyst could play a role in analysis, hence the requirement that new analysts should themselves be analysed before treating patients: a dictum that continues today to be a common requirement in schools of psychotherapy.

Jung went further and put the therapeutic relationship at the very centre of psychotherapy. For Jung, the psychotherapist was not to be thought of as a repository of expert knowledge whose role was to explain to the patient the aetiology of his or her symptoms, rather he was to be right there, 'in' the therapy, as we might put it. If Freud wanted his patients to free associate as a means through which to bypass the defences of consciousness, then Jung wanted his patients to be in dialogue with him. Dialogue suggests something which is two-sided and which is much closer to a meeting of equals. It certainly suggests that the therapy is as likely to influence and affect the psychotherapist as the patient. Jung was not an advocate of silence on the part of the analyst, rather he wanted a dialogic engagement. He puts it like this:

> The intelligent psychotherapist has known for years that any complicated treatment is an individual, *dialectical* process, in which the doctor, as a person, participates just as much as the patient. In any such discussion the question of whether the doctor has as much insight into his own psychic processes as he expects from his patient naturally counts for a very great deal, particularly in regard to the 'rapport', or relationship of mutual confidence, on which the therapeutic success ultimately depends. The patient, that is to say, can win his own inner security only from the security of his relationship to the doctor as a human being.
>
> (Jung, 1951: para. 239; original italics)

Or, put more concisely, 'The personality of the patient demands all the resources of the doctor's personality and not technical tricks' (Jung, 1934b: para. 338). The process of psychotherapy as Jung conceived it is not just an intellectual process. As he neatly summarizes, the whole personality of the doctor is needed, which is to say the whole of the doctor is needed including: intellect, feeling, intuition, creativity, imagination, empathy, care and, of course, the container and vessel for all these elements, the body. We might sum this up by noting that what is needed during each therapy session is the complete 'presence' of the doctor in relationship with the patient.

It also follows from this that the interpretation of a client's material is something that, while validated by the client, arises as a result of the relationship. This marks quite a shift from the position of classical Freudian psychoanalysis with its focus on the expert analyst. Of course, it is also the case that in Jungian-orientated work the psychotherapist brings their expertise to bear in the matter of interpretation. But Jung also stresses that the psychotherapist must not impose an interpretation, as this would be to force the intellect of the psychotherapist on the client. Instead, meaning is something that is brought into being as part of the psychotherapeutic relationship. That said, Jung also struggles with combining the idea of personal interpretation with the collective aspects of images, so he also has a tendency to find in some images collective, trans-historical and trans-cultural meanings. However, the intention is that these benefit from being put to one side, bracketed if you prefer. While acknowledging their significance they should not be allowed to over-determine the interpretation of the client's material. For Jung, therapy as a hermeneutic activity stresses the subjectivity of interpretation of meaning and he regards it as a joint activity. He put it as follows:

> Understanding is clearly a very subjective process. It can be extremely one-sided, in that the doctor understands but not the patient. In such a case the doctor conceives it to be his duty to convince the patient, and if the latter will not allow himself to be convinced, the doctor accuses him of resistance. When the understanding is all on my side, I say quite calmly that I do not understand, for in the end it makes very little difference whether the doctor understands or not, but it makes all the difference whether the patient understands. Understanding should therefore be understanding in the sense of an agreement which is the fruit of joint reflection.
>
> (Jung, 1934a: para. 314)

One of the contributions of this psychotherapeutic clinical theory is to suggest that meaning does not lie just in the 'text', the dream, words, creative act or what we might call the narrative of the client. Rather, psychological meaning is altogether more personal, individual or, to use Jung's preferred term, subjective. Here we have a clear statement of how the production of meaning differs in the humanities and in clinical work. The task of the scholar undertaking the interpretation of a book, a film, a piece of poetry or even a work of art is to stick as closely to the text as possible. For example, in my training I was taught to look at interactions within films, lighting, the use of sound, camera framing and movement, editing, the construction of the narrative and all those other elements of the film that are encoded with meaning. I was never once encouraged to bring my own sense of my psychology, my own feelings or personal responses to understand a film, although I was reprimanded on a couple of occasions for doing so! That said, there are a few instances where cultural theory has stressed the importance of the reader in the act of interpretation, and Roland Barthes's article 'The Death of the Author' (in Barthes, 1977) is one such example. Cinephilia too is no longer consider a mere amateurish interest in movie trivia but is now more widely accepted as a form of engagement with cinematic experience and film culture.

Influenced by the cautious and scholarly approach, Jungian literary theorists such as Terence Dawson have also advocated a procedural approach to the text in which close textual reading is privileged. There is much of merit in his excellent article 'Jung, Literature, and Literary Criticism' (1997) in which he suggests moving away from reductionist interpretations and what he regards as a disproportionate emphasis that can be placed on particular symbols or actions.

> Jungian literary criticism seeks to explore the *possible* psychological implications of the literary text.... the need (a) to establish 'whose' experience is reflected in a narrative fiction, and (b) to view *all* of its events as a representation of a dilemma facing this character.
>
> (Dawson, 1997: 256; original italics)

The implication of this is that it becomes important to be attentive to all events, and hence images too, as a psychological literary reading attempts to mass them up into a single coherent interpretation. Indeed, this is one reasonable and useful way to proceed in a psychological manner with literary texts and it is a scholarly and aesthetically sensitive mode of investigation. However, for me it does not seem to account adequately for the role of the reader in *making* meaning. It instead requires a sort of psychological archaeology in which the various layers of the text need to be carefully excavated as each recovered item is catalogued before a tentative explanation is suggested – as Dawson cautions, before examining the 'possible' psychological implications. But the psyche when it makes meaning does not respect such gentle conventions. Once again, I want to again privilege the role of affect and the body. I would certainly agree with Dawson that when it comes to the negotiation of personal meanings with texts (be they literary or filmic), oftentimes readers do not respond to the key literary or filmic symbols or images. Instead it can be a tiny detail that ignites the affective response.

One of the ways I have learnt to work as a psychotherapist, and my training encouraged this, is bring my own hunches, intuitions, the emotions in my body and the thoughts which spontaneously enter my mind and to reflect on whether these might be helpful in understanding what my clients are trying to tell me. I ask myself, why this image? Why now? How does it relate to the client's history? How does it relate to the client's present life? In doing so I am attempting to locate the image both synchronically (contextually in the here and now) and diachronically, in light of the narrative of the client. In doing this I will consider social, cultural and historical factors. I certainly would not want this approach to be thought of as suggesting the primacy and isolation of the unconscious as the sole location of meaning and insight. Far from it, as what I am advocating is more of a matrix but one in which we see psychological meaning as far more constructed and negotiated than is often realized. Developing this appreciation of the cinematic experience and its psychological meaning involves shifting our attention away from the text onto our affective responses.

Before we do so we need one further piece of theory that was originally developed in clinical psychotherapy. Communication in therapy takes place in a number of simultaneous ways. First there is the communication between the conscious of the therapist and of the client; next there is communication from the conscious of the client to the unconscious of the therapist and vice versa; third there is communication from the unconscious of the client to the consciousness of the therapist, and again vice versa; and finally there is communication at an unconscious level between client and therapist. The result of this is what might be thought of as a force field of communication or a communication matrix in which at any one time each party is only partly aware, or conscious, of the meaning of what is happening between the two of them. Hopefully, the therapist is somewhat more aware than the client, although we must allow for the possibility that this may not in every instance be the case. As you can probably imagine, this situation presents quite a challenge for psychotherapists as it becomes important to correctly identify if a particular feeling or thought relates to the client's material or the therapist's, or possibly both. The activation of a therapist's unconscious complexes is termed countertransference. Sometimes it is easy to recognize, at other times it evades our best endeavours to pin it down, hence one of the reasons why supervision is so important for psychotherapists. Leaving this to one side for a moment, this suggests another way in which meaning arises not just from the 'text' (which in this case is the material of the client) but also from the therapist's reactions and that this meaning might be related to his or her unconscious material.

I want to pause for a moment and consider this idea of countertransference as it provides a helpful way for understanding some of the responses, both intellectual and emotional, that we can have in the cinema. When I am in a psychotherapy session I am sometimes struck by those moments where I find myself saying something seemingly instinctively and often rather too quickly after my client has finished speaking. I notice these times for several reasons. One is that it is my practice to be as thoughtful and considered in what I say as possible. I try quite intentionally to bring my full presence, awareness and intellectual capability in offering something back to the client with the sincere desire that it will be therapeutically helpful. Alongside such considered interventions are those moments when I notice how I can be emotionally moved, sometimes very strongly, and I know why I am having this response. Such moments normally relate to a point of contact between what my client is saying and something that has happened in my own life. These moments of affect enable empathy, care and understanding and I spent quite a lot of time in my training recognizing them and learning to work with them. However, there are those other moments where I am not quite sure why I feel the need to react so quickly and sometimes somewhat incisively. I know these to be my countertransference moments, and on reflection I can often get some purchase or understanding on what was happening between the client and myself. They are strong, laden with affect and often stem from an amplification of what the client has been saying. They are seemingly instinctive and bodily.

If we now shift our attention to the cinema we can probably call to mind films where we have been profoundly moved, or disturbed, elated or perhaps intensely anxious, while others in the audience seemed quite unmoved. I remember one such response to a film which I had found compelling and deeply disturbing while the person I was with by contrast found it boring. I am suggesting here that one of the ways that the cinematic experience works psychologically is by enabling our own countertransference. We have what is a quite irrational response to what we experience in the cinema. Of course, we need to distinguish between the conscious, thoughtful response to a film that actually is disturbing (a parallel to my thoughtful psychotherapeutic interventions) and this altogether more irrational, unpredictable and unlooked-for response. These moments provide us with a great opportunity for personal reflection and insight. They are also quite similar to the way that my clients often talk about films as part of their therapy. Very often they find the film gives them an emotional reaction that may well be odds with the 'actual' or consensual meaning of the film. I recall a male client who found himself crying while watching *Mamma Mia!* (2008), not because of the narrative of the film but instead because he had suddenly realized that he was *never* going to be a father. This film is not about not being a father; actually it is partly about the opposite, as the central character tries to figure out which one of three possible men actually is her father. So the narrative meaning of the film is about the search for a father; my client found in his experience of the film a recognition of the reality that he was never going to be father. If you will, the film activated a father complex in him and much of our work together subsequently involved exploring how his relations, particularly at work, involved unconsciously playing out this previously hidden desire in him; how the workplace became a sort of family in which he assumed a parental role.

What does this suggest about the body–screen relationship?

The way people talk about films in therapy tells us something important about the psychological qualities of the cinematic experience. It quite radically shifts meaning away from the film itself and regards it as something that is negotiated with the film. Sometimes this negotiation takes place at an unconscious level. When it does so, we can be moved by a film in ways that seem surprising to the rational and conscious part of ourselves. On such occasions our bodily responses can be particularly acute, and outside our control. One way to access this type of emotional encoding is through a broadly phenomenological mode, in which we focus on what is happening and in so doing bring the subtle and more marked qualities of the affective response to the conscious parts of ourselves.

However, where I am parting company with the phenomenological mode is that I also want to leave room for the unconscious as an aspect of ourselves that has agency and purpose. This might not surprise psychotherapists as in psychodynamic therapy it is a given that unconscious forces are at work in shaping both the meaning of the conversations we have in therapy and in the felt sense of both client and therapist. Yet film theory is just beginning to come to terms with this possibility. Certainly, cinema theory has been strongly interested in psychoanalysis and in particular its Lacanian variation. As we have seen, this explored the parallels between the internal construction and operation of the unconscious and the mechanisms of cinema. However, from this position meaning is either constructed within the film text itself, or eludes an attempt to locate it more exactly. In this respect, the subjectivity of the self is mirrored in the way that films simultaneously both cohere and fragment.

What I am proposing is somewhat different, namely that the psychological meaning of a film *is* something that is accessible to us. However, that meaning is not fixed or inscribed. Nor is it solely constructed through a network of intertextual signifiers, though they clearly do play a role. Instead I am proposing that we displace the film, so that it no longer takes centre stage, while letting it remain important. In rather the same way the meaning of a dream is not inscribed in its narrative or imagery and is negotiated, or co-constructed, as the client and therapist work together to understand its significance – not the significance of the narrative or imagery of the dream per se but the significance of the meaning that the client finds in the dream. If we approach films and the cinematic experience more generally like this we end up with a perspective on them that requires a new and psychological view of how being-in-the-cinema and being-in-the-world parallel each other. The film theorist Thomas Elsaesser puts it like this:

> Our initial premise of asking film theory to tell us how film and cinema relate to the body and the senses thus may well lead to another question (which we shall not answer here), namely whether – when putting the body and senses at the centre of film theory – the cinema is not proposing to us, besides a new way of knowing the world, also a new way of 'being in the world', and thus demanding from film theory, next to a new epistemology also a new ontology. This, one could argue, is quite an achievement, when one considers how film theory might be said to have 'started' in the seventeenth century as a technical description of movement in/of images, and now – provisionally – ends as a form of film philosophy and in this respect as a general theory of movement: of bodies, of affect, of the mind and the senses.
>
> (Elsaesser and Hagener, 2010: 12)

Of course, Elsaesser and Hagener are right in regarding the way in which cinema seems to propose a new way of understanding how we are in the world as 'quite an achievement'. Yet Jungians might well regard this as less surprising, as one of the insights of the Jungian position concerns the centrality of the image as a meaning-making aspect of the psyche. The translation of a psychic process into a mechanical one was of course by no means necessarily going to retain its initial psychological qualities. Indeed, in the previous chapter we explored some of the pitfalls inherent in such a move. What is striking, however, is the success and longevity of narrative film and I want to suggest that this is partly, but only partly, due to the psychological quality of its image-based narrative form. Freud was alert to the ways in which the analytic process has a tendency to narrativize. At first he was puzzled as to why the scientific accounts of his treatment of patients read more like literature than like an academic paper. His use of medical terminology now reads like a post-modern account in which over-elaboration and deliberate adoption of a particular authorial voice serve both to cover and to reveal the constructed nature of the narrative. This is common in accounts of therapy both as they are told outside the consulting room and, no less, as they are created within its boundaries.

Narrative form and therapeutic enquiry are in a reflexive relationship with each other as though at this cultural point it seems we need a narrative to make sense of our lives. Yet structuralist, semiotic and Lacanian theories remind us that narratives do not hold meaning. There is something of vital importance in this observation about the essential emptiness of narrative and narrative film in particular, as it is this very emptiness that allows for the projection of unconscious contents as a means through which to fill these gaps. If the meaning of a narrative is closed, clear and entirely self-contained, there would be no space available for psychological meaning. As Jung reminded us, it is in the non-psychological novel that we can find the most opportunities for psychological insights, and this also applies to cinema. In these more open narrative (or less psychologically encoded) films, we find that there is more space for the reflexive interplay between the individual and the text and between conscious and unconscious, and it is hard to imagine a space more tightly constructed to allow for such interplay than the therapeutic encounter.

But it is also the case that as well as its narrative form, cinema has found a way of constructing the cinematic in a manner that is particularly conducive to a psychological rendition. Rather than seeing this as a work of translation from the inner world to the cinematic experience, it is more helpfully repositioned as an on-going activity – as a constant coming into being as the involvement of the unconscious with the film shifts the meaning of any narrative. The Jungian idea of individuation, in which we are in a state of becoming fully ourselves, demonstrates how a fluidity of meaning that is neither fixed nor firm is central to Jungian psychology. From this it follows that our own subjectivity and sense of who we are in the world is not static or permanent. Rather it is through our relationships and through our experiences that we become more aware of who we are, even if such insights are partial and relate primarily to the present moment. Cinema provides a defined and imaginative space within which to experience how the fluidity of text and the ebb and flow of unconscious processes can let us explore the central problems of life. It is in the mainstream of narrative films that the unconscious finds an opportunity to present itself, to move us and to affect us. The frame of cinema, its screen and characters are the equivalent of the therapeutic frame, the aspects that as customer or client lie beyond our control. Importantly these two types of frame exist together. Just as to screen is both to make something visible and to protect against it, so too the frame both contains the image and extends beyond the physical limits of the screen to include its viewers; here the psychological frame of the cinematic experience encompasses the auditorium and in so doing provides the potential for psychologically transformative space.

4

BEING MINDFUL OF THE IMAGE

The psychodynamic and the cinematic

At the core of mindfulness is the practice of bringing one's attention to bear on the present moment so that a heightened sense of awareness is achieved. In recent years it has become an increasingly popular and attractive therapy, to the extent that mindfulness is now part of the therapeutic repertoire of cognitive behavioural therapy (Mindfulness-Based Cognitive Therapy – MBCT). It is regularly used by some integrative psychotherapists, and also in existential psychotherapy as described in the previous chapter. The roots of MBCT are in meditative practice and also in phenomenology. This chapter explores how the act of bringing awareness in a focused way into the present moment is not unlike the process of watching a film, where a complex but singular source of light and sound demands the audience's full attention. The suggestion is that the very act of watching a film and of establishing a felt relationship with the screen can be psychologically beneficial. This is especially the case if, as part of the cinematic experience, a 'mindful awareness' is brought to the process. Finally, the chapter will explore if there are parallels between meditative states and watching a film. This is another way of approaching one of the themes which threads its way throughout this book, namely that the experience of the cinema screen can stimulate an affective reaction in the viewer that is personally meaningful. This release of affect is the result of the activation, or expression, of a personal complex – i.e. a part of ourselves of which we are not fully consciously aware. Such affect is meaningful to the extent that the 'intended' meaning of a film is overridden by the new personal meaning that has been found. This is intrinsic to the cinematic experience as a whole, rather than just the aural and ocular act of listening and watching. As it is an unconscious process we are not always aware of the ways in which the individual act of making meaning is taking place. However, it is possible to see this process at work because, if we are attentive to the subtle ways we respond emotionally to films, this reveals how their meaning is actually much more individual than common sense might suggest. While there is certainly something collective, psychological and shared in films (which we might term archetypal) the meaning that we as individuals find in films is personal – though it will of course have shared aspects. The tension between filmic structure and image and between personal and collective is one of the central aspects of Jungian psychology and the cinematic experience replicates these aspects. One of the ideas behind mindfulness is that the meaning of a situation will present itself not in thoughts but as an embodied felt sense of the situation. Perhaps by attending to the reactions of our body when we view a film we might be able to get a more rounded view of what it means for us.

What is mindfulness?

In the UK, mindfulness is now part of CBT, which is among the most widely known of all contemporary therapeutic modalities. Certainly in the UK the first course of psychological therapy that a general practitioner (medical doctor) is likely to offer a patient will be a short, six-week course of CBT, probably delivered by one of the new range of mental health workers trained as part of the national programme for increasing access to psychological therapies (IAPT). It is important not to underestimate the size of this development, which in the UK has seen the training of around 3,000 CBT therapists, often in intensive six-month, or year-long, on-the-job programmes at a cost of several million pounds. CBT sets out to challenge 'automatic negative thoughts' and irrational behaviours and beliefs by 'reprogramming' the brain so that clients have more proportionate responses to life's difficulties. Broadly speaking, there have been three stages in the development of CBT, of which mindfulness forms the final part. The first stage of CBT was established by Aaron Beck in the 1960s. A psychoanalytically trained psychiatrist, Beck was nonetheless dissatisfied with his treatment of patients, particularly those with depression. As a researcher he set up a series of experiments to test the psychoanalytic approach and surprised himself by finding that it was somewhat ineffective. From this basis he developed other ways of conceptualizing depression and the negative thoughts that patients had. Beck discovered that these negative thoughts were related to the core beliefs that we hold about ourselves. This takes us to the second stage of CBT where the focus is on changing those core beliefs or 'schema'. Perhaps the best-known person working in this field (with Beck) is Christine Padesky, whose book *Mind over Mood* (1995) is something of a classic.

I mention this because mindfulness-based CBT exists in a rather different tradition, in fact one that is so different that its association with CBT is rather puzzling. Those with a psychodynamic orientation might be tempted to see this development as something of a compensatory function, in which the systemic, and rational or cognitive approach of CBT needs something more intuitive or non-rational to enter the therapy, stemming as it does from the client's own interior creative and imaginative qualities. MCBT is also predicated on the idea that the individual does not need therapy 'done to them'. Rather, by adopting a mindful approach to life, the mind's innate capacity for healing can be used and this is accompanied by a shift in awareness and orientation.

What, then, does mindfulness entail? Unfortunately it is not easy to give a straightforward answer to this question. Jon Kabat-Zinn and his colleagues at the medical school at the University of Massachusetts developed mindfulness-based approaches to therapy and stress reduction in the late 1970s. Their approach can be summarized as one that helps clients to develop a non-judgemental awareness in the present moment. Behind this simple phrase lies a substantial body of research and theory. Often mindfulness locates its origins in the teaching of the Buddha but in fact what is emphasized in this therapy is a mindful awareness of thoughts, feelings and your body, the world and others in it.

Several key ideas inform this orientation. First is that mind and body are interconnected and form a single interlocked system. This idea certainly has resonances with the insights which are currently being made in neuroscience and also in other more popular and clinical writing such as Gerd Gigerenzer's *Gut Feelings* (2007) and Love and Sterling's *What's Behind your Belly Button?* (2011). In becoming more mindful of what one is feeling, thinking and experiencing the intention is to gain a greater insight and awareness of one's own cognitive processes. As such, mindfulness can be thought of as a metacognitive process. What seems to happen is that as we become increasingly aware of what the mind–body is experiencing it becomes more possible to adopt a proportionate emotional response to a given situation. Here's an example. Yesterday at the university where I work a colleague of mine missed a deadline for getting some paperwork into the faculty administration centre. This was a funding bid to attend a conference. Suddenly he realized he was not going to be able to attend this conference, that he would not give his paper, that his appraisal targets would not be met and that almost certainly he would be out of a job before the year was over. As he told me this story, he explained that his head was pounding, his heart was racing and he felt exhausted. A more mindful approach might have made him aware that giving this paper meant a lot to him, and that he was probably not the only academic to be late with his paperwork. Further, conference organizers want people to attend their conferences, and often there is quite a bit of flexibility about deadlines. As for performance appraisal, his bosses probably didn't even know he was giving the paper. An alternative approach would have involved realizing the importance of the conference, noticing that he often feels overly judged by others and taking some time to sit down and engage in some mindful breathing and bodily awareness. Behaving in this manner involves a type of 'reperceiving' or what in psychotherapeutic circles is sometimes termed 'reframing'. Mindfulness promotes an attitude in which we adopt a kindly inquisitiveness about our own selves. By contrast the depth psychotherapeutic approach would be concerned with where my colleague had learnt to behave in this manner, why his world feels so fragile, and what the role of these responses was in maintaining his inner world. Mindfulness does not directly ask the question, why? Instead it notices what is happening, right now, at this moment in time, in the present.

In particular mindfulness notices how the body continually encodes, or responds emotionally to, life's difficulties. Hence mindfulness training often devotes a considerable amount of time to developing an awareness of our patterns of breathing. In doing so, it becomes possible to pay attention to minute changes in the temperature of breath, to notice the tiny sensations in the nostrils and so forth. A standard exercise involves the body scan which is a similar process but this time it extends from the breath to develop an awareness of the whole body. These exercises typically take between twenty and thirty minutes. Another of the canonical exercises of MCBT is the raisin experiment. Here the participants are encouraged to be aware of the detail of their bodily sensations as they first hold a raisin, then look at it, then smell, place, taste, chew, swallow and finally become aware of the taste of the raisin. It is a simple exercise but it often awakens quite a variety of memories, experiences, images and associations. The 'experiment' demonstrates how meaning is the result of both a collective and a shared experience and the associations that are personal. It shows how the body can both encode such understandings and also act as a means through which to gain access to them. People who undertake a mindful practice regularly report feeling less anxious, less susceptible to intense mood swings, more able to notice, accept and deal with strong emotions. There is also a body of evidence that suggests the usefulness of a mindful approach to dealing with depression (Williams *et al.*, 2007).

Being aware of the mind–body system and in particular of how it embodies emotional responses is helpful to our sense of who we are and how we are in the world. To transfer this insight to the cinema suggests a way of understanding what happens when we watch a film. The experience is rather like what Jungians understand by the creation of an 'image' – a metaphorical constellation of the felt sense of a current of experience that is encapsulated in a moment of intuition or imagination. The cinema offers the opportunity for a rather heightened sense of this experience. For all the reasons that we have explored in previous chapters, the cinema acts as a psychic lens, focusing our psychological awareness onto the film and into ourselves. If we elect to adopt a mindful approach we can, with relative ease, shift our attention to what our bodies are experiencing. This provides a mindful way to befriend our emotions, bringing them into awareness and becoming more fully aware of how the whole of our mind–body system is reacting to them.

We will consider this in more detail once we have explored how mindfulness can usefully be connected to elements of Jungian psychology. This will let us synthesize these two differing perspectives with the intention of understanding how the combination of a non-judgemental approach to our experiences can helpfully infuse a Jungian approach in which the unconscious is constituted with agency and purpose. This is a good point at which to underscore the following. Just as mindfulness does not presuppose a correct or right response to a situation, so it is that the unconscious response to a situation will vary from person to person. While Jung wrote about the unconscious as though it was a single entity in its own right, he also stressed the importance of each individual working out his or her unique path in life. Jungian psychology attempts to hold together in a productive and creative tension a number of seemingly incompatible positions. This is another of those tensions in which Jung suggests the unconscious is personal and collective, actual and metaphorical, essentialist and culturally/socially constructed.

How does mindfulness relate to Jungian psychology?

Without doubt Jung was attracted to the Orient and specifically to what he thought was a particularly spiritual and intuitive approach to life. This is not the place to go into questions of Jung's possible Orientalism. Rather, what I want to note is a tension that runs through Jung's ideas that is derived from an intuitive attraction that was based on what amounts to a fantasy about the Orient. It arose as a consequence of Jung's attempt to find out where myth and the unconscious were thriving in contemporary societies. This was quite a problem for Jung as his radically conservative outlook on life meant that popular culture was excluded from his undertaking. In its place he was attracted to the ideas and practices of the Orient although he also asserted that they were not suitable for Europeans or Americans. Jung sought to identify what he rather problematically thought of as distinctive cultural qualities to which in turn he ascribed psychological attributes and benefits. As such, his view was that we cannot ignore our cultural heritage as it is also our psychological heritage. If we do, we will fail to connect to our unconscious. For Jung, this is a grievous error and one that might actually cause psychological harm. To take a couple of examples, he writes, 'But yoga in Mayfair or Fifth Avenue, or any other place which is on the telephone, is a spiritual fake' (1939/55: para. 802) and:

> There could be no greater mistake than for a Westerner to take up the direct practice of Chinese yoga, for that would merely strengthen his will and consciousness against the unconscious and bring about the very effect to be avoided. The neurosis would then simply be intensified.
>
> (Jung, 1929/57: para. 16)

While some Jungians might still subscribe to these notions I think they are best regarded as rather outmoded. But even so, this line of thought does direct us to something that is important for our understanding of the cinematic experience in terms of an embodied Jungian psychology. The insight that underpins Jung's comments is that rationality in and of itself is not enough to understand psychological life; if the complexities of life are to be understood then the intellect, while indispensable, is not enough. This idea has echoes in Oriental thought, in the allusion to something beyond the immediate grasp of consciousness and in holding and accepting contradictions in life. Jung's writing is full of this type of 'poetic' and expressive formulation. Here are a couple of examples to illustrate the point: 'The least of things with a meaning is always worth more in life than the greatest of things without it' (Jung, 1929/31: para. 96) and 'for in all chaos there is a cosmos, in all disorder a secret order, in all caprice a fixed law, for everything that works is grounded on its opposite' (Jung, 1935/54: para. 66).

For Jung, the idea of a secret hidden world stands as a metaphor for the relationship consciousness has with the unconscious. For him, wisdom lies in becoming aware of the unconscious and letting it do its work of individuation, of living life in an authentic and related fashion. Sometimes, as in the following passage, he suggests that all we need to do is to let the unconscious unfold in our conscious lives.

> The art of letting things happen, action through non-action, letting go of oneself as taught by Meister Eckhart, became for me the key that opens the door to the way. We must be able to let things happen in the psyche. For us, this is an art of which most people know nothing. Consciousness is forever interfering, helping, correcting, and negating, never leaving the psychic processes to grow in peace. It would be simple enough, if only simplicity were not the most difficult of all things.
>
> (Jung, 1929/57: para. 20)

Interestingly, of course in the cinema we are supposed to engage in the act of 'letting things happen'; after all, this is the purpose of the diegetic and narrative aspects of films. The construction of a film should go unnoticed, we should be unaware of how shot follows shot and of the use of non-diegetic music, and the life of characters off screen should go unnoticed. Instead, the structure of the film is designed to draw us into the on-screen world, 'stitching' us into its fabric. Just as with our dreams, we experience films as something that happens to us. Alternatively, we can elect to be more reflective about the experience and we can use films, just as we use dreams, as a means through which to understand ourselves. If dreams are personal first and collective second, then with films it is the other way around. Films are primarily collective products both in their production and reception but the meaning we find in them can also be personal.

While Jung did promote what might at first appear to be a somewhat passive approach to the process of individuation, at other times he stressed the opposite: that it was not enough just to let individuation happen and engaged response is required if we are to understand our inner lives more fully. Part of such an engagement is the experience of affect, the grip of some powerful emotion that indicates the activation of a complex. Similarly, the emotional response that we have to films provides a key indication that we are experiencing archetypal material which is associated with a personal complex. Jung's personal approach to working with these affect-laden psychological complexes can be seen in his *Red Book* (2009) which is a collection of his paintings, imaginative dialogues and musings in calligraphic script. These document his attempt to understand what was happening in his inner world and how his life was psychologically connected to the culture at large. That he used a creative process is no accident as this is a way to access the image-making and symbolic dimension to the psyche. What Jung was aiming for was to expand his conscious understanding of his own personal complexes through the use of creative activity. Jung realized that we want to understand our unconscious selves. Yet at the same time he knew that we are deeply resistant to any such understanding. The reason for this tension is that we believe that the dark side of ourselves contains frightening emotions and shameful thoughts and consequently it has be avoided and kept hidden. However, it is also important to acknowledge these darker aspects to our humanity and their recognition enables their assimilation into consciousness in a balanced fashion.

Interestingly, films provide one way for us to experience the aspects of the psyche which normally we find it necessary to repress and to conceal, including the darker sides of ourselves. For the various reasons we have already identified, in many ways the cinema is an ideal psychological container for strong emotional experiences and powerful unconscious fantasies. As such, it offers viewers the capacity to engage in an exploration of their psyches, much as Jung did with his *Red Book* processes. I am not suggesting that watching a film is the modern equivalent to the years of personal exploration and growth that Jung undertook. However, it remains the case that sometimes people want to talk about films in psychotherapy and they do so because they had an experience while watching a film that was psychologically important, and they want to understand it. If we ignore the psychological qualities of cinema, both personally and collectively, we are missing out on a way of understanding ourselves that has the potential to be enlightening. Jung referred to this increased awareness of who we are as an expansion of consciousness. By this he did not intend a New Age-type rhetoric in which somehow our consciousness was expanded to merge with the unseen mysteries of the universe. Perhaps unsurprisingly, some writers with New Age and mystical inclinations have taken him that way. The work of David Tacey (2001) helpfully redresses this situation. Rather, what Jung was suggesting was that as we become more conscious, so too we become more aware of who we are, secure in ourselves.

An idea that is closely related to this is that increases in consciousness allow the ego to strengthen. As such the ego is the centre of consciousness and has a rather different place in Jung's model of the psyche to the one proposed by Freud. In the way that Jung writes about the ego and consciousness it is difficult to differentiate the two. However, what remains significant is that for Jung consciousness is only ever partial and this means that aspects of our personality will elude understanding. The ego functions as a means through which to distinguish between what is me and what is not me, and it makes it possible to hold the opposition. In theoretical terms this ability to contain two opposing or differing emotions is referred to as the transcendent function. One of the difficulties with the model of the psyche that Jung proposed is that it is actually quite difficult to get a clear grasp of either the mechanisms of the ego or the structures of the unconscious. As Samuels *et al.* (1986: 51) note, 'The role of the ego is to discriminate opposites, withstand their tensions, allow them to be resolved and finally to protect what emerges, which will expand and enhance the previous limitations of ego.'

My contention is that films and the cinematic experience offer the opportunity to understand some of the structures and defences of the ego that normally remain hidden. This is not just a theoretical observation. Jungian theory regards the move towards self-awareness and the strengthening of the ego as the core of the life-long individuation process. Here I have in mind a particular client who, for reasons she did not understand, was attracted to and moved by films that depicted families and childhood in a rather romantic and innocent manner. Indeed, such films, which are normally regarded as somewhat sentimental feel-good films, would always reduce her to a state of uncontrollable sobbing. Yet, despite the predictability of these distressing feelings, she continued to seek out this type of film. In our sessions we came to understand that what touched her was the difference between her own childhood and these idealized representations. This provides us with a clear example of how a personal meaning can be found in a film in a way that is quite at odds with the one depicted by the film-maker. She was not drawn to movies like *Tree of Life* (2011), for example, which explore some of the darker and more primal aspects of growing up. Instead she seemed to need movies that portrayed a perfect childhood. We might say that she was in the grip of a child complex: the realization that there was something that had not matured in her, and that this was acceptable, was quite a relief for her. This insight enabled further reflection on her fantasies about the nature of childhood and for her to become more accepting of the nuanced nature of growing up. She came to accept that childhood is always a mixture of good and bad, light and dark, and that accepting this is actually an important step in preparing ourselves for adulthood. Put another way, she came to see that the incidents from her own childhood that she had believed were exceptional were actually quite a normal part of life. The child complex had done its work in bringing this awareness into consciousness and with a commensurate strengthening of the ego it allowed for a more complicated and accurate view of her own life, and of childhood more generally.

Why being mindful is relevant to an understanding of the viewer–screen relationship

This section of the chapter is going to look at some of the established ways in which psychoanalytically orientated film theory has sought to understand the viewer–film dyad. My intention is to identify some of the strengths of this approach while also noting its limitations. It will conclude by suggesting that a mindful approach is useful in foregrounding the personal relationship viewers have with films. It will tie this into a Jungian psychological view about how meaning is found and created in images and it will explore the role of images and personal meanings in the individuation process.

One of the key ways in which psychoanalytic film theory has sought to understand the viewer–screen relationship is through the idea of *suture*. We have touched on this earlier in the book but a short recap will prove helpful. In 1966

Jacques-Alain Miller (who was a student of Jacques Lacan) proposed the idea of *suture* as a way of formulating the relationship of a subject to his own discourse. The idea was to explore how the subject is produced through the relationship he has to language. Subsequently Jean-Pierre Oudart (1977–8) applied the idea to cinema and in particular to the films of Robert Bresson. His aim was to understand the relationship between the gaze of the viewer and the filmic discourse, in other words how the viewer (subject) is constructed through the structure (or 'language', we might say) of cinema.

Stephen Heath (1981) developed Oudart's position by noting how the editing of cinema, its framing and other acts of narration, both bind (stitch or *suture*) the viewer into the film and also, as shot follows shot, fracture the illusion of momentary wholeness and cohesion. This point of view sits neatly alongside the work of Christian Metz (1982), who notes the illusiveness of the signification of cinema, the relationship between film and dreams, and the cinematic gaze as a parallel for the child's look onto the primal scene. One of the strengths of Heath's approach is that it allows for the construction of the subject both in relation to the screen and also in off-screen space. In other words, the position of the viewer is constructed both in relation to the film itself and to the world outside the film. However, Metz and Heath do not allow for individual unconscious processes. Instead, they focus on the general mechanisms of the unconscious and the techniques and technology of cinema as a means through which to develop a generalized theory of how the subject (viewer) is constructed in relation to cinema.

A variation of this idea is found in Mulvey's now ubiquitous article 'Visual Pleasure and Narrative Cinema' (1975), mentioned in the previous chapter. In this piece she argues that the narrative construction of classic Hollywood cinema is predicated on a male gaze. The function of the shot and of editing is to segment the female body and offer it up as a series of dissected body parts for the pleasure of its male spectators. This suggests that there is a sadistic pleasure in the act of looking, and that pleasure in control and dismemberment is central to the appeal of these films. Of course, I am simplifying her argument but the gist of it is that male pleasure in the cinema is sadistically motivated and patriarchally sanctioned – it serves to perpetuate traditional gendered discourses of power and the tools of psychoanalysis can be used to reveal this hidden discourse. The article is rightly regarded as one of the core texts of psychoanalytic film theory. However as numerous commentators have made clear, and as Mulvey herself acknowledges, the contention is problematic. Not least of the many challenges that the article raises is the question of female pleasure in the cinema, something which Mulvey attempted to address in a subsequent article (1981), arguably with less success. However, once again Mulvey, like Heath, Metz and Oudart, negates the role of the individual in the construction of their own sense of self and their subjectivity. Instead, they concentrate on the mechanisms of cinema, and on cultural and ideological processes. Indeed, Mulvey acknowledges that her project is not a psychological one and that she has appropriated the tools of psychoanalysis as a 'political weapon'. Metz is somewhat less overtly political but again the viewer is treated as a universal given and not afforded space through which to construct or negotiate a personal relationship. To be fair, he does acknowledge this particularly when he is attempting to see how an understanding of the relationship between films and dreams can be illuminating. But, nonetheless, the lack of a personal aspect remains.

Put another way, what is missing in all these theories is a sense of relationship with the cinematic. Instead, films and cinema are positioned as something that viewers experience and as something that is done to them in which their participation is limited to generalized and somewhat universal processes. Of course, films position viewers in certain ways, structurally they encode psychological motifs in a particular manner (castration, the scopic, power, sadistic pleasure, etc.). While these theories do allow for a limited degree of personal interaction there is little room for a personal psychological relationship with film, and certainly there is no talk of it. Instead, the structures of cinema dominate its unconscious signifying practices.

There are examples of more personal writing about films such as Madelon Sprengnether's book *Crying at the Movies* (2002) and Geoff Dyer's *Zona* (2012). Their rather different views of Tarkovsky's films *Solaris* (1972) *and Stalker* (1979) are instrumental in showing how diverse our personal relationships with films can be. Dyer writes at length and in compelling manner about *Stalker*. His cultural and intellectual associations are interspersed with a variety of personal details, ephemera and speculations. It makes for a fascinating account of his life with the film. Sprengnether found *Solaris* caused her to have vivid and powerful dreams and that it was also sexually stimulating. To these accounts I can add another Tarkovksy anecdote – I was having lunch with a writer on Jung and cinema who mentioned to me that he had started to watch *Stalker* but that no other film had him reaching so quickly for the remote control to fast-forward (I'm not sure he actually got as far as the colour sequence). I mention these different responses because they neatly illustrate the diversity of responses that we can have to films that traditional psychoanalytic theory fails to account for. Neither Sprengnether's nor Dyer's book is a work of film theory, except in the most general use of the term, and neither sets out to be. They are, instead, personal accounts of either a single film or, as in Sprengnether's book, a range of films that had been personally and profoundly moving and important in her life. So despite the value of such books there is still room for a more formal psychology of the cinema which both accounts for collective psychological processes and responses, and can accommodate the personal psychological meanings and associations which derive from our cinematic experiences.

One area of film theory that has attempted to explore and track our personal relationship is the detailed work of ethnohistory. I have in mind here the research of Annette Kuhn and in particular her book *An Everyday Magic: Cinema and Cultural Memory* (2002) in which she explores the memories of city and rural people and their experiences of going to the cinema in Britain in the 1930s. This was a time when roughly two-thirds of the UK population went to the cinema two or three times a week. While predominantly a working-class activity, cinema attendance at that time spread to the middle class and was one of the few areas of social activity that both men and women could participate in – another being ballroom dancing. One of the strengths of *An Everyday Magic* is its refusal to privilege the textual aspects of the cinematic experience. As some of the intellectual roots of film studies originate in literary theory, there is often a tendency to emphasize the text and the meanings encoded therein. By contrast, Kuhn draws on the memories of cinema audiences as well as historical and textual sources. While not Jungian or phenomenological in approach, the research nonetheless is suggestive of the ways in which both attending films and the subsequent discussion of the experience can have a psychological and mythological quality. As Kuhn comments:

> The formal attributes of memory texts, too, often betray a collective imagination as well as embodying truths of a more personal salience.... Thus memory texts may create, rework, repeat and recontextualise the stories people tell each other about the kind of lives they have led; and these memory-stories can assume a timeless, even a mythic quality which may be enhanced with every retelling ... [communal] remembering clearly has a ritual quality.
>
> (Kuhn, 2002: 11)

Another writer who explores similar themes is Janet Staiger (1992) who, in *Interpreting Films: Studies in the Reception of American Cinema*, also advocates a contextual approach to understanding films. Her plea is for a reception studies that does not interpret texts but which attempts a historical explanation of the event of interpreting a text (1992: 81). So her emphasis is different – it suggests a historically located approach to textual meaning, as recovered through the work of historical analysis. Certainly both Kuhn and Staiger are undertaking valuable work that is rightly pushing the boundaries of film studies away from the text and towards context. But the issue of the psychological and the personally negotiated meaning is left largely untouched and that this might somehow contribute to a more general psychological theory of the cinematic is outside their frame of reference.

Alongside their work, I am proposing a more explicitly psychological approach to complement the historical and ethnographic orientations of Staiger and Kuhn. Such an orientation would also contribute towards a depth psychological theory of the cinematic. At the centre of this is the importance of the cinematic frame (not to be confused with the 'film frame') as a container of the psychological relationship between viewer and screen. In psychotherapy the 'frame' refers to aspects of the relationship which are somewhat rigid and which are designed to hold the therapeutic relationship. These elements will vary from therapist to therapist and are also influenced by theoretical orientation. That said, they typically include a regular time, payment, non-disclosure by the therapist, the physical details of the consulting rooms and so forth. Interestingly, psychodynamic practitioners tend to have a somewhat more rigid approach to the therapeutic frame which is paralleled in the inflexible conditions of cinema – fixed screening times, costs and so forth. The stable conditions of the frame serve several purposes. First, they create an environment for therapy that is relatively predictable and, within the parameters described, reliable. This is important as it provides the conditions in which it becomes 'safe' to experience the unconscious. My suggestion is that this also happens in cinema where the cinematic frame (rather than the film frame) seems to parallel the environment of therapy.

Another purpose of the therapeutic frame is to provide containment for the emotions, experiences, hopes, fears, anxieties, frustrations and so forth of the client. It is both a relief and a frustration for many clients that each session is fixed in length. It enables them to 'leave' complex psychological material with the therapist and in so doing makes it possible to take down some of their tried and tested defences in the spirit of finding other ways of coping with life's challenges. So, too, the duration of a film is fixed. Perhaps this formal property of the cinema enables viewers to experience repressed material. There is an element of security in knowing that a film is going to finish and that the level of embarrassment, shame, anxiety, tearfulness, or exhilaration, joy and excitement is not going to continue, at least at the same intensity, past the end credits.

From a somewhat different perspective, these ideas have been developed by cognitive film theorists such as Torben Grodal (1997) and Carl Platinga Greg Smith (1999), particularly Smith's own chapter. They propose the existence of a systemic relationship between the activation of mental processes and visual narratives. The result is that the emotions we feel in the cinema are contained through the knowledge that they have been systemically activated by the film. Moods and emotions are 'cued' by the film, and they are held in check by cognitions (we know this to be a fiction). Subsequently the affect dissipates, as we do not act as though the situation were real. The therapeutic frame also enables clients to project aspects of their unconscious onto the therapist. When this happens the therapist becomes for the client some person from their past. One of the great insights of Jungian psychotherapy concerns the manner in which these projections contain both personal and collective material. So the therapist comes to stand for both, say, the client's experience of the negative aspects of their mother, and also the archetypal mother who is experienced as both generative and destructive. Alternatively the therapist may become the love object of the client, and this offers the possibility of repairing damaged parental bonds, reconnecting to a capacity for self-care and a strengthening of the ego. Remember, this happens partly because the client knows very little about the therapist – in a sense the client creates the therapist they need and so too, the therapist creates the client.

Frustration and the frame

One of the key differences between the conditions of cinema and therapy is the relationship. In therapy the quality of the relationship is generally taken to be one of the most important factors at work as the therapeutic alliance that the client and therapist form is crucial to the eventual outcome of their work together. Clearly there is no such relationship in the cinema. Or is there? My contention is that there is a much greater degree of relationship than might be initially expected. We have seen how the therapist can become a person from the client's past. What appears to happen is that the therapeutic frame allows the client to fantasize about the therapist. In so doing they come to relax their psychological defences and this allows the integration of previously unconscious material into ego-consciousness. While this represents the reality of the therapeutic relationship it has relatively little to do with the actual life of the therapist (though it may have rather a lot to do with the personality of the therapist). So too the cinematic frame allows viewers to form a relationship with the characters in the film that is partly based on the narrative but is also the result of a process of personal projection. Here the collective and personal qualities of films are of the utmost importance as when combined with the other aspects of the cinematic frame they provide the optimal conditions for the creation of psychologically meaningful experiences. Thus, the viewer–screen relationship is reflexive.

It is important to be clear about the different types of collective and personal psychological material that we are considering. First, in the film there is its shared collective aspect – what we might designate the narrative of the film as it is understood by most of its viewers, most of the time. For some films, there is also what might be understood as the collective psychological aspect to the film, in other words its archetypal dimension. It is often the case that these aspects are either relatively conscious or at least close to consciousness. We have seen in Chapter 1 what happens if the creative process of filmmaking becomes overly conscious and how what should be affect-laden psychological symbols end up as bland semiotic signs. This is not to negate the unconscious processes which are at work in mainstream narrative filmmaking – even if the production crew do not describe or understand them as such. However, our primary concern is with how the viewer can engage with the film as both a narrative and an archetypal experience. In so doing, viewers also bring their personal psychology, their psyche, to the process. In this regard we have then the personal unconscious of the viewer and also their 'collective unconscious'. These two aspects interact with the film and in so doing shape its contents according to their needs and establish a personal relationship with the film.

The process and state of mindfulness with which this chapter opened offers one way to bring these unconscious processes into a bodily awareness. It suggests a different orientation to the unconscious and a different way for us to understand the meaning of a situation. Without trying to use the intellect to understand what is happening, it becomes possible to notice a 'shift' in the felt sense of ourselves. To be fully understood, the cinematic experience needs to be felt and here a mindful approach has a valuable role to play in bringing bodily awareness to the process of understanding what a film 'means' for an individual.

Perhaps the curious part of this process is that I am suggesting that there exists an element of reflexivity in the viewer–screen relationship. In one sense this is clearly not quite rational, as in a material sense at least the film is not changed as a result of being watched. But in a phenomenological sense the film does change into something else as it becomes more than just the result of its mechanical and electrical projection. Film is the recipient of psychological projections and hence meanings that are extraneous to its materiality. (The last chapter of this book will explore the implications of this in terms of where meaning resides in the cinematic process.) The meanings that are found in the cinematic experience exist partly in the film as text, partly in the environment and partly come about as a result of having been watched. The type of meaning that arises from having been watched is not the sort of meaning that is easy for the intellect to access. It is the type of meaning that is encoded in the body, in a felt sense, in a feeling-tone or a vague sense. Cinephiles are often highly attuned to this type of meaning and talk about the quality of different screenings of a film. It is as though the combination of individual psyches in watching a film together changes the collective experience or meaning of the event. Individuals might also find each viewing of a film evokes a rather different sense of the psychological meaning of the film, for that individual.

For example, in *Frames of Mind* (Hockley, 2007) I wrote about my personal relationship with *Chinatown* (1974). This is a film that regularly comes close to the top of those lists of the 100 best films that are compiled from time to time. Despite a longstanding interest in detective films, I used to find *Chinatown* boring. When I say this at film conferences there is a collective gasp of shock and disbelief. Yet I did. I did not just find it slightly uninteresting and dull, I found it boring and almost unwatchable. I got achy watching the film, I couldn't sit still. If I watched the DVD of the film I would invariably turn it off before the end. My body was defending me against something in this film that I found deeply distressing and unpalatable. Many of you will know that the crime committed in *Chinatown* is not, as in most detective films, a murder (though it contains those too) but is the crime of incest. This only comes to light in a violent scene in the film where the detective J. J. Gittes (Jack Nicholson) beats the truth out of Evelyn Mulwray (Faye Dunaway). It is a shocking scene and it is the first time in the film where as viewers we get to know with any certainty what has been happening. This dreadful moment of revelation happens towards the end of the film and so it does not really help to explain my boredom which set in much earlier.

It took me months of work and time reflecting on the imagery of the film to come to see how, throughout the film, images are denaturalized, corrupted and perverted. Symbols do not work in the way we expect. Noah Cross, with his name combining both Old and New Testament saviours, is actually the perpetrator, and this type of mythological and symbolic inversion runs throughout film. Now that I realize this whenever I watch the film I do so almost dispassionately. To pick up an idea referred to in Chapter 1, what has happened for me is the move from a symbolic experience to a semiotic one. The psychological experience and hence meaning of the film have changed for me. I can now appreciate the film aesthetically and intellectually, but my personal and psychological relationship with it has changed, and something has been lost. It is no longer the same film for me and it never can be again. As my relationship with the film has changed, so too phenomenologially has the film. Reflexivity is a central part of the cinematic experience; the unconscious relationship that as viewers we have with films is crucial. By 'unconscious relationship' I do not mean that the viewers are somehow unaware that they are in some way connected to films. Most people know that certain films have a special meaning for them. Rather, I want to suggest that the psychological relationship that viewers have with films is one of the defining characteristics of the cinematic experience, as in my relationship with *Chinatown*. It is the difference between watching a film and experiencing the cinematic.

The interplay between the audio-visual surfaces of the film and archetypal structures provides a rich environment for the unconscious material to flourish. Importantly, what arises from these two elements is something new and fresh: not just an image from the unconscious of the viewer, not just the image on the screen, but something new that comes into being as a result of their interaction – or, as I would prefer to put it, their relationship. This new image I have termed the 'third image' and it exists in the space between viewer and screen (cf. my chapter 'The Third Image', in Hauke and Hockley, 2011). It would be mistaken to regard this image as a type of suture, as it performs quite a different function. In the processes of suture, the viewer is both stitched into the film and simultaneously constructed as a subject by the film. It is the film, its structure and the mechanisms of cinema that replicate the 'machinery' of the unconscious and so facilitate a process of self-recognition and identification – undoubtedly this is further facilitated by the mimetic qualities of cinema. The third image, on the other hand, arises from a relationship in which the unconscious of the viewer co-opts the film to create a meaning that is honed, bespoke and specific for each viewer. Of course, there are also collective meanings and sometimes these sit alongside the personal. But more often than not, the activation of personal unconscious material is so strong that it overwrites the inscribed, consensual and collective sense of the film's narrative.

In this model, the viewer and the film are not stitched together. There is no sense in which some sort of temporary and illusory cohesion is sought. Rather, the third image holds the transitory, shifting and elusive psychological meaning of the film for the viewer in that moment. This meaning is partly available to consciousness but it is also felt, as the psychological meaning that each film has for each viewer is bodily encoded. One of the benefits of mindfulness is that it lets us become aware of what the body is experiencing without seeking to impose a fixed or predetermined meaning on it. From this perspective the psychological response of the body partially erodes the gap between the viewer and the screen, and it does so unconsciously as a response to what is experienced in the cinema – a response that is composed of personal and archetypal qualities. By accessing the imaginative image-making qualities of the unconscious it becomes possible to become mindful both of the psychological image as it is in the body and of how it might contribute to the third image which is the personal psychological meaning we have negotiated and found in the film.

Being mindful of the body helps to bypass the defences that the conscious part of the mind mounts, and adopting a mindful orientation helps to access the felt sense of the film. Again, to be clear, this is not necessarily related to the narrative meaning of the film – at least not in a direct way. Instead, this is more concerned with how films move us in ways that we are not always fully conscious of and which are unexpected. It is about how we can gain access to the unconscious's psychological images as a means of understanding the reality of our psychological situation and of developing a sense of what is happening for us emotionally. Accessing this information causes a shift in the sense we have of ourselves and also of our relation to a film. This shift is a felt sense that arises as a result of the movement of unconscious material into consciousness. This does not necessarily mean we understand what is happening but instead it offers the chance to change our emotional awareness through accessing what our body is telling us. Here the body can be thought of as integral to the cinematic experience. Chapter 6 will explore how film theorists such as Sobchack and Barker have theorized the viewer–screen relationship in a phenomenological manner with the use of bodily metaphors such as touch and skin. For the moment, however, we are concerned with the way in which adopting a mindful approach to the body's emotional responses can help to reveal the unconscious psychological processes which are integral to the cinematic experience.

You might be wondering if, therefore, watching films is psychologically beneficial. Or perhaps you had the opposite thought, that accessing the unconscious in such a direct fashion might be psychologically dangerous as raw unconscious fantasy invades consciousness. This latter point is certainly a view that is promoted by the tabloid press in the UK which likes to suggest that watching violent films causes violent behaviour. Take the headline: 'Rambo Killer gets Life in Jail' (*Sun*, 2 August 2009). The headline leads the reader to believe that in some unspecified way there was a direct connection between the *Rambo* movies and the murderer's behaviour. This suggestion is enhanced with a line in the body copy which described the murder scene as like 'something you would see in a horror movie'. What the *Sun* did not report was that at the time of the dreadful stabbing the murderer had been taking crack cocaine. What is striking, however, given how many people watch films, is how little negative effect there is – if indeed there is any at all. This area has been well documented by researchers into film, television and the media such as David Gauntlett (2005), David Buckingham (2003), Martin Barker (1998), Julian Petley (Petley and Barker, 2001) and many more.

However, from the psychological perspective here the parallel with dreams is again instructive. While dreams might be distressing, terrifying even, they do not cause us to behave in a particular manner. Yet, following tabloid logic, they should. It seems that the psyche is able to distinguish between reality and delusion both in dreams and in the cinema. Christian Metz wrote about this in *Psychoanalysis and Cinema* (1982) where he put forward the interesting argument that the 'delusional coefficient' of cinema is actually greater than that of dreams. The reason for this, he posits, is that films are delusions we have when awake, while we are unaware that we are dreaming. In some ways this is an attractive suggestion but what it does not account for is the individual and bespoke formulation of dreams as images that are fitted to the specific life of each dreamer. Where Metz is helpful is in reminding us that all films are a type of delusion. It is not that films that set out to depict dream states are particularly delusional. It is more that all films create in viewers mildly delusional, dream-like states. This type of temporary psychological condition is understood by the psyche as just that. Should we come to experience the delusion as permanent then we would be in a psychotic state. Put slightly more technically, the psychological function of dreams, and I would argue films too, is to activate unconscious defences and to integrate their material into ego-consciousness. This requires a degree of ego-strength if we are not to be overwhelmed by the affective, collective power of the images. If people end up acting out in an uncontrollable manner fantasies from films or dreams it is because the ego has been unable to hold and integrate this archetypal material.

Despite tabloid speculations and their appeal to common sense, there is little evidence to support the view that these permanent invasions of consciousness by the unconscious happen as a result of watching films. What is clear from the way that clients talk about films in therapy is that films activate our unconscious defences and offer the opportunity to experience the dark side of ourselves, our aggression, violence, capacity for hate, the power of our sexuality, our contrasexuality and such like as part of the mechanism of ego-consciousness. This raises the interesting question of whether we should work on the psychological meanings that films have for us, or, if we should instead just let the images do their work. In *The Dream and the Underworld* (1979) James Hillman argues for the latter, at least with regard to dreams. His clear suggestion is that it is enough to hold the dream images in consciousness (i.e. remember them and keep remembering them) and that this will let the image do its work in the strengthening of the ego, as the archetypal contents of the unconscious are integrated. While there is therapeutic value in this approach it denies the role of the thinking-orientated part of the psyche. Entering into the delusion of the film in a quasi-hypnagogic manner will certainly allow for a psychological relationship with the film as its images and sounds unfold. But attending to how our body responds gives us another way to access still further levels of unconscious responses.

If we are to get the most from the experience we need to be conscious of how our unconscious processes are replayed as part of the cinematic experience. Here

I wish to distinguish between the way in which the formal structures of the unconscious are replicated in the cinema and ways in which our personal psychology interacts with the narrative of the film to make meaning. Without doubt, the psychological landscape of films is meaningful to us because we are already familiar with its topography. The Lacanian position argued this convincingly and from a somewhat different perspective, so too did Metz. However, paying attention to the scopic and aural regimes is not enough. As will have become clear by now, I am arguing that while the audio-visual aspects of cinema are self evidently central, attending to just this is not enough if we are to understand the psychology of what is happening as viewers watch a film as they engage in the act of meaning making. It does not adequately account for and what Jean Mitry (1963/98: 75) refers to as the 'logic of contradiction' – that cinema both resembles the outer world yet signifies the inner world; that it is both representational and yet the shot and edit also dissect and dismantle; cinema is both personal and collective, its meanings both inscribed and negotiated.

If attention to the aural and scopic, the audio and the visual realms, is not enough, neither is the act of detailed textual reading or interpretation in and of itself sufficient to understand what is happening when we watch a film, particularly in the cinema. Again, while this important, and I would not want to suggest otherwise, cinematic meanings also result from individual experiences. The act of eating a raisin can give rise to markedly different experiences: it can *mean* different things to different people. So too cinema is a medium that is designed to evoke meaning and it is particularly effective in awakening personal associations. As a psychological medium, cinema can and does, awaken psychological complexes and this is one of the reasons why we react so strongly to films. This is what it means to consume images psychologically and it is a form of commercial retail therapy that does not have to buy in to the other aspects of capitalist and materialist ideology.

To summarize, I am suggesting that the meaning of film lies in the following elements. First, is the act of going to the cinema that includes expectation built up from previous cinematic experiences and from inter- and paratextual experiences. The physical setting is also significant: the building, the seating, the forward-facing orientation, etc. Second, comes the shared experience of watching the film which offers a collective experience of the *séance* where the focus is on the inscribed textual meaning of the film, and our aesthetic and intellectual engagement with its narrative. Finally comes our responses to the film, both conscious and unconscious, in the mind and in the body, and in the creation of the psychologically meaningful third image. Put another way, and more simply: we find ourselves in films – and the ambiguity in this statement is intended.

5

SEEING THE IMAGE

With the screen dominating the auditorium this might seem rather obvious, but narrative films exist to be looked at. While the film industry might regard the primary role of films as making money, for audiences films are things that are watched. This apparently simplistic observation about the need for films to have an audience disguises some other latent and more significant concerns. It turns out that we need to look more deeply into the screen as a means to discover what is actually going on in the cinema. For example, while the cinema screen exists in two dimensions, the images on screen are actually full of depth cues that invite the viewer to gaze 'into' the screen, and not 'at' it. This is significant as the way the screen suggests a three-dimensional space is one of the formal properties of cinema that helps to draw viewers into the narrative of a film. While the screen is two-dimensional, the cinematic experience allows viewers to access the depths of the cinematic image and in so doing it provides access into the interior psychological landscape of films. The act of looking bridges the gap between viewer and screen and is assisted by the diegetic construction of film, which encourages this elision. It is part of my contention that what also happens in bridging the screen–viewer gap is that the inner psychological images of viewers are brought closer to consciousness. The depths of the cinematic experience are mirrored also, allowing the move from images in the 'depths' of the unconscious to come to light. This goes some way to explaining the rather dream-like nature of some films, as dreams are also a place where we encounter our unconscious selves.

This chapter is concerned with looking in the cinema and with the cinematic look. It explores the ways in which looking into films and the look of the camera both construct a particular point of view. We will see how these different points of view are central to the cinematic experience. Related to this, the chapter will examine how the collective narrative aspects of films facilitate the creation of new individual narratives and how such narratives emerge as a means to understanding what is happening in our lives. This suggests a type of reciprocal relationship in which the physical projection of images in the cinema facilitates the psychological projection of personal unconscious images. Without doubt cinema is the medium of projection par excellence. Not only does it require the actual projection of images but it also seems to assist the psychological process of projection. The way in which cinema can assist the process of personal awareness can be seen in the privacy of the consulting room where it is possible to observe the strength of the emotional reactions we have to films.

The to-be-looked-at-ness of the cinematic image

The starting point for this exploration is Colin McGuinn's (2005) claim that the acting of looking is not just about sight, it is also metaphorically concerned with the search for meaning. We might paraphrase this by saying that looking is an activity where sight meets insight. To briefly recap McGuinn's argument (introduced in Chapter 2 above), he notes that looking is not just about discovering physical information about the world around us, though of course that is an important part of its function. For McGuinn, what is more important is that we look to find meaning. An obvious example of this is the way we notice the facial expression and body movements of other people and we use these to understand the emotions and meaning that are being conveyed. But more than this, McGuinn suggests that the very to-be-looked-at-ness of an object has the function of investing it with meaning. While he does not make the following point explicitly, it is clear that this 'invested' meaning is not intrinsic to what is being looked at, but rather comes from our relationship with it. In other words, meaning arises from the interplay of object and look. Examples that he cites include looking at or into a river or lake, looking into the night sky and its stars, and looking into the eyes of a loved one. In all cases we are looking with the expectation of finding something that will be relevant to ourselves. Sometimes we also imagine this meaning connects us to a wider reality, to nature and the world. While what we see is individual, what we imagine we find has a collective and archetypal quality.

This is a helpful starting point for our exploration of looking in the cinema. I want to distinguish the act of looking from 'the cinematic look' which is concerned with how the 'eye' of the camera records, represents and constructs the object of its gaze. That type of look is discussed later on in this chapter. Instead, we are going to start with the human act of looking, and from there reflect on just what it is that is being looked into and also the significance of the search for meaning.

Stanley Cavell provides a strong counter-argument to McGuinn's position regarding the hermeneutic significance of looking. For Cavell, the psychological significance of films does not come from their to-be-looked-at-ness. Instead, he suggests that films draw out of us our longings or, as he puts it, what our 'heart desires'. The cinema is a safe place for this because its fantasy worlds are premade, already constructed and available for our psychological habitation. This means that rather than withdrawing into ourselves, films make change seem possible and positive. It is as though the imaginative worlds of fiction films somehow make longing for a different life and different types of relationships acceptable. To put this in more Jungian terms, films engage the image-making capacity of the psyche, and because of this give the cinematic experience an archetypal dimension. As Cavell puts it:

> movies seem more natural than reality. Not because they are escapes into fantasy, but because they are reliefs from a private fantasy and its responsibilities; from the fact that the world is *already* drawn by fantasy. And not because they are dreams, but because they permit the self to be wakened, so that we may stop withdrawing our longings further inside ourselves. Movies convince us of the world's reality in the only way we have to be convinced, with learning to bring the world closer to the heart's desire ... by taking views of it.
>
> (1971: 102)

I would add to Cavell's touching image of how the movies bring the world closer to our heart's desire by noting that it is not just the desire of our heart that is moved by films. Actually films can move us closer to all our unconscious desires and wishes and also to our fears and fantasies. We will see in one of the examples of psychotherapy work later in this chapter how films can provide access to these unconscious parts of ourselves. Sometimes the desires that we bury deeply in ourselves, alongside the hopes and anxieties that we also do our best to hide, are released in the cinema as emotions and affects flood our bodies. Even if the film has little to do directly with such emotions it is as though the film is co-opted into the service of the unconscious. Here our personal and individual psychology will have an important role to play. Some people will find that films which have a fantastic setting, perhaps in outer space or Middle Earth, facilitate the release of inner fantasies and desires. Others will find no such attraction and will instead prefer more romantic movies; others still might find such release in almost any type of film.

Another way of thinking about this involves reframing, or repositioning, the mimetic qualities of cinema. Cinema films look rather like reality and it is tempting and all too easy to overplay their mimetic qualities. Yet, as we will see, the mimetic, while it does offer a useful way to think about cinema, only gives us part of the picture. In fact it is necessary to see cinema as both mimetic and symbolic – as both a screen onto which an image is projected and a mirror that also reflects. This observation by Baudry (1974–5: 352) neatly encapsulates this ambiguity: 'The paradoxical nature of the cinematic mirror-screen is without doubt that it reflects *images* but not "reality"; the word *reflect*, being transitive, leaves this ambiguity unresolved'.

If, as Baudry comments, cinema reflects images but not reality, then what is it that cinema reflects? To answer this question, Baudry suggests that the screen reflects the self. By 'self' he means the reality of the viewer as a transcendental subject who is not in the film but who instead exists outside the constraints of the cinematic frame. While it is not actually shown on the screen, the viewer recognizes his or her world as it is portrayed. As such, Baudry's suggestion is that the viewer does not identify with the representations on the screen but instead with the position of the camera.

> The 'reality' mimed by the cinema is thus first of all that of a 'self.' But because the reflected image is not that of the body itself but that of a world already given as meaning, one can distinguish two levels of identification. The first, attached to the image itself, derives from the character portrayed as a centre of secondary identifications, carrying an identity which constantly must be seized and reestablished. The second level permits the appearance of the first and places it 'in action' – this transcendental subject whose place is taken by the camera which constitutes and rules the objects in the 'world'. Thus the spectator identifies less with what is represented, the spectacle itself, than with what stages the spectacle, makes it seen, obliging him to see what it sees: this is exactly the function taken over by the camera as a sort of relay.
>
> (ibid., 353–4)

There is no doubt that the position of the camera, and the way it moves and frames, influence our emotional responses to what we experience in the cinema. But there again, so too do all the other elements of filmmaking: music, mise-en-scène, editing, casting, lighting and so forth. Yet for Baudry, identification is with the camera alone. However, this does not seem to capture the actual experience of watching a film, which is more complex and multi-layered than identification with the camera, or indeed with any single part of the cinematic apparatus. Nonetheless, what is important about Baudry's position is that it preserves the agency of the viewer in making meaning. This is crucial, as it is in the making of meaning, the finding of meaning and the experiencing of meaning that we encounter the psychological aspects of the cinematic. These various types of hermeneutic activity might not be conscious and are more likely to be bodily, felt and intuited. In short, the psychological value of the cinematic lies in our personal affective and 'heartfelt' responses.

Despite Cavell's reservations, it is still possible to suggest that what we see in the cinema is not so different to what we see in our dreams. The psychological meaning of dreams comes not from what they depict but from what they symbolize as their meanings are not mimetic but symbolic. That means that any attempt to understand a dream from a logical and rational point of view will end in failure, as the meaning of dreams comes from our associations, our emotional responses and our intuitions about its contents and also from our overall emotional response to the dream as a whole. The same holds good for the cinema:

> taking into account the darkness of the movie theatre, the relative passivity of the situation, the forced immobility of the cine-subject, and the effects which result from the projection of images, moving

> images, the cinematographic apparatus brings about a state of artificial regression. It artificially leads back to an anterior phase of his development – a phase which is barely hidden, as dream and certain pathological forms of our mental life have shown.... Following this line of reasoning, one may then be able to understand the reasons for the intensity of the subject's attachment to the images and the process of identification created by cinema. A return to a primitive narcissism by the regression of the ego.
>
> (Baudry, 1975: 773)

The 'depth' of the cinematic image and 'depth psychology'

Analytical psychology is a depth psychology. This slightly curious term is not widely used in the UK but has more currency in other parts of the world notably in America. It is mentioned here because this chapter is exploring the apparent 'depth' of the image on the cinema screen and some of the implications of this for a psychological understanding of the cinematic experience. Depth psychology (*tiefenpsychologie*) refers to those approaches which incorporate an understanding of the unconscious. The term itself was coined by Eugen Bleuler, when he was director of the Burghölzli Institute at the turn of the twentieth century. The term is a suggestive one in the way that it hints that underneath the conscious part of the psyche there are unknown regions that have the capacity and power to influence the behaviour of the whole person. As Jung comments:

> Consciousness is like a surface or a skin upon a vast unconscious area of unknown extent. We do not know how far the unconscious rules because we simply know nothing of it....
>
> The conscious mind moreover is characterized by a certain narrowness. It can hold only a few simultaneous contents at a given moment. All the rest is unconscious at the time, and we only get a sort of continuation or a general understanding or awareness of a conscious world, the *succession* of conscious moments. We can never hold an image of totality because our consciousness is too narrow ... all the rest is dark and we are not aware of it at that moment (emphasis as original).
>
> (Jung, 1935: paras 11, 13; original italics)

I am going to suggest that there are some points of similarity between this idea of a deep unconscious and the apparent depth of the two-dimensional image in the cinema. It is also important to hold on to the idea that the conscious mind cannot hold an image of totality. To go further, I would say that the conscious mind cannot ever *fully* hold any psychological image; in other words, our psychological understanding and awareness of any given situation is always partial and incomplete. In both the cinema and the unconscious, depth is taken to imply that there is something meaningful about the act of looking into the depths of either the unconscious or the cinematic.

Here it is necessary to make a distinction between films and the cinematic apparatus, although at other times we will seek to blur this distinction as the image and the mechanisms which bring it to life are both integral parts of the cinematic experience. Perhaps the most significant theorist in this field was Jean Baudry (whose ideas we have already encountered in this chapter). In two important articles (1974–5 and 1975) he wove together Platonic philosophy and Freudian ideas, as developed by Lacan and Metz, with a technological understanding of cinema. For Baudry, cinema is primarily a medium of technology and not of narrative or realism. He traces the origins of cinema back to Renaissance perspective, Cartesian optics and the camera obscura – a lineage that is often recalled, for example by Mulvey (2006) though there are many other examples. Of particular note is Heath's work on the *quattrocento* (1993) and the emergence of perspective in painting in fifteenth-century Italy, and its relationship to visual culture of the time and eventually to the contemporary conventions of modern cinematography. It is this history that for Baudry influences the development of the cinematic apparatus and the relative positioning of the projector, screen and audience. Importantly, the construction of the apparatus of cinema is predicated on the history of a particular way of looking and is therefore ideological and cultural. So, for Baudry, the apparatus of cinema is physical, ideological and psychological, with each element replicating or mirroring the other. The way this works in practice is that the individual believes he or she has mastery of the image as it plays out in front of them. In fact, the viewer and the image are both being constructed by the machinery of cinema. This specular illusion heightens a sense of false consciousness and promotes an illusion of control while at the same time it negates the agency of the audience. This is neatly summarized by Elsaesser and Hagener:

> In the cinema, the specific set-up of projection, screen and audience, together with the 'centering' effect of optical perspective and the focalizing strategies of filmic narration, all ensure or conspire to transfix but also to transpose the spectator into a trance-like state in which it becomes difficult to distinguish between the 'out-there' and the 'in-here'.
>
> (2010: 68)

However, Elsaesser and Hagener find this view of events somewhat problematic. They refer to Crary's critique (1992) and the objections raised by Penley (1985) who commented on the issues surrounding its fetishistic approach to technology. Finally, Elsaesser and Hagener critique Baudry's reliance on the centrality of the Lacanian mirror stage in understanding the cinematic. As Crary indicates, there is little evidence that in early cinema the audience were still, central or immobile. In many of the entertainments of pre-cinema the audience walked around, as in the phantasmagoria. Alongside this the more magical aspects of cinema and early optical entertainments are marginalized to allow room for a more technologically determined and structural understanding of specular relations. Further, Baudry's theory allows little room for the individual and instead it operates on the level of the ideological and within the certainty of the universality of the mirror phase. However, what remains appealing in his account is his attempt to bring together an ideologically informed view of the composition and technological creation of film in a way that retains a correspondence, or connection, between the unconscious and the mechanisms of cinema.

What I am suggesting arguably goes too far in the opposite direction. Nonetheless, I want to stress how relatively small a role cinema theory has historically found for the personal. The subjectivity of the self in determining meaning has been an issue which film theory has not managed to embrace fully, and instead it tends to see individuals as somewhat determined, constructed and positioned by the cinematic. I also want to preserve the sense of illusion that is so central to the experience of watching a film. This gives the cinema greater proximity to the world of magic than to the material world, and it is not difficult to see why this was, and remains today, unappealing to ideologically informed criticism. It is equally easy to see why such a repositioning is helpful when adopting a view of the unconscious that regards it as symbolic, metaphorical, ultimately unknowable: this is to privilege the personal and the non-rational over the determined and technological. Yet at the same time it is important not to lose sight of the cultural location of cinema. I am not arguing for an abandonment of the historical and cultural aspects of representation and its associated technologies. They are important and they too play a significant part in the construction of cinema as a psychologically meaningful experience. However, crucially these material factors need to be seen in relationship with the individual and not just the collective; they need to be seen as part of a process of creating meaning and not as the sole determiners of meaning. In other words, we need a psychology of the cinema which is relational and contextual, both synchronic and diachronic, for, as Jung reminds us, the image provides the best possible encapsulation of the psychological situation – both its history and its current articulation. It follows that there is something archetypal about the cinematic experience in as much as archetypes have both a historical and a cultural dimension, but are also personal and current in the ways they address the particularity of the psyche in a given moment.

An echo of the idea that we need a psychology which is aware of material and cultural conditions, and which also allows for a personal psychology, can be discerned in Baudry's work. In the following quotation he explores what he thinks of as the 'language' of the unconscious but significantly his emphasis is on the structural elements of the unconscious and not its contents. In identifying the mechanisms that are at play Baudry elucidates a set of correspondences between: the structures that are work in the unconscious; the ideological structures of society; and the machinery of cinema.

> We might not be far from seeing what is at play on this material basis if we recall that the 'language' of the unconscious, as it is found in dreams, slips of the tongue, or hysterical symptoms, manifests itself as continuity destroyed, broken and as the unexpected surging forth of a marked difference. Couldn't we thus say that cinema reconstructs and forms the mechanical model (with the simplifications that this can entail) of a system of writing [*écriture*] constituted by a material base and a countersystem (ideology, idealism) which uses this system while also concealing it?
>
> (Baudry, 1974–5: 349)

Baudry goes on to argue that the physical conditions of cinema allow viewers to relate to films as though they were dreams. The other significant factor in this process is what he terms an 'overcathexis of representation' which he suggests is another psychological quality that films share with dreams. Cathexis is the psychological term for the process by which libidinal energy becomes associated with an object or body part. It also refers to the way in which energy can become attached to the internal representations of psychic processes. To use a more Jungian terminology, cathexis describes the mechanism by which psychological images become laden with affect.

> The cinematographic apparatus reproduces the psychical apparatus during sleep: separation from the outside world, inhibition of motoricity, in sleep, these conditions causing an overcathexis of representation can penetrate the system of perception as sensory stimuli; in cinema, the images perceived (very likely reinforced by the setup of the psychical apparatus) will be over cathected and thus acquire a status which will be the same as that of the sensory images of dream.
>
> (ibid., 1975: 775–6)

There is not an entirely clear answer to why Baudry thinks this experience is over-cathected, but it seems to revolve around the accretion of psychic energy in bodily representations of internal psychological states. However, it might also be reasonably argued that in fact the cinema provides the optimal optical conditions for the experience of affect and that as a result it is not over-cathected. Because cinema is both mimetic (sign) and symbolic; external and internal; personal and collective, and highly boundaried, it can contain what would otherwise be an over-cathexis – this is part of what constitutes the *temenos* of the cinematic experience.

In *Psychoanalysis and the Cinema* Christian Metz explores these ideas where, among other topics, he shows how the mechanisms of dreams (dream work and so forth) are replicated in the cinema. This observation leads Metz to suggest that films have a similar relationship to consciousness as dreams. What Baudry and Metz leave unexplored is the bespoke nature of dreams. People's dreams are theirs and theirs alone, and they are personal and private experiences. Dreams also address the specific psychological situation of the dreamer and as such they are tailor-made by the unconscious to fit each individual perfectly. As Jung comments, 'It [the dream] shows the inner reality of the patient as it really is: not as I conjecture it to be, and not as he would like it to be, but *as it is*' (Jung, 1934a: para. 304). This raises an interesting problem. If dreams present the inner reality of the patient and films work in a similar way, then what inner reality do films reveal? Of course, there is no single answer to this question because films can reveal a plethora of different aspects of culture, in their production, their historical location, their appropriation by fans and so forth. But I am going to suggest that films are at their most dream-like when we find in them personal and individual meanings. Put another way, when we are moved unexpectedly, suddenly and uncontrollably by a film then the likelihood is that we are experiencing the film as a psychological image, as a symbol whose meaning is not fully understood by consciousness. Chapter 7 of this book explores how this type of psychological relationship with films leads to the release of an affect in the formation of a psychological image – a process which is analogous to the experience of what happens in the consulting room. This should not be taken to mean that the cinematic apparatus is not important, as we have already explored in some detail how it is an essential part of the way that cinematic meaning is made. But the psychological relationship we have with films and our ability to make or negotiate personal meanings with films is where we treat the film as though it were a dream. It is on those occasions that we relate to the film psychologically and the process is certainly facilitated by the material construction of films, and the physical conditions surrounding their viewing. Put another way, films can indeed resemble dreams and they also illuminate aspects of our cultural lives. But for viewers, films become most like dreams when psychologically we relate to them as though they were our dreams. In so doing, we forge a unique symbolic relationship with films as in our experience of them they come to represent aspects of our inner lives.

In a move that is reminiscent of a deconstructive approach, what I am advocating is the disrupting of an established interpretative hierarchy in which the inscribed meaning of the film is privileged. There is a hint of Derrida's thinking in the approach, in so much as we are not attempting to synthesize opposites but rather are attempting to understand the interplay between the inscribed meaning and the negotiated meaning of a film. Where we depart from Derrida is by focusing on the unconscious and the personal aspects of this undertaking. This in turn emphasizes the emotional affect of the cinematic experience and the body's encoding of it. That said, affect creates a kind of trace (in Derrida's terms) which itself signifies difference. In this case the difference is between the personal and negotiated meanings that are intrinsic to the cinematic experience, and also to the inscribed narrative meaning of the film.

If we are to access these personal meanings we need to pay attention to the affect and as a result to temporarily preserve it. In doing this, we hold on to the affect, we stick with the affect, and notice how it moved us, without trying to analyse, comprehend or fix the meaning of the experience. This is letting the image do its work (in a manner which would be familiar to readers of James Hillman, who advocates holding the dream image in mind without attempting to fix its meaning). Next comes any sharing of the process, of being more conscious and rational about what we have experienced, as we must let consciousness do its work too. This is the work of discriminating, understanding and supporting the strengthening of the ego.

Of course, meaning here is somewhat slippery and it needs to be so, because what we are trying to access is something that is non-tangible and something that is also non-rational yet it is here that the psychological meaning is felt and articulated. What we have is a blurring of the signifiers of internal psychology and also of external films. To put this another way, this chapter started by noticing how cinema needs to be looked into and how the image with its implicit depth cues promotes the sustained act of looking. I suggested the activity of looking is purposeful and that we are looking into the image with the expectation of finding meaning. We also saw how this type of looking is predicated on existing fine art practices and in particular the development of perspective in Renaissance painting. As we explored this further we began to see that this is just one view of the history of cinema, and one that has ignored bodily-based affects. It privileges a history of perspective over the expression of experience. This might be altered if the phantasmagoria, diorama, zoetrope and similar optical entertainments are also taken as the starting points of cinema alongside painting. While they are often acknowledged, it is the technology of projection or movement that is of value and not their ability to release affect. This capacity of films to mobilize affect is crucial, however. Films are successful in mobilizing affect because the experience of cinema blurs the boundaries between the conscious and unconscious parts of the psyche and consequently it is not clear just what it is that viewers are looking into – while films appear to be external and mimetic they are actually internal and symbolic. Meaning in the cinematic experience is in flux and changes and the interplay of the psyche's relationship with the film means that the significatory surface of the film actually shifts as the trace of meaning moves; such is the transitive work of signification and meaning making in the cinematic experience.

Audiences, cinephilia and the pleasure of looking in detail

In his work on cinephilia Greg Singh (2011) has identified two specific areas where it is possible to see this shifting surface of signification with particular clarity. The first concerns the significance of discussing films once they have been watched. The second involves the way in which meaning for cinephiles is found in what appear to be trivial details in films which, while significant for them, go unnoticed by casual viewers. It might seem curious to want to pay attention to these aspects of a film. Nonetheless, Singh convincingly suggests that these tiny details can have a determining influence on the meaning that we take from films. More accurately, Singh makes the point that these fleeting visual images and brief moments actually offer film viewers the opportunity to develop and cultivate a personal relationship with films. He observes the way these precious tiny moments are variously shared with other cinephiles or retained as a source of private and solitary pleasure. In highlighting the use that cinephiles make of films, Singh draws our attention away from the film itself, to the manner in which film viewers extrapolate those elements of the film which have personal meaning for them. This is a significant shift, as it makes it clear that the narrative of the film is not the only way in which films have meaning. Singh's overall project is a grand one and it is nothing less than to dethrone the film as text and in so doing to challenge its dominant place in film theory. It is his contention that film theory has failed to adequately account for the everyday pleasures of cinema. In its emphasis on structure, both institutional and cinematic, film theory has largely forgotten the seemingly more mundane enjoyment that is gained from films. While he does not focus on the complexity of the film or on the intricacies of the cinematic apparatus, he does not dispute them either. Rather, for him, the cinephile (which as he quips sounds like a psychological diagnostic category) is someone who quite simply finds pleasure in watching films and in all those linked activities that form part of a relationship with cinema. Following a film star, tracking the work of a director, collecting movie memorabilia are all part of cinephilia. But so too are some of the other more mundane aspects of cinema.

As part of his discussion of pleasure and the cinematic, Singh reflects on the importance of what happens after we have watched a film. Far from seeing the post-movie chat as a piece of irrelevant communication, he suggests that talking about a film after the event has the capacity to be even more emotional than watching the film itself. It is as though the act of recollection serves to invest the experience with a heightened sense of affect.

> we tend to recall events that happened in the film in a highly narrativised way. Often, this recollection is accompanied by heightened emotional responses, and the recollections of how the film made us feel as we watched. This recollection, this retelling, adds to the 'making-sense' of the film.... Not so much a disorder then, I would argue that cinephilia is a useful term for thinking through a normal pathology of film-viewing that captures something of what people experience through their everyday encounters with film.
>
> (Singh, 2011: 164)

The affect-laden retelling of important events is of course also a central feature of psychotherapy and it might be that what Singh has identified is a process of cathexis in which the libidinal energy of the psyche gets channelled, or reinvested, into the creation of a new narrative. This fresh narrative aims to make sense of the event and also to understand our response to it. In therapy these are the narratives by which we come to understand our lives. So too in the cinema these narratives are ways of preserving our affective relationship with films and of holding on to the emotion of the experience once the film has ended. They 'make sense' of the film and of our emotional responses to it. As Singh puts it:

> It is this aspect of Jungian psychology that proves the most effective in negotiating what actually happens in contemporary cinephilia: in the re-telling of our encounters, active imagination stirs and drives the emotional intensity of the encounter. The power is in the recollection. This may in the event be slight and unimportant – trivial even – in its manifestation, but is a potential site of transformation that compels the theorist to concentrate analysis on meaningfulness and the recollective experience, rather than on the screen and its images as somehow repositories of archetypal material.
>
> (Ibid., 178)

Here it seems that Singh is using the term 'active imagination' both in the general sense of a lively imagination and also in the technical Jungian sense. In Jungian therapy active imagination is the process of engaging the inner world in dialogue. For example, in working with a dream a client might imagine they were a figure in the dream and speak from that point of view, or they might imagine themselves as the river in the dream and wonder what it is like to have a stranger dive into you. Of course the images that are the starting point for active imagination do not have to originate in a dream. Indeed, Jung's own process of imaginative engagement with his inner world is detailed in his *Red Book* and records his personal dialogues, paintings and internal discussions with the characters of his imagination which he uses as a means to tease out his relationship to the world. Of course the process of active imagination in recalling a cinema film is not quite so formal and elaborate, nor does a psychotherapist guide it. But what it shares with active imagination in therapy is the use of psychological energy to create stories that open up new possibilities and new meanings that in turn allow for a fuller understanding of how we are in the world.

Like cinema itself, active imagination is an immersive technique in which the inner world of fantasy and creativity is treated as though it were real. Engaging with and treating a fantasy in this way opens up the possibility of a dialogue with the unconscious and in doing so it provides a means to sidestep the defences which consciousness erects in an attempt to keep the unconscious at bay. The process of using intuition to engage imaginatively with images is important as it provides new avenues for psychological understanding. In a move that might appear contradictory, I am arguing that an increased awareness of the inner world of imagination helps us to become more fully connected to the psychological realities of the external world. In some ways, the role of active imagination is not so very different to the psychoanalytic idea of free association in which one idea, thought or feeling leads in a spontaneous but meaningful manner to the next. However, the important distinction is that active imagination is a narrative process. In active imagination personal creativity and images are used to create new narratives through which to understand personal experiences. In developing this way of working with images Jung discovered how it can connect people not just to a personal unconscious but also to the archetypal aspects of humanity. So again, for Jung, a personal and conscious activity helps us to establish a relationship to unconscious concerns that are personal and collective. Perhaps the same holds good for the recounting of our cinematic experiences. Here too, the creation of a narrative and the development of a new understanding of the film derives from the relationship that we have with the film. In this context, meaning comes from what we opt to do with the film and the psychological work we undertake in cultivating our cinematic experiences.

Internal and external images – projections from psyche to screen

Cavell, whose work we encountered earlier in this chapter, approaches the issue of meaning from a rather different angle. Without needing to invoke the full weight of the philosophical positions he adopts we can nonetheless take his main point: at any one moment, and at any given point in time, the camera and the viewer combine to create meaning. He arrives at this conclusion via a consideration of the Kantian position that our own involvement in an event is the only way we can 'know' it. He combines this with the Hegelian insight that our involvement in the event is determined by our experiences leading up to the event. In other words, the meaning of films can change over time. The way this happens depends on our relationship with a film. It might be in therapy; in the case of cinema, with other cinephiles, or perhaps as a solitary cinephilic experience. More subtly and importantly, the meaning of films changes as a result of changes to our own psychology. As our psychology changes so too we remake and renegotiate our relationship with films and in so doing films come to mean something different and fresh each time we watch them. While Cavell is arguing a slightly different point, he nonetheless recognizes the importance of personal experience and of the role that subjective experiences and personal histories play in the creation of meaning in the cinema.

> if the camera must acknowledge itself … for it recognizes the hard Berkeleyan-Kantian truth that an event in which we participate is not knowable apart from our knowledge or our participation in it. Yet it neglects the Hegelian truth that the actual consciousness of our participation is not assured *a priori*, but can be won only though the paths over which we have arrived at this event, and at this specific placement toward it. The camera cannot in general merely declare itself; it must give at least the illusion of saying something.
>
> (Cavell, 1971: 129)

Stating that the camera has at least to 'give the illusion of saying something' is to invest it with a degree of agency. Of course, the camera is not autonomous, it has to be put to use by a team of camera operators. But the final effect in the finished film is that the camera is positioned within the film as something which frames and selects, and which through depth of field makes implicit links between the different elements of the scene. A similar point applies to the use of and interconnection between long shots, close-ups, point-of-view shots and such like. Unlike the human eye, the camera must select whether to have all elements in a scene in focus, or whether to have a narrow plane of focus in which a single object is sharp. It has to frame an object in the distance or close up. It either lets the scene unfold in front of the lens or it adopts the point of view of a character. The effect of this is to interpret the scene and to imbue it with meaning. Objects are either related or separated though these depth cues, and we interpret these associations psychologically. To this extent, the camera is the first point at which the images that will form the final film are created. It is not the set itself or lighting that drives this, it is the moment the image is created that is significant. It does not matter if the camera here is real or a computer in a digital studio. What does matter is the birth point of the image and the origination of a point of view and of an interpretation. This is the creation of the collective and narrative dimension of films and it is the mechanism by which it becomes possible to share the narrative meaning of the film. While the narrative of a film is composed around an implied point of view, and it is inscribed with what are broadly shared collective meanings, it also allows for a highly personal response.

Put another way, viewers respond to the filmic flux and its evocation of the cinematic experience as though they were the unconscious. Of course it is a curious type of unconscious because it is collective and yet it also acts as a mirror of our own internal unconscious life but does so effectively enough for us to relate to it as though it were our personal unconscious. Importantly, we do not relate to films as reality. We do not believe that what we see on the screen is happening or has actually happened in the world. We know the difference between illusion and reality.[1] However, we do relate to films as representatives of the unconscious, personal and shared. Films are the collective without the personal and it is when we as individual viewers actually watch a film that we develop a personal relationship to it, and in doing so we create the cinematic experience. It follows that there is a psychological sense in which viewers complete cinema, and by doing so they find in films psyche. Another way of putting this would be to note that the viewer turns the film into the cinematic experience, and it is that experience which embodies the psychological. This is what I think of as the 'cinematic frame' in distinction to the film frame.

Film needs the viewer, as without viewers there is no cinematic experience. Contrary to Cavell in *The World Viewed* (1971), the world of the film is not whole and complete – it only lives when viewed, and the act of viewing changes the film. More accurately, every viewing of a film reconstructs the cinematic experience anew. The accretion of meaning that occurs as a result of repeatedly watching a film is like the laying down of sediment as layer rests upon layer. However, unlike sediment, this is not the deposit of some external silt; rather, it is the gradual building up of precious personal experiences and meanings which are found, treasured and stored as memories, experiences of the fleeting images of our felt self.

Negotiating meanings with films

To illustrate the way that the cinematic experience can create a meaningful psychological experience I want to introduce Sally, a client of mine whom I have written about elsewhere (Hockley, 2010). But I want to write about her again here in the context of exploring how the act of looking into the cinematic from a psychological perspective can show how meanings found in popular films may also be quite personal. Sally was in her thirties when I first met her. She was so dependent on alcohol that it was almost impossible for her to work, even on a part-time basis. Her life was made even more complicated because she often had the idea that men were following her. These might be her previous lovers, or men encountered in the street or men she thought were watching her from parked cars. These men were all spying on her and without exception they meant her harm. Sally also frequently heard the doorbell ringing when no one was there and similarly the telephone would ring but the caller remained silent. Sally was also certain that she was a clairvoyant. Spirits would come and visit her, but unlike the men in her life these tended to be benign, more on the side of the angels.

The early years of Sally's life were characterized by violence. Her father was mostly absent from home and when he did periodically return he was physically violent towards both Sally and her mother. Both her parents drank heavily. From a very early age, Sally learnt that one of the ways she could keep herself safe from the violence and anger in the house was to make herself sexually available. Her early sexual experiences were extremely distressing.

When I first met Sally she was in the process of separating from a long-term relationship. Like her childhood experiences with men, this relationship had been typified by aggression and violence. She became convinced that her previous partner was spying on her, paying neighbours for information about her, entering her flat when she was not there, and following her. Needless to say, she found life exceedingly distressing, full of worry and for her large quantities of strong alcohol provided a temporary respite, even though often it would also intensify her anxiety.

Our relationship was one in which she regarded me as a man in authority who was also kind and caring and someone who was interested in her as a person. To use a technical vocabulary, she developed an idealizing transference in which I became an unattainable object of desire. During one session Sally wanted to talk about a film that she had been to see. This was unusual, as we had not talked about films before, though Sally had often talked about the books she like to read. Also, to the best of my knowledge, she was unaware of the particular interest I have in films. The film in question was a *Happy-Go-Lucky* (Dir. Leigh, 2009) and the character in the film that had most struck her was Poppy (Sally Hawkins). Poppy is a teacher at an inner-city, north London primary school. She has an indomitably optimistic outlook on life that can be exasperating to those round her. Even so, it was this aspect of Poppy's character that moved Sally. Unlike her, Poppy seemed to triumph in the face of life's difficulties and Sally was moved to tears, both in the cinema and as she told me about the experience. The next part caught me slightly by surprise. Sally suddenly announced that she thought it would be fun if we could watch the film together. As she put it, 'It's really a woman's film but you're not a typical man and you'll be able to understand it, and then perhaps we could go for a picnic!'

In the context of this discussion about looking into the cinema image and finding something other than that which is apparently there, what I want to stress here is that the reason why Sally identified with Poppy is that their lives were so very different. Poppy was not an identification figure in a traditional sense, rather she became a source of psychological inspiration – almost like an inner spirit guide or psychopomp. In looking at the film Sally found something other than herself. While many viewers might find Poppy on the rather irritating side of enthusiastic, for Sally she embodied much of what she hoped for herself. The film also became a vehicle for her fantasy image of seeing me outside the consulting room. I put it to Sally that going to the movies was not unusual as a date. She looked truly horrified at the prospect and it was absolutely clear that no such thought had entered her mind. I suspect she was right, that the thought had not entered her mind consciously. Indeed, while Sally's thoughts about me might have been erotic, they were not directly to do with sex. For her, sex was associated with violence, violation and physically aggressive men. Sally wanted something else from me. She wanted me to be 'not a typical man'. Instead my role was to be capable of understanding 'a woman's film' and by implication someone who was also capable of understanding her. Part of her idealizing transference to me meant the castration of my sexuality – the idea that I was a man like other men was so intolerable to her that it became necessary for her to destroy my sexuality altogether and to render me as what she imagined to be her ideal man – caring, soft and incapable of hardness in any form.

The film gradually became a source of psychological transformation and insight for her. In a sense, the therapy mirrored the film and acted as a container, a *temenos*, for her hopes, thoughts and fantasies. As the weeks went by we explored the extent to which a part of her actually was a little like Poppy, although it was deeply repressed. This is the part that kept her going, even when thoughts of ending her life seemed like a logical relief from her constant anxieties. A significant aspect of what we were able to do together was to explore what a life in a relationship with her 'ideal man' might be like for her – a committed relationship of two people, not one that was characterized by pain, abuse and violence.

So I am arguing here that Sally was psychologically moved by the way the film was quite unlike her life. But nor in a psychological sense did she simply see an idealized form of herself on the screen. What happened for her was that an image formed that was in part based on the film but was highly augmented by the narrative of her own life. Sally found in the film a personal meaning that is not a direct part of the film's narrative and she found herself profoundly moved and in tears at a film that is ostensibly a comedy, a film that while attempting to capture a sense of life in north London, does so gently. The only character to exhibit any powerful emotions is Poppy's driving instructor – and he is more of a caricature than a character. What Sally saw in the film, what she found in that particular cinematic experience, was something that was the product of her own unconscious hopes and it was these personal psychological fantasies that were animated by the film. In this context 'animation' is very much a double-sided term which suggests movement and life in the cinematic frame. This is not so unlike the therapeutic frame where unconscious desires and materials can be animated through the process of therapy. Animation in the context of Jungian psychology takes on an explicit double meaning as Jung used the term 'anima' to mean both spirit and the contrasexual aspect of the male psyche (the equivalent in women he termed 'animus'). In explicitly referring to animation here I hope to suggest a use beyond that, particularly in the general philosophical sense of life-breath in the way the cinematic experience is alive.

What emerged in the consulting room from Sally's spontaneous remarks about going to the movies and having a picnic was the possibility of a relationship with a man that was not violent or physically sexual. This was the first time in her life that she had entertained such a possibility and it pointed the way towards the possibility of a new type of relationship for her with men. It also offered her the hope of developing a new type of more harmonious relationship with her own inner life. In a way the example of Poppy's life and the fantasy of an impossible relationship with me opened the way for her to accept how deprived her life had been and to accept the depth of the abuse that she had experienced. As the therapy progressed the vans that were following her became fewer and fewer. The doorbell did not ring so regularly and when it did, there was someone there. The telephone rang only when someone was actually trying to get in touch with her. She reduced the amount of alcohol she was drinking, though it remained excessive. By the time we stopped working together Sally was working part-time, and enjoying it. She was still troubled by periods of anxiety and depression but these were less intense and less frequent.

In his *Notes on the Cinematographer* the director Robert Bresson observes that the function of the cinema is the 'production of emotion determined by a resistance to emotion' (Bresson, 1975: 126.) That is what happened for Sally and the capacity of the cinematic to evoke emotion in the face of personal resistance is one of the reasons why cinema is a powerful psychological medium. This is not simply a replaying of internal psychological structures but arises instead from the complex interplay of personal and collective material in creating an insight, or image, which encapsulates the psychological reality of the situation. This is facilitated by the action of seeing the image, not just the image on the screen nor just the image in the mind, but this new image that gives expression to those aspects of psychology which the conscious mind alone cannot.

Personal meanings and collective inscribed images

Here is another example from psychotherapy which illustrates how clients can find personal meanings in films which are psychologically beneficial. This example shows how tending to an emotionally encoded bodily response to film can provide a way to access unconscious but active complexes.

John had reached midlife, being about 50 years old. He had been taken to the cinema to see a film that did not really appeal. His new wife had chosen the film, which she thought they might both enjoy. It was *Mamma Mia!* (2008), whose story is built around a series of songs by Abba. The narrative of the film concerns Sophie, who is about to get married on the Greek island of Kalokairi. She doesn't know who her father is but on discovering her mother's diary she realizes there are three possibilities ... She invites them all to the wedding where they meet for the first time. Each of them think they are Sophie's father and there is competition and confusion, yet true love triumphs in the end.

As John was telling me about being 'dragged' to see what most people would find to be a generally innocuous 'feel-good' film he started to sob uncontrollably. He told me what had happened in the cinema. These were the sort of tears through which it was almost impossible to speak. Temporarily they prevented verbal communication between the two of us. Some might think of these as tears of defence which try to keep something unpalatable at bay, to avoid something extraordinarily painful. At first we just sat with the weeping until gradually it faded. At this point I enquired if John knew what was behind what had just happened. He told me that he had no idea, that it was distressing and mystifying to him and that he was generally puzzled about why he was having such an uncontrollable and unexpected (not to say unwelcome) emotional reaction. Gradually we shifted to a more mindful orientation. This helped to bring some sense of relief. I got John to focus on his breathing, noticing the details of whether it was deep or shallow and then gradually moving from that to an awareness of other feelings and sensations in his body. The important point to note here is that neither of us tried to interpret what was happening for John. Instead, we got closer to the bodily expression of the experience.

As the session progressed John began to become somewhat more focused. Then he started crying again. These tears felt different, more like tears of release. He said, 'I'm never going to be a father.' John had recently remarried following a childless first marriage, only to discover that children were not going to be a possibility in his second marriage. Of course, intellectually he had known this for a while, but the emotional reality of it was less evident to him. The film had triggered a deep emotional connection to this sense of loss.

What is interesting about this is not that John had been emotionally moved by the film – this is not at all unusual, as viewers are regularly moved by films. Rather, there are two factors that I want to focus on. First, John did not know why he was responding in the way he was. To him, it was a mystery. It made no sense to him because he was experiencing something powerful and unconscious in his own personal psychology or psyche that could not be grasped by the intellect alone. This sense of being out of control, as though life is something that is happening to us and is beyond our control, can be an indication that the conscious part of our mind has been overwhelmed by something quite unconscious. When this occurs it is as though the rational and conscious part of the psyche has been temporarily invaded by the unconscious. Putting this to therapeutic use, the challenge is first to recognize that this has happened and second to hold the contents as something that needs to be integrated into consciousness. If this portion of the psyche remains split off, then the complex will return another day, probably in an intensified form. If we remain 'stuck' in the complex, then the opportunity to makes conscious rational sense of it is lost. Using responses to films in therapy like this provides a powerful way to access unconscious fantasies. It is not so much that this is better or worse than the imagery in dreams but our cinematic experiences are more conscious (as we are awake, to recall Metz) and so the affect is somewhat easier to access, to recall and to work with.

Second, if we cry in the cinema it is generally because something sad is happening on screen. We have already explored some of the technicalities of how the apparatus of cinema enables this type of psychological identification to take place. But what is significant here is the disjunction between the narrative on screen and John's overwhelming emotional response. Of all the things that *Mamma Mia!* might be about, it is certainly not about being fatherless. Indeed there is a surfeit of fathers in the film. It would be a mistake to regard this in semiotic terms as an 'aberrant decoding' or even, to use a more Humanities-style terminology, as a 'creative misreading'. Rather, John's response shows the psychological and phenomenological meaning that was central to his experience of the film. Significantly, John's cinematic experience was one in which a deeply rooted sense of personal loss was experienced at a bodily level. John found in the film a personal meaning that was his and by attending to the way his body encoded this we were able to acknowledge and experience a painful and significant part of his life.

The example of John, like most of the clinical examples in this book, serves several purposes. One is that it shows how our emotional responses to films can be used effectively in personal psychotherapy. Second, I am suggesting that while these are fairly clear and extreme examples, this type of personal negotiation with films is actually much more commonplace than might be suspected. To put it more strongly, it seems that the negotiation of personal meanings is central and intrinsic to the cinematic experience. For far too long, film theory has focused on either the psychological and hermeneutic construction of the text or the effect of the cinematic apparatus and narrative in the construction of the subject. I am arguing for a much greater degree of individual intervention in the construction of identity as an activity that emerges from the interplay of a viewer's unconscious with film. I remarked in a previous chapter that we find ourselves in films – perhaps it would be more accurate to observe that we become aware of ourselves through a relationship with films, and that this reflexivity is central to the cinematic experience.

6

BEING TOUCHED BY THE IMAGE

Vivian Sobchack (1992, 2004) has eloquently and persuasively noted how film theory has been ocular-centric. Experiencing films, or being in a relationship with a film, is a full-body experience that is not just a matter of sight and sound. As viewers, we have a range of tactile responses to films that go beyond the visual and the auditory: goose bumps, tears, laughter, gut-wrenching feelings, joy, along with a range of other responses and emotions, are all part of the cinematic experience. Whatever the feelings we have when we are in the cinema they are both heart-felt and genuine, and these emotions tell us something that is important about ourselves.

Sobchack's idea is that the senses do not work in isolation. While she does not make this point directly, it is implicit in her argument that it is the filmic diegesis that makes it possible for the 'look' of film to pave the way for other sensory and meaning-making responses. These arise from the body's sensory and felt relationship to the screen. Sobchack uses the work of Merleau-Ponty to explore the interconnection of the senses and also to reflect on the manner in which cinematic experiences and life experiences can reinforce one another. However, in her debate she does not take into account the unconscious and as a result she misses a key way to understand the phenomenology of the cinematic experience.

This chapter attempts to take the undoubted strengths of Sobchack's phenomenological approach and combine them with the idea that the unconscious maintains a psychological agency in creating and finding meaning in the world. Again, taking examples from the consulting room makes it possible to see how the unconscious inflects and structures the cinematic experience and the meanings that are created.

The tactile flow of films' images and sounds

Daniel Frampton in *Filmosophy* (2006) sets out the case for using philosophy to understand what he terms 'film-thinking' and he does so in a lucid and convincing manner. Yet he is also doubtful that phenomenology will be of great use in this enterprise. While phenomenology is a philosophy of experience, Frampton concludes that once it has been subjected to philosophic argument it becomes clear that phenomenology is of little use in helping to understand what it means to 'be' in the cinema. Of course Frampton is right that if what is wanted is a way of engaging with film-thinking, then phenomenology is indeed of little use. However, the main part of this chapter is going to approach this topic from a different angle. It is concerned with how a phenomenological approach can be used to understand the ways in which psychological and affect-laden meanings are created when we view films. In other words, we are going to use phenomenology not as a way of understanding film-thinking, but as a way to comprehend what it means to 'be' in the cinema and what it means to exist in relationship with the cinematic. In doing so, we will assert the primacy of the psychological image and our relationship with it as a way of being aware of how we are in the world: both our world and the world of the cinematic. In support of the argument, and towards the end of this chapter, we will reintroduce the role that unconscious processes play in the meanings we find in psychological images.

The phenomenological film theory of Sobchack and also of Janet Barker finds its origins in the phenomenology of Merleau-Ponty and not in the transcendental phenomenology of Husserl. The reason for this preference in orientation is that for Merleau-Ponty human consciousness is embodied. In other words, there is a materiality to how he understands the 'lived experience' that at first sight appears to sit well with film theory's focus on the materiality of cinema. Alongside this is film theory's need for a historical and materially located understanding of meaning and experience. Again, Merleau-Ponty's suggestion that 'appearances' are not something which cover or mask a reality, and that they are in themselves real, is pertinent. So too is his focus on the appearance of form and structure both as the carrier of meaning and also as the building blocks of experience.

> The idea we have of the world would be overturned if we could succeed in seeing the intervals between things (for example, the space between the trees on the boulevard) as objects and, inversely, if we saw the things themselves–the trees–as the ground.... The perception of forms, understood very broadly as structure, grouping, or configuration, should be considered our spontaneous way of seeing.
>
> (Merleau-Ponty, 1964: 48–9)

Typically the emphasis he places on structure is taken to refer to the perception of forms in the world, as in Merleau-Ponty's example of the trees-as-ground. Here he is referring to the patterns that are formed between figures and the ground they are drawn on, in much the same way that Gestalt theory conceives of figure–ground relationships. But Merleau-Ponty is also foregrounding the experience we have of the representations of reality. For example, when watching a film we might see a tree in two dimensions but we infer, or create, a third dimension: we do not need to see behind the tree to know it has depth as we directly experience it that way. However, a slightly different take on this idea is to think about the perception of form in the cinematic experience. In the relationship that the viewer has with the screen something like Merleau-Ponty's desire for the reversal of figure–ground relationships occurs. Instead of experiencing ourselves as sitting in the cinema and watching a film, we find ourselves experiencing the film as though it were real. As we are coming to understand, this is because the film *is* psychologically real and this reversal occurs as a result of some deeply unconscious processes. To clarify, I am not using the term unconscious in a phenomenological sense where it would mean something of which we are not aware. Instead, I am using the term psychodynamically to suggest that something at a formal, structural and procedural level takes over consciousness. To use Jungian vocabulary, part of the cinematic experience can involve the activation of the deep structures in the unconscious whose presence is characterized by affect, namely the archetypes, and these temporarily invade consciousness. When this happens we bridge the gap between the viewer and the screen (the space between the trees, if you will) as we are possessed by the affective experience.

An 'invasion' can be recognized because consciousness stops articulating the details of what is happening and the experience becomes embodied. Such moments have a strong affect and understanding them has a crucial role to play in seeing how individuals come to create meaning from experiences, cinematic and otherwise. In many ways this is perfectly congruent with the position that Merleau-Ponty proposes. Where it differs is in the suggestion of unconscious agency, which we will return to at the end of this chapter. What it shares is the observation that perception does not occur solely through sight, or hearing, or touch, rather the whole experience is embodied in a given moment. In a way it parallels what we have been describing as the psychological qualities of the cinematic experience in which no single element of either the film or the cinematic holds the key to understanding. Rather what matters is the bodily experience of the whole. For Merleau-Ponty, this involves the comprehension of 'a unique structure' that we might say is the experience of an archetype or archetypes in an embodied manner. As he puts it:

> My perception is therefore not a sum of visual, tactile, and audible givens: I perceive in a total way with my whole being; I grasp a unique structure of the thing, a unique way of being, which speaks to all my senses at once.
>
> (Merleau-Ponty, 1964: 50)

Being overwhelmed while simultaneously feeling connected to both the world and our inner selves is characteristic of archetypal experiences. Jung hypothesized that the deep unconscious archetypal structures in the psyche regulate our psychological lives, and at any moment they keep us in touch with what is happening both in the world and in ourselves. Archetypes, then, are not so much about psychological health as they are about personal insight and understanding, both individual and collective. What Jung shared with some existential thinking was a concern with living life in an authentic manner: as he might put it, being fully the person you are and not the person that life has turned you into. He regarded this as the life-long process of 'individuation'. It was one of his insights that images, and the meanings we find in them, are an important and integral part of the process of living life authentically as an individuating person.

Of course, Freud was alert to this as well, and his work on dreams in particular had a powerful impact on Jung. Where they differ is that that for Freud the dream was an indication of something that had been repressed, while for Jung the dream talks to the present situation. Indeed, for him, this is the function of all psychological imagery and we see this most clearly in his personal imaginative work in the *Red Book* (2009). Freud used a logical and rational approach to understand the hidden meaning of dreams. He thought that the process of 'dream work' could be reversed through intellectual engagement and that the disguised meanings of dreams could thereby be revealed. This rational approach was of little use to Jung, as for him dreams were not full of concealed meanings. Instead, they depicted the condition of the unconscious and the social reality of life as it actually was.

We might summarize these differences by noting that for Freud dreams could be used to deconstruct the patient's fantasies while for Jung dreams are reconstructive; they show what is happening and in so doing suggest a way forward. For Jung, this meant that understanding dreams cannot be just an intellectual process. Instead he suggested that the best way to work with dreams is to bypass the defences of consciousness and to engage in the creative and imaginative process of interpretation. Again, here we find a point of connection to the ideas of Merleau-Ponty who stressed that perception and the subsequent meaning that arises from it is not the prerogative of the intellect alone. The way he writes about recovering a 'presence in the world which is older than intelligence' is reminiscent of the way that Jung writes about the experience of the unconscious. For both theorists it is important to find an embodied way of being-in-the world. As Merleau-Ponty observes:

> Nor do I give it [perception] this meaning through thought. Perception is not a sort of beginning science, an elementary exercise of the intelligence; we must rediscover a commerce with the world and a presence to the world which is older than intelligence.
>
> (Merleau-Ponty, 1964: 52)

What then might this mean in terms of our project of trying to understand how meanings are made when we watch films? Here some psychotherapy thinking can be of use. When working with a client from a psychodynamic perspective it is necessary to use more than just the intellect to comprehend what he or she is trying to say. The theory that underpins this concerns the ideas of projection and transference. Projection is the attribution to inanimate objects of internal psychological distress and associations, while transference is a similar mechanism, but with people. These mechanisms are dealt with in detail by Jung in Volume 16 of his *Collected Works* (*The Practice of Psychotherapy*) and in many ways they have become the cornerstone of psychodynamic psychotherapy. (They are dealt with in some detail in Chapter 5 above.) In coming to a view of unconscious processes for the client, the therapist will of course engage intellectually. But it is also important to sense, feel, attend to aches and pains, or unexpected responses in the body of the therapist. The appearance of the client, a shared sense of the client's personal history, the knowledge of what is happening right now for the client are all held and felt. I consider it my role to offer back my experience of being with the client in as simple and clear a manner as I can, and one which speaks to the emotional reality of the situation. In other words, I try to use all my senses and my intellect too as I attempt to sense a pattern or, as I would prefer to put it, an image. This is an image which comes not solely from my client, not just from my psyche – it is something we create together, a third image if you will, which distils the psychological meaning at that moment in time. Such images are often difficult to grasp, temporary and fleeting, but they are always characterized by the presence of strong affect.

There is more than an echo of this when Merleau-Ponty writes, 'Let us say right off that a film is not a sum total of images but a temporal gestalt' (1964: 54). He goes on to develop this idea, noting that when meaning is found in an image it arises not from the content but from the arrangement of the composition. He makes this technical point about composition to shift the argument away from representation and towards perception. For Merleau-Ponty, it is the act of perceiving a structure that creates meaning. By becoming aware of the gestalt of an image and how we have learnt to read it, and also by realizing the extent to which this 'reading' is culturally bound, we are able to invert many of the formal elements of the world and perceive them fully, as if for the first time.

The proposal that we should perceive unconscious structures and reverse normal modes of understanding is something which sits comfortably alongside Jungian psychology. After all, one of the functions of therapy, at least from the depth-psychological point of view, is to come to an awareness of how unconscious material and processes influence our everyday lives. The purpose of this is not to remove these processes, or fully to understand them, but rather it is to perceive them differently. Here I am referring to the archetypal structures of the unconscious and the function they have in the formation of images that encapsulate what is happening psychologically in life. Jung suggested that even though it turns out to be impossible to understand these unconscious patterns fully they still show something significant about our lives. Consequently, it is vital that we pay attention to them and, in particular, to the feelings that we experience as they are manifest. Indeed, therapy is one way to encourage the activation of the archetypes, and for us to experience them in a safe and potentially positive manner. Even when such imagery can be terrifying it is important to see it as part of the psyche's attempt to keep the whole person, body and mind, safe. (A particularly clear example of this can be found in the work of Donald Kalsched, 1996.)

I want to suggest that something similar can happen in the cinema. Rather than approach this through psychotherapy thinking, I want to work up to the idea through the notion that the meaning of a film comes not from what it represents but instead from how we perceive it; to which I would also add, how we perceive it *psychologically*. I am going to use a rather long extract from Merleau-Ponty here because in it he introduces a number of significant points. First, he notes that meaning in films comes about through relationship with the film; second, that films are 'finer-grained' than real life or, as I would put it, films offer a more contained and focused experience than real life; third, film is not understood by the intellect alone but arises from the senses as a whole. In other words, it is the relationship we have with films that gives rise to meaning.

> The meaning of a film is incorporated into its rhythm just as the meaning of a gesture may immediately be read in that gesture: the film does not mean anything but itself. The idea is presented in a nascent state and emerges from the temporal structure of the film as it does from the coexistence of the parts of a painting. The joy of art lies in its showing how something takes on meaning – not by referring to already established and acquired ideas but by the temporal or spatial arrangement of elements. As we saw above, a movie has meaning in the same way that a thing does: neither of them speaks to an isolated understanding; rather, both appeal to our power tacitly to decipher the world or men and to coexist with them. It is true that in our ordinary lives we lose sight of this aesthetic value of the tiniest perceived thing. It is also true that the perceived form is never perfect in real life, that it always has blurs, smudges, and superfluous matter, as it were. Cinematographic drama is, so to speak, finer-grained than real-life dramas: it takes place in a world that is more exact than the real world. But in the last analysis perception permits us to understand the meaning of the cinema. A movie is not thought; it is perceived.
>
> (Merleau-Ponty, 1964: 57–8)

Some of the examples I provided earlier in this book, and in particular the examples from clients like Sally and John in the previous chapter illustrate how psychological meanings in films are created that have little to do with their narratives. This is typical of the way that clients talk about films in therapy. Clients do not want to talk about the narrative meaning of a film: they want to talk about how they felt and about the images that came to their mind. They also want to understand their fears, anxieties and sometimes the hope and inspiration they felt. It is quite possible for two clients to be moved by the same film in quite different ways, one finding it depressing, the other inspirational. I have one client who finds the *Harry Potter* movies sources of inspiration and stability, and constant reference points over a difficult period of her life. I have another who finds them tedious in the extreme. The reason for this difference is that the meaning of films is not as fixed as we often assume. This is crucial as it shifts the site of meaning away from the sensory signifying surface of the film and takes it towards the viewer.

As discussed, while films are not dreams we appear to relate to them as dream-like. Just as we find personal meanings in dreams despite cinema being a mass medium we also find personal meanings in films. We seemingly cannot help but have an unconscious affective response to the films we watch and part of that process is the way the cinematic experience brings to life our own experiences and our personal unconscious fantasies. This is not really a question of identifying with the characters on the screen, though that does happen. What I am referring to is the way that we negotiate a unique psychological relationship with the films we view, and the ways in which the meanings that arise are affect-laden and whole-body experiences. While Merleau-Ponty would not find the idea of the unconscious necessary, he nonetheless gets to a view of films that is remarkably close to the one that I am suggesting when he notes:

> Well, the movies are peculiarly suited to make manifest the union of mind and body, mind and world, and the expression of one in the other ... contemporary philosophy consists not in stringing concepts together but in describing the mingling of consciousness with the world, its involvement in a body, and its coexistence with others; and because this is movie material par excellence.
>
> (Merleau-Ponty, 1964: 58)

My claim is that the concept of the unconscious is needed in order to explain how personal meanings are derived in the cinema. Of course this is not fresh territory and Vivian Sobchack and Jennifer Barker have both explored this topic but, as will become evident, like Merleau-Ponty they find the idea of the unconscious unnecessary. However, as we examine the views set out in their variant of phenomenological film theory, it will become clear why a concept of the unconscious remains indispensable to understanding the psychological meanings and relationships we have with films.

The work of Sobchack and Barker and the insights of the phenomenological approach

In her phenomenological-orientated film theory Vivian Sobchack attempts to bring the viewer back into the theoretical picture, so to speak. Her argument is a complicated one in which she thinks her way into a phenomenological understanding of the relationship that viewers have with films. One great advantage of her approach is that it accounts for the role that the body has as a site of meaning in the cinematic experience. Sobchack suggests that films and viewers have a great deal in common, and that this sense of communality is at the core of how meanings are made in, and with, films. Elsaesser and Hagener neatly summarize her position:

> Building on Maurice Merleau-Ponty's phenomenology, Vivian Sobchack has developed a film theory in which intellectual understanding and cognitive skills are complemented by a strong bodily component. The process is circular or self-reinforcing: film is the expression of an experience, and this expression is itself experienced in the act of watching a film, becoming as a consequence the experience of an expression.
>
> (Elsaesser and Hagener, 2010: 116)

To be clear, Sobchack argues that film is an expression of an experience of the material world. As we will see, when she develops this into the idea that film is a conscious articulation of a particular view of the world, her argument becomes increasingly involved. For the moment, it is enough to notice that for Sobchack film presents a particular and specific view of the world. Like film, the viewer too has a view of the world and the experience of watching a film brings these two different views together. Daniel Frampton most helpfully divides Sobchack's phenomenological account of the experience of film into different components, commenting:

> There seem to be four levels to Sobchack's phenomenology of film's 'experience': that film sees and expresses its seeing; that it is subjective; that it is embodied; and that the filmgoer feels this presence, this other. For Sobchack film is both an '*instrumental mediation* necessary to *cinematic communication*' and 'a *direct means* of having and expressing a world', that is given to itself 'as the immediate expression of consciousness'.
>
> (Fampton, 2006: 41; original italics)

Of course it is the case that the consciousness of film is not the same as the consciousness we have as humans. Nor, as we shall see, is the 'body of film' the same as the flesh of the human body. Nonetheless, Sobchack argues that films possess a certain type of consciousness, and for her they represent a specific view, and understanding, or position, on the world. Consequently she endows films with a certain type of collective consciousness which emerges from the collective creative act of filmmaking. This is what she terms the 'viewing-view'. Frampton (2006: 41) explains this idea, noting Sobchack's claim that 'Film simultaneously has vision and intention, it sees objects and expresses intention about those objects'. Thus she formulates Merleau-Ponty's observations about the reversibility of the frames of perception, in which there is expression–perception and also perception–expression.

The idea that somehow in the cinematic experience films, at least to some extent, replicate the internal human processes has a long history in film theory, and its appeal is one we have already alluded to. It finds its fullest expression in Lacanian film theory where the machinery of cinema is regarded as replicating the conditions of the mirror phase. Academically appealing though this account might be, the problem is that it does not seem to actually correspond with the experience of watching a film. Viewers do not feel alternately fractured and whole, nor do they feel deconstructed as viewing subjects. Instead of regarding films as replicating human processes, why not allow them to have a somewhat more ambiguous status? Films look a little like the material world, but also they are quite unlike it. Representationally, we recognize a world that is somewhat familiar to us. However, it is not the same as our world, nor do we perceive the world in frames, edited, lit, scripted and seen through a camera lens. We recognize something of ourselves in films, but also something quite unlike ourselves. While clearly there are elements of human psychology such as emotions and character traits that are familiar to us up on the screen, there are also elements that are quite alien. For example, characters in films live fantastic lives that are contained in impossibly condensed time-frames which are quite unlike daily life.

A further problem with Sobchack's account lies in the idea that films possess consciousness. The question this raises is exactly what is it that films are conscious of. As humans we have a certain degree of consciousness of the material world and of our experience of it and of being in it. But take away from film lighting, sets, music, camera, editing, actors, script and so forth and what is left? Sobchack is also clear that films do not possess self-consciousness. As this chapter unfolds we will see why assigning consciousness to films is actually unnecessary. Further, Sobchack concedes that when we watch a film we are not aware of the filmmaking, the very conditions of its view of the world which provide film with its consciousness. Instead we are aware of being with the film. Film is a fiction, and it is my contention that it is this fictional quality which is of particular importance because, as I will argue later on, it is that fictional quality that facilitates the active and imaginative function of the unconscious which is the ability to create images that have psychological meaning. This is what Jung is pointing towards when he notes that:

> the psyche consists essentially of images. It is a series of images in the truest sense, not an accidental juxtaposition or sequence, but a structure that is throughout full of meaning and purpose; it is a 'picturing' of vital activities.
>
> (Jung, 1926/31: para. 618)

This is an idea that occurs frequently in Jung's writing, though his definition of exactly what he means by an image is never quite pinned down. However, we get close to it in Volume 6 of his *Collected Works* (*Psychological Types*), much of which is concerned with definitions, where he writes:

> When I speak of 'image' in this book, I do not mean the psychic reflection of an external object, but a concept derived from poetic usage, namely, a figure of fancy, of *fantasy-image* which is related only indirectly to the perception of an external object. This image depends much more on unconscious fantasy activity … it never takes the place of reality, and can always be distinguished from sensuous reality by the fact that it is an 'inner' image.
>
> (Jung, 1921: para. 743; original italics)

While films and viewers do not have parallel processes there are certainly points of similarity and difference but what they do have in common is that both are involved with the process of creating 'fantasy-images'. Greg Singh in his book *Film after Jung* (2009) raises a cognate point in his exploration of the longevity of the work of Hugo Munsterberg, who was one of the early pioneers of film theory. In particular, Singh examines the relationship between the inner image and outer experience of embodied emotions. Developing this, I would argue that films and viewers share the capacity to create fictional images, both material and psychological. These images allow us to understand a psychological reality, and what matters in meaning making is the relationship we have with those images. This relationship is based on our capacity to hold together inner and outer meanings and this entails acknowledging the inscribed meaning of the film (its narrative), and also the meaning that we find as a result of our relationship with the film. We might say that images facilitate a dialogue between the unconscious and consciousness, and that in so doing the ego as a sense of self, or a way of being-in-the-world, is strengthened. Something akin to this is also intrinsic to the cinematic experience in the way that films can activate unconscious fantasies and in so doing offer an insight into what is actually happening, or has happened, in our lives. Cinema is fantasy that connects us to reality. As we have already noted, in both therapy and the cinema, the psychological image is a full-body experience. Films and therapy are not just intellectual undertakings. Important though the intellect is, by itself it is not enough. Just as no amount of describing therapy can actually prepare you for what it is like, so too reading about a film is not in any way comparable to the experience of watching it.

For Frampton, one of the strengths of Sobchack's approach is that she acknowledges that films have to be experienced to have meaning. In a moment we will return to the body of the viewer as the site of such meanings but first I want to explore the idea that film, like the viewer, possesses body. For Sobchack, this is an important idea because irrespective of whether the body is a virtual or fleshy body, it remains the site of experience of the world. Thus films build their implied bodies from their representation of the world as shot, scene, frame, music and so forth. This is the body of film and it is a body of which film itself can never become aware. Even though film is without a sense of self-consciousness, Frampton makes it clear in explaining Sobchack's thinking that the body of film is socially and historically located; this constitutes for him, and

Sobchack, a certain awareness of experience. This is a highly particular and specific type of consciousness as it is one that embodies a set of social relations, of being in a certain place and time. It also embodies a particular way of having been made, and the way films are made varies over time. Cinematic conventions, techniques and technologies change and so too it follows that the 'look' of films onto and in the world also changes. For Sobchack, it is the body of film that holds together the reality of the world it depicts, much as our own corporeal bodies act as the interface between our sense of self and our understanding of the world. Frampton neatly summarizes the role of the film-body for Sobchack:

> This film-body (invisible in its own vision) is the subject of the film's image and space and dynamism, inscribing 'its presence to, at, and in the world in the visible motility of its viewing view'. What is important about Sobchack's move to seeing film as a body is the way that it allows for social meaning – allows for a historical, situated film: a body that intends in relation to the world and other films.... Marking film as a body allows for a coherence of the cinematic. Body is to reality as film is to its world.
>
> (Frampton, 2006: 43)

Of course, it is not necessary to conceptualize film as body for films to be historically and social located. That said, my main concern with this approach is that again it does not seem to relate to the phenomenological experience of actually watching a film. Take a 1940s American *film noir*. It is a perfectly reasonable exercise to understand such a film in relation to the terrible world events of the time, America's role on the world stage, and the possible effects of this on the American psyche. We might also choose to look at the migration of German film directors, composers, cameramen and other film industry professionals to Hollywood and notice the stylistic and thematic influence they had on American film-making in relocating the German Expressionism of the Weimar period and the aesthetics of psychological realism. Now some academically inclined film viewers might watch a *film noir* and see it in that light. However, most viewers, I suggest, are not that detached when watching film. Indeed, we might go further and say that actually the 'academic viewer' is analysing the film while the other viewers are experiencing the film. While clearly films do contain meanings that are social, historical and cultural, to analyse films in just that way is to approach them through the intellect alone. However, the phenomenology of the cinematic experience would suggest that much of the meaning we find in films comes from the emotional relationship that viewers have with them. Such an emotional relationship does not necessarily correspond to the film's material reality: that it was made in 1941; is about a statue of a Maltese falcon; that it stars Humphrey Bogart; and was directed by John Huston. What matters is how we relate to the film. No amount of academic argument is going shift us from hating a film to loving it, from being enthralled to being bored, or from being enraged to being placid. Perhaps we might eventually begrudgingly come to admire a film and to understand more about what it is trying to communicate and the sophistication of its aesthetic and narrative techniques. But in this shift we have moved from film as cinematic experience to film as intellectual appreciation. While clearly the academic understanding of films is important and has a role to play in appreciating the changing social, cultural, economic and political functions of cinema what we are doing is shifting from the whole-body dimension of the cinematic experience and into the intellect.

Of course, we can psychologize about such matters too. Indeed, I have used the phrase 'therapy thinking' elsewhere in this book to encapsulate how we can use the terminology and approach of psychotherapy to understand processes that are not strictly clinical. However, again this takes us away from the embodied experience of films and the emotional meanings they have for us. Here I disagree with Sobchack as her insistence on the film-body as conscious and as replicating the viewer's internal engagement with the world remains somewhat confusing. Frampton summarizes as follows:

> To name this presence for the filmgoer Sobchack settles on simply conceptualising the film-body as 'an animate, conscious "other" who visually, audibly and kinetically intends toward the world or toward its own conscious activity in a structure of embodied engagement with the world and others that is similar in structure to our own'.
>
> (Frampton, 2006: 44)

There seems little to be gained from such a formulation as clearly the apparatus of film constitutes a set of conventions through which meaning is encoded but this does not mean that film can, or needs to, possess consciousness. The shot, framing, editing, camera movement, lighting are all ways that films are constructed in which reality is not. While film has a certain mimetic relationship to reality is it that which actually facilitates our psychological relationship to films? A clear example of this is animated films which tend not to look particularly like the world we live in, yet they are capable of awakening in us deep and heart-felt emotions. This suggests that what seems to happen when we view a film is that an innate need to find images psychologically meaningful is activated. These meanings might be concerned or connected to the narrative of the film, or they might be something that is strongly influenced by our personal psychology.

There is no guarantee that the personal meanings we find in the cinema will correspond to those 'intended' meanings, indeed frequently they are in opposition to the narrative of the film. Our personal response might be a question of intensity. For example, the slow zoom to the face of an actor has the effect of increasing the intensity of our identification with a character. For some, this might be too much to bear while for other viewers the trope of this particular cinematic technique might be overly clichéd. For still other viewers, the device might be compelling. At other times our affective engagement with a film is not just a question of intensity or degree. In such moments our personal psychological concerns subsume these inscribed and codified meanings, and something from our personal psychology takes over. Let us put this more technically and from the perspective of analytical psychology. In Jungian psychology complexes are characterized by the presence of strong affect and we tend both to project them onto inanimate objects and to transfer them onto people. As such, the complex conforms to Jung's definition of an image. This might be an actual image, a dream image or a felt image. One of the ways in which the complex is dissolved is for us to become conscious of it and for the unconscious fantasy to be replaced by a more overt recognition of life's realities. We might say that the function of both projections and complexes is actually to situate ourselves more fully in the reality of the world. In therapy, this comes about through the therapeutic relationship and the ways in which client and therapist work together to understand what is happening for the client. Such moments of understanding are likely to be felt as a shift or change in the client, though they can also be articulated as conscious thought or new insight. Importantly, it is the fantasy function of projection and of image making that as a personal process also allows for a fuller engagement with social relations and collective concerns.

As complexes have both personal and collective elements one might experience, say, a father complex, to contain aspects of an actual human father and also collective aspects of the archetypal father. Cinema as a medium offers ideal conditions for this image-making capacity of the psyche to thrive. It is both collective and individual, it deals with transitory fleeting images on the screen, yet these images resemble us as humans. We recognize our world, yet the filmic worlds of cinema are also quite unlike our everyday experiences. Cinema provides an opportunity for unconscious content to briefly invade the conscious and we experience these moments in a spontaneous and affect-laden way. It is not so much that internal psychological processes are replicated or mirrored by the cinema. Rather, cinema provides a contained environment that facilitates the psychological process of making images that are full of personal psychological meanings. Other art forms do this too, including literature, theatre, painting and photography. Indeed, we might say that wherever there is a creative act, the psyche can be creative in the meaning it finds. But I want to make the case for us having a distinctive relationship with cinema that is different to those we have with other media forms and artistic artefacts. It follows from this argument that the fantasy worlds of cinema have the capacity to help us experience the world and our role in it in a more engaged manner.

Limitations to the phenomenological approach and the lack of the unconscious in critical work today

It will be clear by now that while there is considerable merit in the phenomenological approach offered by both Sobchack and those who have developed her line of argument there are also some problems. The main one concerns the particular type of phenomenological investigation that she deploys. Indeed, a different type of phenomenology might well offer up a rather different response. Sobchack starts from an intellectual position but what happens if we start instead from experience?

As I have argued up to this point, one of the phenomenological aspects of the cinematic experience is that it is unlike our experience of being in the everyday world and, even though it is also a little like it, I have suggested that we do not experience films in the same ways that we experience the world outside the cinema. This sense of the cinema as being both like and unlike the actual world, as a liminal place, is one of the reasons why it is so potent in awakening our unconscious complexes and fantasies. The point is that the film world is not real and we know that to be the case, yet at the same time it corresponds to the real world. Frampton puts it neatly when he makes the following observation:

> Phenomenology concerns human engagement with reality. Film-being is not human, and the film-world is not real. Film is its own reality, its own world, and the *attention* of any possible conceptual film-being must be theorized as being part of that world, not separate and observational. We are subjective beings, but film seems more fluid in its place of intent.
>
> (Frampton, 2006: 46; original italics)

We experience films differently precisely because they are not real. Yet we also treat the cinema as a place where we can experience the reality of our personal and unique fantasies. (Here I am using the idea of a fantasy-sense in a technical psychological manner as an expression of an unconscious.) A phenomenological approach to the cinematic experience can help us to become aware of how the meanings we make in the cinema arise from the individual and personal relationships we have with films. While we have a core narrative to our life, just as films have a central narrative, this narrative changes as a result of the relationships we have, be they relationships with other people, ideas, or indeed films. So, too, the meaning we find in films changes depending on the relationship we have with a film. My understanding of *Blade Runner* (Dir. Scott, 1982), a film I started writing about in 1985, is now different. I am different, and so too when seen through a phenomenological lens, *Blade Runner* is not the same film. Here I do not refer to the numerous different versions of the film that have been released, rather my psychological relationship with the film simply means it is now, for me, a different film. And when I watch it I have a different cinematic experience, each and every time.

Phenomenological film theory has identified how the experience of the cinematic is a full-body experience. In doing so it has rightly noticed that images carry an affect that we respond to before we consciously process the image itself. While phenomenologically orientated film theorists choose not to use this language, what they observe is that viewers have an affect-laden response to images which happens quickly and before consciousness can intervene. Elsaesser notes: 'We take in films somatically, with our whole body, and we are affected by images even before the cognitive information processing or unconscious identification addresses and envelops us on another level' (Elsaesser and Hagener, 2010: 117).

In her essay 'What my Fingers Knew' Sobchack (2004) provides an elegant and detailed account of her experience of watching the opening shots of *The Piano* (Dir. Campion, 1993). She explores how her own fingers seemingly recognized the close-up blurring of colour and light on the screen as a point-of-view shot of the character's fingers: her body knew something before her mind could process and recognize the image. This echoes some of the ideas of Merleau-Ponty (1962), especially when he writes about the perception and motility of the body, and in particular the idea of tacit procedural knowledge – which in the example he provides involves a reflection on how we use a typewriter keyboard. The type of embodied mimetic representation that Sobchack refers to is imbued with knowledge derived from experience and this might well be one of the aspects which influences the types of meaning we find in the cinema. Indeed, Sobchack's moving account of watching *The Piano* appears to be just that. However, I want to look at a somewhat different type of meaning. Not the representational meaning of what we experience in the cinema but the psychological and unconscious responses and meanings that we create. At times this interest in making meaning gets close to what also interests Sobchack. Indeed her formulation of the separateness of the reality of the filmic world and our own reality is most helpful and argued persuasively.

> We never watch a film as if, in fact, 'we' as our bodies weren't engaged in the watching. Thus, although our interest may be dominantly and transcendently There, our bodies are also irreducibly and imminently Here. The film's Here, although it is always understood as such, always remains a There for us – for our Here is uniquely our own. It is where we are situated, where we're 'coming from' as we intend toward the viewing-view/viewed-view we are watching and toward the intentional presence we feel constituting it for us in its particular significance.
>
> (Sobchack, 1992: 287)

However, Sobchack goes further. As previously mentioned, for her it is important that film possesses its own body and its own consciousness. Sobchack argues that film needs a body because without it there is no interface to the world, and equally film needs a consciousness because otherwise it cannot articulate its position, which is to say its own view of reality. In the following quotation Sobchack starts by noting that interpretation of the film experience only makes sense as it is perceived by the viewer, that it is intellectually perceived and also that it is perceived by the body of the viewer. So far so good. However, she then goes on to argue that this requires film to be both embodied and conscious. Further, she suggests that the structure of the film's embodiment needs to be in some way similar to our own.

> This interpretation [of the film] is meaningful only insofar as it emerges from our understanding of the film (and its intelligibility) as it is originally perceived by us in the film experience – that is, as an animate, conscious 'other' who visually, audibly, and kinetically intends toward the world or toward its own conscious activity in a structure of *embodied* engagement with the world and others that is similar in structure to our own.
>
> (Sobchack, 1992: 285)

The question of similarity is an interesting one. Certainly the structure of film needs to be 'in some way similar to our own' because otherwise it would be unintelligible to us. Without a point of reference we would not be able to recognize the film for what it is. But actually this only needs to be a 'sense' of recognition, not one of similarity. In fact Sobchack goes on to argue a seemingly contradictory point, noting that it is at those moments when the structure of the film is most unlike our experience that we find meaning, as it is at those points that we become most conscious of the film as other. She comments, 'It is in moments of disjuncture and divergence that the film reveals itself most obviously to the spectator as an "other's" intentional consciousness at work' (Sobchack, 1992: 285). There is something that is almost Socratic in the way that Sobchack positions film as a type of interlocutor: the film constructs itself in dialogue with and in opposition to the viewer, and in so doing film challenges the viewer to become more aware of how meaning is embodied and made. Such hermeneutic activity for Sobchack is activated as a result of what amounts to a challenge to the perceptions of the viewer – something which appeared to be similar; a point of recognition, agreement and even identification is revealed to be something which challenges, is different and which is actually other. This point of recognition of otherness occurs when the need to make meaning is activated and we subsequently become more conscious of who we are and how the totality of ourselves is situated in the world.

> If the cinematic experience were intentionally one-sided and we took the film's vision not merely *into* our own but *as* our own, there would be no moments of discontinuity and rupture, no need for hermeneutic activity – that conscious seeking to disclose what is understood as meant but whose meaning presently eludes us.
>
> (Sobchack, 1992: 286)

I agree that the meaning of films comes partly because they are not like us. However, I disagree that meaning requires moments of rupture and discontinuity. What Sobchack is getting at is the way that films are made according to certain rules, which when followed mean the material form of their construction goes unnoticed. Collectively these techniques form the diegesis, and the way they cover their tracks I like to think of as diegetic deceit. It takes a subtle and attentive reading to appreciate the ways in which some films adopt a different type of looking, and in so doing position the viewer rather differently. (Such films tend not to be mainstream 'Hollywood' productions.) Even allowing for these detailed and sensitive interpretations, moments of filmic discontinuity are not necessary for hermeneutic activity. Indeed, to suggest they are reminds me more of structuralist and semiotic discussions than it does of what it is like to be in the cinema. Both those modes of analysis placed a particular value on films that set out to deconstruct the cultural norms. Both structural and semiotic approaches to films also emphasized the way films could 'embody' such self-reflexivity in their structure: jump-cuts, handheld camera shots, the use of natural light, intertextual references to other films, long tracking shots and so forth are all typical techniques used by the filmmakers to draw attention to the material construction of film. Less 'aware' films codified and embodied cultural norms and were offered up as examples of how cinema hegemonized cultural and ideological positions. Of course, moments of discontinuity occur in a more subtle way in films all the time, and Sobchack's account of her reactions to the first two shots of *The Piano* (1993) provides a good example. So too do her reflections on the significance of the ink-bottle in the opening of Krzysztof Kieslowski's *Dekalog 1* (1989). In her article Sobchack (2004) describes how the ink-bottle exists both as a material object and also as something that exceeds the bounds of its materiality. In the context of the film's narrative it acts as an analogue, or index, of some dreadful other as the opening of the film suggests an impossible connection between ink leaking from the bottle and the death of Pawel who while ice-skating has fallen through the ice. In different ways the character of Krzysztof (whose name doubles with the director's) and the viewer have their gaze expanded beyond the materiality of the moment. This leads to the 'existential conjunction of logical contingence and emotional turbulence' (2004: 87) that for Sobchack is at the core of the phenomenology of the experience of the film, a position she develops in her essay on pedagogy and Derek Jarman's last film *Blue* (1993) (Sobchack, 2011).

An interesting aspect to her argument is that paradoxically it is at the point when we are drawn into the film, and when we enter its fictional world, that we have the greatest opportunity for finding our own meanings. This marks something of a development of her earlier position, and it is closer to the one that I am adopting here. So while our reaction might cause a moment of discontinuity with the film's narrative, it nonetheless binds us into the subjectivity of the cinematic experience. The film seems to activate in us a certain type of fantasy function. I would describe it as the 'third image' and as an embodied experience of ourselves in relationship with the film. Here we need to be clear because in Jungian theory the function of fantasy is not to distance ourselves from the psychological reality of a situation. Instead, it is the opposite. Fantasy offers us an insight into the reality of our own interiority as it partially bypasses the defences of consciousness and the limitations of the conscious mind. Just as we experience the affect of an image before we consciously understand its meaning, so too fantasy can connect us with something that the rational mind has yet to grasp. This is something that films share with dreams and to find the meaning of the experience we need both to be aware of how our body is responding emotionally and also to think ourselves into the meaning. To argue this is to provide an alternative view to the Lacanian construction of the decentred and fragmentary self. It is one that suggests that the relationship with the cinematic is broader even than Sobchack's 'expanded gaze' and that the viewer and the film construct each other as subjects within the cinematic experience.

The importance and role of the unconscious and its agency in structuring relationships

It will not have eluded you that for my argument to make sense it needs the existence of an unconscious part of the psyche. By the unconscious, I do not mean just a part of the self, the psyche, of which we are not aware, though it is certainly that too. I have in mind a sense of the unconscious that is much closer to how Jung uses the term. Here the unconscious functions with intention: it seeks to bring into the conscious mind those aspects of the psyche that have for whatever reason been repressed. These might be unpalatable or they might be more attractive but, irrespective of their appeal or otherwise, they are essential to an understanding of who we are, and of what is happening in our lives.

To reach the point where we can recognize the importance of the unconscious in making meaning in the cinema we first need to reflect on the question of identification. Remember I am arguing that meaning does not come from identification with the film, nor does it arise from a sense of difference or otherness. Instead, it involves containing these different elements in the form of a composited psychological image. Sobchack's view of spectatorial identification comes close to what I am suggesting but it is also rather different.

> Thus, what is often taken to be the spectator's *identification* with the film's discretely embodied 'address of the eye' is, in fact, the spectator and film's *identical directedness* toward the same intentional object. That is, the spectator and the film often share the same *interest* in the world. They do *not*, however, share the same *place* in the world, nor the same *body*.
>
> (Sobchack, 1992: 286)

It is difficult reconcile Sobchack's claim for identical directedness with her instance on difference. This is particularly so as one of the tenets of the phenomenological orientation is that the possibility of an identical position is ruled out. So I think it easiest, and indeed more coherent, to suggest that films and spectators do not share the same place, body or, indeed, directedness towards the same 'intentional object'. Instead, the meanings, which viewers find in the filmic experience, are more helpfully thought of as being in a state of flux in which they are more individual and negotiated than Sobchack suggests, even allowing for her identification of and with the 'expanded gaze'. In this scenario what happens is that the unconscious overrides any attempt to direct, or to fix and to share interest, and instead it imposes its own meaning on the film. Of course, in part this arises from the film but it is not the sole result of the film. Rather, as I have stated repeatedly in this book, it is the result of a psychological relationship with the film. It is this relationship which gives rise to a meaning that is not just from the narrative of the film, or from the objective components of the cinematic experience (the apparatus of cinema), or solely from the psyche of the viewer. Instead, this psychological need for a creative and personal response to films results in the third image: an affect-laden response to the cinematic which is both deeply personal and yet also contains shared collective components. While the narrative of the film might be a matter for collective experience, the meaning of the cinematic experience is personal and psychological, if at times also archetypal. Of course, suggesting the sense-making aspect of the unconscious is rather different to the general position adopted by Sobchack.

Elsaesser and Hagener draw our attention to another issue in the stance that Sobchack takes and they use it to illustrate a more general concern about phenomenological film theories. For them, despite the claim that the body is the central site of meaning, phenomenological film theory also wants to hold onto its roots in a theory of representation which originates from cultural studies and in particular in a broadly Marxist-informed critique of culture and its signifying practices. I alluded to the issue of the dominance of this mode of film theory above. However, such is the weight of this theoretical position that much film theory finds it difficult to move away from concerns with material form, structure and ideology. Psychoanalytically informed film theory is no different and historically it has emphasized structural relations including intrapsychic structures, such as the mechanisms of id, ego and superego and the formal processes of dream work that were identified by Freud. From the 1970s up to the present day, Lacanian concerns with image, form, mirror phase and the realms of the 'imaginary', 'symbolic' and the 'real' have come to dominate psychoanalytic film theory. Elsaesser suggests that phenomenological film theory's interest in the body and its role in meaning sets up a tension between meanings that are 'embodied' in a form of materialist commodification and meaning that is more literally embodied in the viewer of the film:

> the continuous rhetorical invocation of the body as a central element of any given theory does not automatically undercut the distance between film and spectator in terms of phenomenology. Indeed, there are a number of approaches that constantly talk about the body but

> nevertheless cling to the representational paradigm familiar from Cultural Studies, whose ideology critique cannot be unproblematically reconciled with the phenomenological experience of the body.
>
> (Elsaesser and Hagener, 2010: 119)

To be fair, Sobchack is aware of this pull and tension, and she attempts in her argument to move away from what she rightly identifies as the ocular-centric view of film theory. For her, the embodied gaze is pre-reflective and pre-representational, at least at its most basic level. That said, she retains an interest in body politics that is somewhat similar to the paradigms used by cultural studies. However, Sobchack develops a different focus because she is rooted in the existential philosophy of Merleau-Ponty. Broadly speaking, Merleau-Ponty's affiliations were with French Marxism, although he was influenced by the Hungarian Georg Lukács and also by Leon Trotsky. To an extent Sobchack is reading Merleau-Ponty through this political filter,[1] yet to my mind she does not fully reconcile the difference between the materialist theories of representation and the emphasis on the body which is both a site of meaning and also the place where film is transformed into the cinematic experience. Another phenomenological film theorist Laura Marks adopts a slightly different position in solving this problem. For her, both sight and the act of looking, exist outside the realm of the visual. Much as Jung's idea of the image is in fact a whole-body experience, so too Marks suggests that seeing should not be divorced from the other senses, and in particular touch:

> *The Skin of the Film* [the title of her book] offers a metaphor to emphasize the way film signifies through its materiality, through a contact between perceiver and object represented. It also suggests the way vision itself can be tactile, as though one were touching a film with one's eyes: I term this *haptic visuality.*
>
> (Marks, 2000: xi)

This helpfully directs us to the way in which meaning is not the product of a single sense or activity. This seems to correspond to the experience of psychotherapy. The meaning of what a client talks about is not fixed, nor is the meaning of a dream or indeed of any material that is introduced into the consulting room. Nor are the meanings of the therapist's words fixed. It is not uncommon for me to make an intervention or offer an interpretation to a client and for them to 'mishear' what I have said, only to say what an accurate observation I had made. Being alert to these moments in therapy helps to identify times when the unconscious is particularly active. Meaning is not something that is static, as is generally assumed, a point which Marks also makes:

> In revaluing haptic visuality I am suggesting that a sensuous response may be elicited without abstraction, through the mimetic relationship

> between the perceiver and a sensuous object. This relationship does not require an initial separation between perceiver and object that is mediated by representation.
>
> (ibid., 64

Here I want to argue both for and against the particular phenomenological position that is suggested by Laura Marks. When she writes that a 'sensuous response can be elicited without abstraction' I am sure she is correct. Where I disagree is that this comes about as a result of a mimetic relationship. As Elsaesser reminded us, the roots of film studies are so firmly intertwined with a historical materialism that it is extremely difficult to step outside that mode of understanding. Even so, it is important to move past these arguments because the quality of psychological relationships is not solely predicated upon a set of material relationships. Instead, the quality of the experience of being in a psychological relationship is derived from an affect-laden felt sense in which questions of materiality have less of a role to play than is normally supposed. If we pause for a moment, then actually it is easy to see that the cinematic experience is set up to be something other than reality. While notions of materiality, substance, text, encoding and so forth are important for academic film theory, they do not reflect the way that we actually experience films. This is quite a problem as what we need is a psychological way of understanding the feelings we have when we watch films, but not a psychoanalytic theory rooted in structure. Nor do we want to use psychoanalytic theory as a means to deconstruct the ideological implications of the cinematic. While both these approaches are of course legitimate, and indeed insightful, they do not help us to make sense of the sensuous and the affective responses we have which are integral to our experience of the cinematic. Instead, we need a way to understand how our bodies encode emotions when we watch films. It is here that psychotherapy can be of use because one of the things that it knows about is how meanings arise from relationships, how our bodies unthinkingly and unknowingly respond to such meanings, and what happens when we become conscious of what is occurring. To understand the psychology of what happens, we need to attend to our own affective responses in relation to the cinematic.

To summarize, the intellect will not suffice in understanding the cinematic experience, though it is of course essential. We have also seen that it is the very lack of mimesis in the cinema that points us towards the psychological meaning of films. Such meanings lie not in their materialism, nor just in their narrative, but in their ability to constellate in us a desire to understand ourselves in relationship with the world through the psychological images that we create. It is this sense of otherness that turns out to take us towards a psychological reality, not a material one, in which affect has a crucial role to play in creating meaning.

7

FEELING THE IMAGE

This chapter focuses on the therapeutic dyad and how meaning is constructed between client and therapist. It does so as a means to understanding the viewer–screen relationship. It is by no means self-evident that ideas that relate to one discipline, in this case psychotherapy, have value and utility to another, namely film theory. While keeping this in mind, this chapter is going to explore if the way in which Jungian-orientated psychotherapy understands the idea of image, and also the meanings of those images, can be used to illuminate the emotional responses we have when viewing films. The intention is to reflect on how our bodies encode those emotions. In psychotherapy the intellect, feelings and bodies are all used to help in understanding the psychology of a given situation. Central to this is the idea of the intersubjective field which is an imaginal space that is constellated between client and therapist and which contains meaning at an unconscious and bodily level. As a paradigm for the viewer–screen relationship, the intersubjective field suggests that far from meaning residing solely on the screen, or just in the mind of the viewer, it is possible that meaning exists in a space somewhere between the two. This, and the space where it resides, I refer to as the 'third image'. It is characterized by apperceptive responses to films in which collective, inscribed, narrative meanings are subsumed in unexpected personal and emotional reactions.

To a greater and lesser extent, the third image is always present when we view a film. At times it is palpable, and when this is the case the result is a special and personal relationship with films. This is one of the reasons why a film might enthrall one person and bore another; psychologically, these two people have not seen the same film – they have not had the same experience. It is also why someone can become obsessed with a film, be quite literally in love with it, while everyone else is mystified about its appeal. This is the apperceptive response to film in which personal meanings are created even though such meanings are often at odds with more consensual views. I think of this as 'losing the plot'. Of course, it is losing the plot that lets us gain an insight into ourselves.

The client and therapist relationship and the intersubjective field

One of the cornerstones of psychodynamic psychotherapy theory is the curious process of transference and countertransference; we have discussed some of the technicalities of these processes earlier in the book. To recap, the two terms are similar: transference is an attempt to understand how the client's emotions can be felt by the therapist, while countertransference is a way of distinguishing the therapist's emotions from those of the client. As we will see, this is not always as easy at it might first appear. Behind this idea there is a growing body of scientific research concerning how we convey and learn about emotions. For example, the possible existence of 'mirror neurons' that are activated when we see a recognizable behaviour being performed by someone else has been of interest in psychotherapy research. Other researchers, most notably Allan Schore (2003), have written about mirroring behaviour more generally, and the role of this in affect regulation. Slowly the biochemistry of these processes is becoming clearer, especially the role that oxytocin, the so-called 'empathy' or 'trust' molecule, has to play in mother–child bonding, physical contact and the pleasure we have when looking at another person, and how it can act as an anti-depressant and so reduce stress. This relationship between neuroscience and psychotherapy has been well documented and from a Jungian perspective two of the key exponents are Margaret Wilkinson (2006) and Ginette Paris (2007).

However, I am more concerned with the experience of being in the consulting room than with the neuropsychology of the experience. In particular, I am going to try to present what happens for the psychotherapist in a session. In doing so I want move away from a mechanistic model in which the client in some way 'transmits' emotions into the therapist. Quite often, the theory of transference and countertransference is taught to trainee psychotherapists as though this were the case. When this happens trainees are encouraged to 'tune in', or to gain therapeutic attunement to the client as a way of enabling the process of transference to take place in an optimal manner. They are told to 'work in the transference' or sometimes to work in the 'negative transference'. Sometimes, this way of working therapeutically is referred to as the 'blank screen approach', though as is probably already clear the term is something of a misnomer. At one level this is respectful of the client as it attempts to gain the fullest possible understanding of what the client is trying to communicate. The role of the therapist is to help the client locate the sessions' narratives in the context of broader life narratives. This act of interpretation is not unlike the process of consciously engaging with and understanding the narrative of a film. This should not be taken to suggest that interpretation of the transference is only an intellectual process. Clearly, the feelings of the therapist (or viewer) have a role to play in understanding what is happening.

The problem with the theory is that it downplays the role of the therapist in *creating* meaning with the client. It tends to impose an interpretative scheme onto what the client is saying. Transference interpretations focus on the way two people appear to transmit emotions and thoughts in the therapeutic relationship. However, rather than seeing this as a process of transmission it is more helpful to imaginc thc relationship as a matrix, or field, of conscious and unconscious interactions. Here I do not mean to evoke Kurt Lewin's ideas from the 1940s in which he emphasizes social and cultural factors and behaviour. Instead what I am suggesting is that in the consulting room communication between therapist and client constitutes a psychological field in which meaning is constellated or co-created. The 'presence' of the therapist is crucial to the way that these meanings are made in therapy. Here I am going beyond the often stated claim that 'it is the relationship that heals', which, leaving aside the question of whether therapy is about healing, has a certain truth to it. Instead I am suggesting that the same client with a different therapist will arrive at a different understanding of his or her life. This is not just a question of theoretical orientation on the part of the therapist (an existential therapist might see things differently to a Rogerian, for example) though that does play a role. Rather, it is the 'being' of the therapist which interacts with the 'being' of the client as together they create and understand what the client is talking about. This is going to prove important, as I want to suggest that something remarkably similar happens when we view films.

To shed a little light onto the processes of transference and countertransference, here are a couple of examples from therapeutic work which will give a general sense of how I think the therapeutic field works in practice. One of the interesting aspects to this process is the way in which a client's material intermingles with the susceptibilities and concerns of the therapist. Learning to sift out the two and to cope with the emotional demands this imposes on the therapist is one of the reasons why training in psychotherapy is lengthy and often requires the trainee to be in therapy for its duration. Here is my first example. A colleague of mine who is a psychotherapist was telling me of his persistent anxiety that he might not be a very good therapist. Recently a client was telling him how well his own career was going and how successful he was. My colleague's thoughts began to wander. As they did so he found himself thinking that he was doing a particularly poor job in this session. In fact, he thought, he was being useless. Then it occurred to him that actually it might be best if he gave up working as a therapist altogether as clearly he was not suited to this type of work. These troubling thoughts were accompanied by a sinking feeling as though something heavy, grey and large had sunk to the very pit of his stomach. Reasonably quickly, he noticed what had happened and pulled himself back into the session. At the end of the hour, the client thanked him for a really good session and mentioned how insightful and helpful it had been! The therapist had realized at the time that this sinking feeling of self-doubt was only partly due to his anxieties. One of the clues to this was the intensity of the experience in which he was almost overwhelmed by thoughts of his own incompetence as a therapist. Something unconscious was on the loose. It also became to clear to him that while the client had been telling him about how successful he was at work. He was also unconsciously voicing deep concerns about his ability to do his job well and indeed to live life in a successful and whole manner. This is an example of a transference which activated in my colleague a mild countertransference. I say mild, because while the feelings were strong, they were quite containable. He also found it interesting that the affirmation from the client seemed to be another unconscious way of signalling to both of them that it might be best if they did not explore this any further as both of them were doing a great job. (Of course, they did return to this topic in many future sessions.) Something that was partly unconscious in my colleague and largely unconscious in the client had come together and presented itself with some weight because it needed to be addressed. I am certain that a different therapist would have understood what was happening differently, and the client would have gained a different perspective. But this is the meaning the two of them made that day, at that time.

To these psychotherapeutic ideas of transference and countertransference I want to add the specifically Jungian notion of 'apperception' which is what takes us closer to the idea of a psychological field. Apperception is a way of understanding how psychological changes happen. *A Critical Dictionary of Jungian Analysis* defines it as follows:

> A process by which a new psychic content (recognition, evaluation, intuition, sense perception) is articulated in such way that it becomes understood, apprehended or 'clear'. It is an inner faculty which represents external things as perceived by the registering, responding psyche: therefore, the result is always a mixture of reality and fantasy.
>
> (Samuels *et al.*, 1986: 25)

Jung identified two different types of apperception that arise as the result of conscious self-reflection: active and passive. Active apperceptions require the purposeful and deliberate engagement of the senses and also of our critical faculties. By contrast, passive apperception arises from the unconscious, or is forced on the senses. In the first instance the activity comes from the ego and in the second, with the self-enforcing content, from the unconscious. The cinema, then, provides a most interesting situation where visual and auditory information is 'forced' on the viewer and where the viewer also has the opportunity to engage with the process in an imaginative manner. The result is a mixture of reality and fantasy in which the role of fantasy is to make a psychological reality available in ways that consciousness, thinking and the rational part of the psyche are not able to. In this way, the 'fantasy-image' we explored towards the end of the previous chapter connects us to an image that encapsulates our inner psychological reality.

While cinema can be therapeutic, of course it is not therapy. That said, the way to approach those qualities of cinema that have the potential to be therapeutic is through an understanding of how we create meaning in the cinematic experience. In therapy the meaning of any event in life becomes clear as client and therapist work together to understand what is happening for the client. Something similar happens in the cinema where meaning arises from our unconscious interactions with what is seen and heard. Its origin might be the film on the screen but the psychological meaning of the experience comes about as a result of the interaction between the viewer and the film. Such interaction involves both transference and countertransference and it arises from the psychological field of felt, intuited, thought in which imagined and embodied experiences exist.

The third image

In psychotherapy the physical space between client and therapist is part of an intersubjective field. I think that it is helpful to think of this field as including the physical boundaries of the consulting room, the arrangement of furniture and other objects, even the temperature and lighting. It also includes the social boundaries that form part of the 'therapeutic contract' which is established with the client: non-disclosure by the therapist, the client not asking direct questions about the private life of the therapist, a non-judgemental attitude on the part of the therapist are common parts of such agreements. All these elements play a role in the creation of the intersubjective field. However, what I want to explore is the ways in which psychological meaning is experienced in this somewhat boundaried/framed space. This is actually quite difficult to put into words because such meanings are fleeting, difficult to grasp and hard to sense. It is a meaning that is encoded in the body of both client and therapist, it is almost as though something that is both conscious and unconscious at the same time comes into being as both parties meet psychologically. This is why the metaphor of the field is more appropriate than one of transmission. It is not that emotions are being broadcast, it is more that new understandings are being created. It has to be said that this is not always a pleasant experience. I described above how fear and terror can be part of this meeting. So too there can be a palpable sense of shame, envy, jealousy, anger and sadness, as well as more uplifting emotions. When we transfer this idea to the cinema, at first it does not seem to make much sense to think about an intersubjective field. As explored in the previous chapter, despite the claims of some phenomenological film theorists, film does not possess a subjectivity, a consciousness or a body, other than in the most abstract sense. Quite simply, film is not alive. However, what is very much alive is the relationship that viewers have with films and it is this relationship which animates the film and derives meaning from it.

There are numerous ways to view a film and each involves forming a different type of relationship. The following description explores three different ways of finding meaning in films. They are presented as somewhat separate but in fact they overlap and the question is really which aspect of the viewer–screen relationship is emphasized at any given moment. The most obvious way to watch a film is to let its images and sounds unfold in front of us. When we do this the locus of meaning is predominantly on screen and in the representational qualities of what it is that we see and hear. In this mode of film viewing we go along with the narrative of the film. This is the 'first image'. Even here, in the first image, meanings other than those of the narrative can arise, yet the focus of meaning remains on the representational aspects of the image and the narrative of the film. Of course, there is an unconscious aspect to this mode of viewing too. Typically in the first image, viewers are not consciously aware of how the film is communicating; they do not consciously register lighting, framing, editing, music and so forth and yet this cinematic apparatus is clearly central to how the narrative of the film is created and conveyed. It is through these conventions as they combine diegetically that the viewer understands the film is a constructed fiction.

A second way to watch a film involves consciously trying to understand and interpret it. This is an intellectual and intuitive activity that incorporates an aesthetic sensibility, and it follows that it is both conscious and unconscious. Here we engage with the film conceptually and are also sensitive to what it is that we feel when we watch the film. In so doing we form an understanding of the film, its narrative and the way meaning is encoded in its structure – shot, editing, lighting, etc. The object of understanding is the film and the approach is one of conscious hermeneutic activity which deconstructs the film's diegetic and representational aspects. I call this the second image as it is the image that we create in our mind of what the film is about, of what the film is trying to explore and how we understand it. Here we draw on our own subjectivity, our intuitive capacity and our ability to empathize with the on-screen characters to help in understanding the film. In the creation of the second image we pay particular attention to the use of formal narrative devices such as metaphor, symbol, allegory in the film. We interpret the meaning behind the editing, the framing, lighting, etc. For example, we might notice how music in the film reinforces the emotions of the scene, or subverts them, or how it alludes to emotions and characters other than those on the screen, to other genres, and makes extra-textual references.

A third way to watch a film involves becoming aware of the ways in which viewing a film is a whole-body experience; in other words, that it is both a conscious and an unconscious process. Arguably, in this mode we are not viewing the film at all. Instead we are entering into a cinematic experience where meaning does not reside in the narrative of the film or its audio-visual structure, but instead rests in our experience of the film. As in therapy, and with the intersubjective field, this type of relationship emphasizes those meanings that are intensely personal and deeply felt. This is a response to film that bypasses the intellect and in which the viewer is momentarily overwhelmed. This is the third image. It should not be confused with suture or diegesis. As already mentioned, diegesis refers to the techniques that are used to make the on-screen world coherent and believable. These techniques are used by filmmakers in order that viewers do not notice edits, the change of scene, the auditory enhancements of the soundtrack and so forth. They are the 'tricks of the trade' and they belong to the first and second images. By contrast, *suture* refers to the way in which the unconscious of the viewer can be 'stitched' into the structure of the film. This somewhat complicated theory suggests that the structure of film replicates intrapsychic structures and that is why we identify with films and their characters. These intrapsychic structures (ego-ideal, for example) are inherently unstable; so too the structure of films is unstable as it offers a potential unity (of the body) which framing and editing cannot allow as they dissect the body into separate parts. Seen in that light, film replicates our own search for wholeness while at the same time it negates that possibility.

In the third image, what we experience is not a direct result of the techniques of cinema, though they might well be a contributing factor. What we experience is a personal affect as our unconscious temporarily invades consciousness. We no longer know why we are reacting in the ways we are. We do not understand where these tears have come from, why we are so afraid, why we are embarrassed or shameful. Meaning comes from the intermingling of our individual psychology with the film, its narrative, images and sounds, in order to create a new meaning. This new meaning does not come directly from the screen, nor does it come from the intellectual investigations of consciousness. To repeat, this is the third image and it takes the form of an unexpected, powerful emotional response, almost as though we have lost our mind and have been taken over by something else. We are losing the plot, yet as the narrative of the film fades into the background, so the narrative of our life comes to the fore.

One of the ideas that runs throughout Jung's work is the desirability of holding together competing thoughts or feelings at the same time. So it is not surprising that while he wants to comprehend the unconscious, at the same time he proclaims its fundamentally unknowable qualities. An interesting facet of this is the way in which Jung often constructs the unconscious as an autonomous entity that behaves in a manner that is independent of the ego. Of course, this is reminiscent of the way in which Sobchack thinks about the film as something that has an identity, perception and a body of its own. However, it is important to resist the notion that the psychological qualities of cinema are predicated solely on their replication of internal psychic structures. The reason why films have a certain proximity to the unconscious is largely because they operate at the level of metaphor and allusion, of feeling and affect, which are qualities cinema shares with the psychological image of the intrapsychic field. As Jung comments:

> We have no knowledge of how this unconscious functions, but since it is conjectured to be a psychic system it may possibly have everything that consciousness has, including perception, apperception, memory, imagination, will, affectivity, feeling, reflection, judgment, etc., all in subliminal form.
>
> (Jung, 1947/55: para. 362)

Cinema has the capacity to trigger these responses in viewers as it brings back forgotten emotions. It helps us to imagine our life experiences laden with affect and it offers viewers opportunities for reflection and judgement, 'all in subliminal form'. Such subliminal qualities are experienced as a result of the passage of the film's images and sounds and are encoded in our bodily response to this unconscious material. Jung puts it as follows:

> Beside things that have been forgotten, subliminal perceptions form part of the contents of the unconscious. These may be sense perceptions occurring below the stimulus-threshold of conscious hearing, or in the peripheral field of vision; or they may be apperceptions, by which are meant perceptions of endopsychic or external processes.
>
> (Jung, 1918: para. 9)

While these are not terms that Jung used a great deal he nonetheless conceived of two psychological systems: the ectopsychic and the endopsychic. The ectopsychic contains the main components of consciousness (sensing, thinking, feeling, intuition – seeing possibilities). He later came to develop these aspects into a theory of consciousness and of personality type. Together, these two systems form the most accessible and observable psychological parts of ourselves, though they are not without unconscious qualities. In particular, the endopsychic system points towards the psychological aspects of the self that are orientated towards unconscious contents. For Jung, this includes: memory; subjective orientation; emotions and affect; and invasion.

What I want to suggest is that the cinematic experience is a place where we are able to experience temporary affect and its less conscious and more intensive counterpart, invasion. We are able to do so in a manner that is relatively safe as it is controlled and containable. Of course, we can experience psychological invasion and affect in many ways that are not overly anxiety-provoking. However, cinema sets out to create such experiences, in a time-limited and focused form, and in a way that is both personal and collective. Most forms of cultural invasion are about the individual losing their identity. Large sporting events, open-air concerts, rallies or demonstrations are all occasions when the individual becomes part of the collective. This is not to say that they lack a personal dimension, more that the emphasis is on the collective.

By contrast, cinema offers the chance for an individual and highly personal response, as does theatre. But cinema sets out with a large screen that occupies the field of vision, sound that is immersive to envelop us with its unrelenting parade of shot following shot, and scene after scene. What it offers is a personal intensity of affect that is experienced at a physical level which we find difficult, and sometimes impossible, to control. Cinema is not alone in creating such strong emotional reactions – I have been at my most terrified when upside down on a roller-coaster. But the affect in the cinematic experience is much more variegated than my experience in the theme park. What cinema seems to offer is something really quite bespoke and individual in which our own psychological needs shape the meaning of the experience. While not writing about the cinema per se, Jung notes how these affective experiences originate in the unconscious and how they can overwhelm, or take over and possess, the ego.

> Then we come to the *affects* and *invasions*, which are only controllable by sheer force. You can suppress them, and that is all you can do. You have to clench your fists in order not to explode, because they are apt to be stronger than your ego-complex.
>
> (Jung, 1935: para. 90)

We can have somewhat similar responses in the cinema. Our heart rate goes up as the action increases, we can feel sad or angry for the characters on screen. But more significantly, we can experience feelings that we did not expect and that do not seem to come directly from the narrative of the film. For no apparent reason we feel uncomfortable, guilty, ashamed, worried, fearful. Somehow, it seems the film is exposing something that we have tried to keep hidden. The sense of being taken over leads us into the psychological territory that Jung has termed apperception and invasion. These psychological states will illuminate the 'between' space in the cinematic experience. They help to reveal how the third image exists between the film's effects on the viewer and the viewer's own affects and projections onto, and into, the film. This is the field of the cinematic experience.

One way in which to understand what is happening in such a situation is to regard the experience as the failure of the psyche's mechanisms to repress some unpalatable contents. If this is right, then what appears to happen is that the sheer intensity of the audio-visual experience overwhelms the psyche and, as the systems of repression break down, the unconscious contents find their way into consciousness. This is not so unlike the mechanism of parapraxis, where, evading the control of consciousness, some inner fantasy, thought or fear 'slips' unwittingly into the light of day. It might also be reasonably argued that this process is facilitated by the physical conditions of cinema, which are particularly well suited to the experience of unconscious affect. Let us allow this as a possible explanation but it might be that something else is happening as well. Here, it is important to remember that for Jung the psyche is teleological, which is to say that the innate tendency in the psyche is towards a greater awareness of its unconscious contents. Sometimes this is formulated as the movement towards an expansion of ego-consciousness; alternatively, we might say that when the ego is strong enough to assimilate the contents of the unconscious, the unconscious enables a move into consciousness. This is marked by an affective shift. It is important to remember that these unconscious contents were kept in the unconscious for a reason, namely because they were too painful or unpalatable for the conscious part of ourselves to deal with. It therefore follows that sometimes the affective shift is typified by unpleasant and seemingly unwanted emotions but their appearance also offers the opportunity for their integration into consciousness.

When we watch films a complicated psychological process is at work in the way the unconscious finds meaning. The idea of the first image suggested that we need a sense of recognition and that what we hear and see in the cinema can be taken as a depiction of events which we accept through the diegetic as in some way believable. These events adhere to an established mode of representation which is close enough to our experience of reality to allow us to accept them as 'believable' but in which they are also codified as different. The second image suggests that we then interrogate these representations in an effort to understand their aesthetic and emotional meanings. This is a conscious attempt to use our life experiences and our intellectual and aesthetic sensibilities to understand the narrative of the film. The third image is where the unconscious parts of ourselves, memories, experiences we have tried to forget are brought to the fore by the passage of the images and sounds of the film. Equally, the reality of our current psychological situation of which we might not be consciously aware is activated. When this happens a highly personal and individual meaning is experienced as an outpouring of affect. These processes broadly correspond to what Jung describes as the act of 'apperception' in which an experience of affect is released by a sense of recognition. Importantly, this act of recognition is not based in any mimetic similarity. Instead, it is the recognition that something we did not know about ourselves is coming to light and as such this act of psychological recognition is also an act of psychological interpretation.

> As is well known, the act of apperception consists of two phases: first the perception of the object, second the assimilation of the perception to a preexisting pattern or concept by means of which the object is 'comprehended'.... Every new representation, be it a perception or spontaneous thought, arouses associations which derive from the storehouse of memory. These leap immediately into consciousness, producing the complex picture of an 'impression', though this is already a sort of interpretation.
>
> (Jung, 1939/55: para. 776)

The experience of these affects can be so powerful that it appears as though temporarily we are not ourselves. Such affects can be strong and, if experienced outside the confines of the cinema or some other psychologically contained environment, they are also quite frightening. Nevertheless, in the safety of the cinema we have little difficulty in witnessing murder, death, violence and such like. These affects can also take the form of love, romance, erotic attraction and other fantasies. What seems to happen is that emotions which we normally repress are able to find an 'acceptable' outlet in the cinema. Our first psychological and defensive strategy is to displace these unconscious contents onto the characters and narrative of the film. In such cases we feel a strong sense of identification with the characters as we let them experience 'our' emotions. However, sometimes the affects are so strong and so personal that displacement is not possible. When this happens we experience them in a powerful somatic manner and our body encodes the experience and, without thinking, it responds. As Jung comments:

> You experience sometimes what you call 'pathological' emotions, and there you observe most peculiar contents coming through as emotion: thoughts you have never thought before, sometimes terrible thoughts and fantasies. For instance, some people when they are very angry, instead of having the ordinary feelings of revenge and so on, have the most terrific fantasies of committing murder, cutting off the arms and legs of the enemy, and such things. Those are invading fragments of the unconscious, and if you take a fully developed pathological emotion it is really a state of *eclipse* of consciousness when people are raving mad for a while and do perfectly crazy things. That is an invasion. That would be a pathological case, but fantasies of this kind can also occur within the limits of normal. I have heard innocent people say, 'I could cut him limb from limb', and they actually do have these bloody fantasies: they would 'smash the brains' of people, they imagine *doing* what in cold blood is merely *said* as metaphor. When these fantasies get vivid and people are afraid of themselves, you speak of invasion.
>
> (Jung, 1935: para. 65)

Of course, cinema is full of experiences just like those described by Jung – at least popular cinema is, and this is one of the reasons why this book, like much Jungian-orientated writing on films, tends to focus on mainstream popular cinema. There is something immediate, visceral and earthy in popular cinema that speaks to the darker aspects of the unconscious. It is not that other films are without these qualities but popular cinema seems particularly direct in its psychological affect. It is in a temporary 'state of eclipse of consciousness' in which what might be characterized as pathological states outside the cinema can be experienced in relative safety and in what is potentially a psychologically beneficial manner. Much as our dreams can express the psychological reality of our lives, so too these moments where the cinematic experience invades us offer another opportunity to experience what we do not know about ourselves. These momentary and affective cinematic invasions have a psychological relevance when the meaning we find in them comes from the narrative of our own lives and not the narrative of the film. While intensely personal, such moments are also archetypal, as the affect connects us to the inner workings of the objective psyche, which Jung conceived of as the foundation of the unconscious.

This interplay between the individual and the collective, and the unconscious and conscious parts of ourselves, is at the core of psychodynamic psychotherapy, and it is also at the core of the cinematic experience. Clearly, psychotherapy and viewing a film are not the same. Nor are dreams the same as films. However, a Jungian understanding of 'image' reveals how psychological images are the result of intellectual engagement and experience. Importantly, they also arise from dialogue. In therapy, it is an actual dialogue between therapist and client, with all the complexities of conscious and unconscious interactions which that situation suggests and, indeed, requires. In dreams, the dialogue with the unconscious is mediated through images and sounds, while in the cinema the dialogue is facilitated through our bodies and the way they encode our conscious and unconscious engagement with the film. In this immersive environment we simultaneously experience the cinematic as body, concept, feeling and intellect.

The psychological meaning of these experiences, in therapy, from dreams and in the cinematic occurs when two different elements interact, and this gives rise to a new meaning that is not inherent in either. Jung terms this mechanism the transcendent function. Some might understand this term somewhat mystically, but actually it is better understood as our capacity to hold contradiction and to find meaning in the tension between differing perspectives. The transcendent function operates at moments of psychological insight and when we come to accept competing and different understandings of what a situation means for us as individuals. What is particularly confusing about the term is that it suggests a removal from the here and now, along with a type of escape from the pressing realities of the present moment. This is unfortunate as Jung observes how the ability to hold together these competing tensions actually serves to connect us more securely to our psychological reality.

The element of transcendence is concerned with the ability to 'rise above' the competing views of consciousness and the unconscious and in so doing we become what Levi-Strauss (1966) terms an anomalous character. This is a character who can straddle the divide between good and evil – a nuanced character who when influenced by situation and ethics can proceed in a manner which is authentic, socially aware and also culturally situated. Of course, we do not need the moral language here that Levi-Strauss employs to understand how the ability to contain different psychological dynamics is at the core of being. This is not a question of just being oneself, it is being oneself in relationship – and this relationship is intrapsychic as it involves the dynamic between the conscious, the personal and the collective and unconscious aspects of ourselves. It also embraces the individual and the social with the personal and the historical. All these elements inform and shape the language and discourses we use to articulate our understanding of our lives. Put another way, the psychological image is: visual and intuited; felt and thought; personal and collective; individual and archetypal; subjective and historically located; personal and part of a shared discourse.

Images are formed in the psyche partly as a result of structure and agency, but also as independent and semi-autonomous entities. As such, images are both the object of knowledge and the object of knowing and they serve as the fulcrum between past and future. To be clear, there is nothing mystical in this statement. Indeed, we can observe the same structure at work in the narrative of films where at any moment the viewer is aware of how the current situation has arisen, what is happening in the present, and what the future might hold. This is what Jung means when he writes that the psyche is Janus-faced – any image, visual or otherwise, holds the competing needs of the individual and the collective, the desire to be in the present right here and right now, and the pull of the past alongside the call of the future. In microcosm, this is what happens whenever we view a film as our own being intersects with the narrative of the film and in so doing the narrative is diverted and becomes intertwined with our personal story. When this happens we create a new image, a new narrative and a new way of feeling what it means to 'be'. The impossibility of reconciling our personal narratives with the realities of life is temporally transcended and in these moments we also experience a greater sense of immanence. This is a type of *enantiodromia* in which, contrary to expectation, opposites do not pull away from each other but instead run together. It helps to explain why the cinematic experience as a fiction has the capacity to connect us physically to our bodies and psychologically to our whole selves: it is the ability of the cinematic to contain contradictory qualities which makes it such a profoundly psychological medium.

Cinema is sufficiently like reality for us to recognize what we are seeing and it is also quite unlike reality. This discrepancy gives us permission to fantasize and to imagine. Equally, it is an experience of the liminal as cinema is both real and unreal, it is both individual and collective, it has a shared meaning and a personal meaning, it is both psychological and mundane. The cinematic experience is an experience of profound tensions yet one of its most remarkable qualities is that, unless we pause, it appears unremarkable.

The non-rational and psychological reading

The following is an account of an episode from psychotherapy. It is included here as an example of how in psychotherapy the imagery of films can have a meaning that is quite divorced from the narrative of the film. Up to this point in the book I have illustrated the third image with reference to clients in psychotherapy, but now I will describe how my own film-watching experiences have directly informed my practice as a psychotherapist. The following example demonstrates how one of my own third images related to the psychological situation in which the client found herself. It illustrates how I evolved a non-rational understanding of the imagery of the film and how it also provided me with a way to connect to the client's unconscious anxieties.

I do not want to suggest that there is a direct causal relationship between the particular film I was watching and what the client was experiencing. The idea of the psychological field clarifies this point as it offers a metaphorical way to understand how the unconscious aspects of a situation arise in therapy from the client–therapist relationship, and subsequently how they take the form of an image. Like therapy, films provide a particularly fertile ground for this type of apperceptive response which, as we noted, is based partly in reality (the life of the client) and partly in the illusion that is the world of film. As such, the apperceptive response is a psychological fantasy and it is an image that captures a reality. Such images are akin to dream images, whose meanings are not fixed but are negotiated, felt and embodied. These images might be felt in the room, or they might be found in art, drama, literature or in some other fortuitous manner. What matters is not the site of the original image but the ways in which the context of therapy inflects the meaning of the image, and in which the image can inform the therapy. This is what forms the field of influences in which client, therapist, external image and internal image are all bound together.

Rebecca's entrance was remarkable as in her first session she announced, 'I can seduce any man!' It was one of those memorable starts to therapy in which an initial claim provided the basis for the next couple of years of work. Despite the power and bravado of her statement, Rebecca was in a highly distraught state and she believed that her marriage was in crisis. She no longer felt as erotically attracted to her husband as she once had and she described him as stable, solid and dependable. She was also upset by the loss of a close male friend, Richard, with whom she had formed a bond. She would describe Richard as exactly like herself – effervescent and full of life. There was a powerful 'buzz' about their time together that felt intoxicating and joyous, even as she was retelling the evenings of dancing, the beautiful meals and cocktails.

When I met her, Rebecca was a somewhat unselfconsciously self-absorbed person. Her self-love took the form of a glow, and ability to animate people round about her as they quite literally fell under her spell. While she did not recognize this as a narcissistic quality, she did know how to quite consciously use and manipulate relationships. She once described to me her 'tools of seduction' and they were well honed.

Our work together developed quickly. A few months later Rebecca's distress had quite considerably alleviated. As we explored her upbringing and childhood, her tendency to binge-eat subsided. The sessions did have a tendency to get a little academic and as Rebecca is exceedingly bright she unsurprisingly showed a considerable appetite for psychological self-examination. She also took to praising me, to thanking me for my insights, expressing gratitude for the work we were doing and such like. She was highly resistant to my suggestion that this was a type of seduction, and indeed that some of the ways she behaved with me were a type of intellectual eroticism.

After a year, Rebecca had something of a transformative experience. While travelling abroad she discovered personal meditation, a practice that became an important part of her life although she remains somewhat surprised by this development. Meditative practice did not fit with her self-image which was of a highly polished professional and well-educated woman and not, as she would put it, 'a tree-hugging charity worker'. During one guided meditation in which she imagined sending out love and kindness into the world she astonished herself. Out of the blue she had an image of a large ball of glowing power that she was holding and then released, as she watched, it floated out across the countryside and into the sky. For Rebecca, this was not an act of imagination, as she actually saw and felt the warmth that emanated from this ball of light. Interestingly, she was not perturbed by the experience but instead internalized the glowing sensation. It left her feeling uplifted for quite some time.

As if this image and the experience were not striking enough, as Rebecca recounted her experience an image from a film that I had watched the previous day leapt into my mind. The film was *Burnt by the Sun* (Утомлённые солнцем, or transliterated, *Utomlyonnye solntsem*) (Dir. Nikita Mikhalkov, 1994). Outside Russia and people with a particular interest in Russian film, it is not particularly well known. The film is set in a dacha near Moscow in 1936 and is shot in a fairly naturalistic style with high production values, and it emulates something of the style of contemporary American films of the 1990s. On closer inspection, *Burnt by the Sun* turns out to be more ironic, self-knowing and critical of Russian society than it first appears. However, as is the tendency in this book, once again the narrative of the film need not detain us too much. While most of the film is realist in style, there are two moments when a large fireball appears and it is these that I want to concentrate on.

During its first appearance the fireball emerges over a river, then collides with a falcon and finally burns down a single tree. All this takes place while the character of Dimitri or Mitia (Oleg Menshikov) tells a fairytale to a little girl Nadia (Naclezhda Mikhalkova). The story he tells concerns a good singer and musician called Yatim and his adopted father, a magician called Sirob. Sirob also has a daughter Yasum, and they all live happily until the outbreak of war when Yatim has to leave for the front. He is subsequently injured and stays abroad. Nadia claims to know the end of the story – Yatim and Yasum will marry. However, Mitia has another ending in which Yatim returns home but an important man (a sort of bogeyman or ogre) arrives and he sends Yatim away. While Yatim wants to be happy he knows that he is not allowed such bourgeois thoughts. Yasum cries, and ends up marrying the important man whose name Yatim cannot remember. In this story Mitia is actually describing the complexities of the triangular relationship between himself, Kotov (Nikita Mikhalkov) and Marusia (Ingeborga Dapkunaite). The second and final time the fireball appears is at the end of the film when it coincides with Mitia's suicide. On both occasions the fireball goes unnoticed, although near the start of the film its appearance is reported in a newspaper article read by Philippe (André Umansky).

Now it has probably struck you that the fireball in *Burnt by the Sun* has a somewhat destructive quality to it that seems at odds with how Rebecca described her experience. Even so, as she was talking, the image from the film stuck in my mind, along with its somewhat jarring associations. Gradually I discerned very clearly that Rebecca's narcissistic glow had both a positive and a negative quality to it. To put it another way, I became aware of how life-affirming she could be both to herself and to others, and yet also how this had the potential to be destructive, especially as her affirmation was frequently built in and around her manipulation of other people. It seemed to me that this was something we were going to explore in the work and I wondered whether Rebecca would be able to acknowledge this contradiction in her behaviour. It also crossed my mind that identifying this quality in her might mean that its grip on her would be weakened, and I wondered whether this would be entirely welcome.

A few weeks later I was talking to a Russian friend about the film *Burnt by the Sun*. She pointed out to me that the translation of the title was not accurate and that in Russian Утомлённые (utomlyonnye – burnt) actually means 'tired'. So a more precise translation of the film's title would be 'Tired by the Sun' – I checked with her to see if this had a particular meaning in Russian and was told, clearly (!), that it meant just the same as the English – 'The Sun was responsible for us being tired'.[1] This made me wonder just how much energy Rebecca might use up in fuelling her own iridescent qualities and in igniting that glow in others. I find that a useful way of thinking about psychological energy (what Jung called libido) is to imagine it as a fixed quantity. All psychological activity requires energy, be it anxiety, anger, depression, worry, an escape into fantasy and so forth. If any one of these elements is lessened, the affect becomes less intense and it is then possible to redirect the libidinal energy. In so doing, the natural tendency we have towards health means that this redeployed energy is now used more fruitfully as we feel more content and able to cope with life. This seems to fit rather well with Jung's view of the mind–body system as something which is homeostatic, teleological, and behaves in a compensatory manner as a dynamic system which strives for balance, but which attains it only momentarily.

What then would it mean for Rebecca if my associations to the image from 'Tired by the Sun' were indeed right? The initial phases of withdrawing energy from a psychological fantasy are often characterized by a feeling of weariness or fatigue. This was something I also occasionally felt in the sessions and I had shared this sensation with Rebecca. At first she found the idea that anyone could sense or embody the feelings of someone else rather curious. Yet as time progressed Rebecca gradually came to realize that her capacity for compassion and empathy were much greater than she had expected and that she too was capable of understanding how other people felt. It was interesting that as she became more aware of her feelings and her desire to care for others, the glow of her narcissistic aura dimmed, and it surprised her just how visible this change in her was to other people. Gradually she found the personal strength to question the core values around which she had come to build her life. Some remained, others altered in their importance, while some disappeared completely.

Up to this point we have been considering how clients negotiate or find meaning(s) in films. Here we have my associations with a film and what a client was telling me. It would be possible to take this material and go back to the film to see if its meaning had changed for me but I have not done so. Instead, I have chosen to focus on the curious coincidence of a fireball appearing in an otherwise naturalistic film and Rebecca's unusual experience of a glow of warm loving energy appearing, unlooked for and unbidden, in the midst of her everyday life. From a Jungian perspective it might be tempting to see this as an example of synchronicity, which Jung thought of as an acausal but significant coincidence. In other words, such events are coincidences that have a psychological meaning for the client and therapist. It would be perfectly possible just to notice that I had seen a film with a fireball in it the day before my client wanted to talk about her experience. On the other hand, there is an unlooked-for opportunity to engage in a creative and imaginative way with these 'found' images and in therapy I like to use whatever presents itself. My own way of thinking about this is simply to notice what has happened. I also take time to pause and wonder about the imagery. Why was I attracted to this film at this time? What was happening for me in my life that drew me to this film? Does it raise in terms of countertransference anything that needs to kept in mind about the work? Is my reaction alerting me to something I had not previously noticed in the consulting room, and so forth? I do not find the idea of a formal mechanism, such as synchronicity, necessary here. Nor do I find that it adds much to my understanding of my experiences and those of my client. Instead I prefer just to note the psychological experience that I am having and to be as aware of it as possible.

As I began to work with the story which Mitia tells Nadia I watched the extract (not the whole film) numerous times and I gradually discovered all sorts of other meanings that seemed relevant to Rebecca. The fairytale has three central characters, Yatim, Sirob and Yasum. To help his storytelling, Mitia uses three dolls: Yatim, whose doll is small and naked; Yasum's doll is taller and clothed; while Sirob's doll is an old disfigured male, who also looks somewhat primitive and archaic. There were a couple of points about Mitia's story that particularly struck me. First, it is Yasum's father, Sirob, who is ill. Second, Yatim does not initially recognize the now beautiful Yasum, and asks if she is the same person who 'used to pee in your pants and fall asleep on your father's knee while he was teaching me music?' She affirms it is indeed her. Finally, Nadia thinks she knows the ending of the story which is that Yatim will marry Yasum, but Mitia has a different ending in which Yatim is banished from the country with the threat that if he remains he will be beheaded.

As mentioned, in the film the fairytale is an allegory of the relationships of the key characters in the room. To ensure the viewer does not miss this point, the shot cuts to each person when his or her character appears in the fairytale. For example, at one point Nadia enquires if Yatim has been summoned by Koschei (translated in the subtitles as a Bogeyman) and the shot cuts to Kotov. Importantly, Koschei is not really a bogeyman at all but a well-known character in Russian folklore with an indestructible soul who abducts, or steals, the hero's wife.[2]

Prompted by these associations it was a short step to thinking about the characters in the film and in the fairytale in relation to Rebecca and myself. I do not intend at this point to offer a whole clinical picture, rather what I want to show is how my own personal associations with the imagery of the film were closely related to the work that Rebecca and I were engaged in. For example, I found myself wondering if the sick old Sirob who gets pushed to one side was reminiscent of Jung. In the film the doll looks primitive and old, as though it might have been fashioned in a remote Russian village. It seemed a fitting figurine for Jung. The questions kept coming: did I think there was something sick (wrong) with Jung, or did Rebecca? Why did he need to be banished? Why did he need to be out of the picture, so to speak? Was he the man whom through his physical absence she could never seduce? Was it significant that the doll of Yasum is somewhat taller than the naked doll of Yatim? Did Rebecca see herself as in some way towering over a naked version of me with nowhere for me to hide in this story? Did I feel exposed before her, or was I perhaps the purveyor of the 'naked truth'?

The neat inversion of the character of the adulterous Koschei and Rebecca's boast that she could seduce any man was of course ringing in my ears. What I want to stress is how all this is at odds with what the film is mostly about. It is important to remember that the fireball and the fairytale form only a tiny part of the film, indeed so tiny that film theorists have not paid them much attention. This might be because there is a wealth of ideological and political material that is much more accessible in the film. Yet it is precisely the oddity of the fireball and Mitia's story that I find appealing. Certainly it activated for me a series of associations and personal meanings that would not be available to any other viewer. In a very real way I negotiated my own set of meanings with at least this portion of the film. Even now the affect of those sequences stays with me and colours my understanding of the psychology of the film's characters. Similarly, my associations from the film inflected my understanding of what was happening for Rebecca.

The interaction between personal meanings and the narrative of films is a central problematic for film theory. The unconscious mechanisms of projections, identifications and complexes are always at work when we watch film. Central to this is the way that the cinematic experience offers an excellent environment in which to experience feelings that are otherwise repressed in everyday life. No doubt other art forms can offer something similar. But I want to suggest that the opportunities provided by the cinematic experience for these types of psychological process are actually greater than those afforded by other media. Occasionally clients will want to talk about theatre, television programmes, or current events in politics, the news and so forth. But without any doubt the desire to talk about emotional experiences that take place while watching films and during subsequent reflections is more common.

This takes us closer to one of Rebecca's central beliefs, namely that the glow of her narcissistic energy was necessary for her life, yet it was also destructive. She thought that if it was withdrawn then she, and those close to her, would be harmed. More particularly, if I really got to know her, it would be intolerable to me – perhaps I would not have the energy to live: coping with her would be too exhausting and I simply would have been ‘tired by the sun’. So too in the film the final appearance of the fireball occurs as Mitia ends his life. To be clear, I do not mean this to be taken literally, rather the destruction that took place for Rebecca was a metaphorical destruction. My challenge was to be strong enough to hold these energies and to provide a space where Rebecca was safe and contained.

It would be possible to reflect in much greater detail about how the symbolic qualities of these extracts are relevant to the therapy. But the central point I want to make is that my film-going practices were helpful in providing a new understanding of Rebecca. The interpretations I made acted as a kind of amplification of her experiences. Significantly, my psychological relationship with the film formed a type of third image which came from a highly personal experience of the film in which the meanings I found were somewhat (though not completely) at odds with the film’s narrative.

CONCLUSION

Throughout the course of this book I have been arguing in a variety of ways that the meaning of films is not something that is fixed. To suggest this, I have used the term 'cinematic experience' as a shorthand device to encapsulate the way in which each one of us has a separate and a distinctive relationship with the films we view. I have also stressed the changing nature of this relationship, and the way in which it is both our sense of who we are and what the films mean that changes. Of course the idea of 'experience' as a creator of meaning is, at least from some perspectives, a problematic one. After all, one of the historical foundations of academic argument is that understanding does not require experience and that instead it arises from enquiry, investigation and argument. From this standpoint it is not necessary to have experienced an event in order to understand it and to appreciate what its implications might be. The foundations of this approach are hundreds of years old, stemming as they do from the Enlightenment of the seventeenth and eighteenth centuries. As a twentieth-century thinker, one of Jung's insights, although he was hardly alone in this endeavour, was that psychological understanding sometimes requires experience. Like psychology, music demonstrates how experience can give a different insight to the one offered by the intellect. A piece of music might be described to me in great detail and I might well study the composer in order to understand the historical and cultural contexts in which he or she was working. However, it is not until I hear the music that it becomes possible for me to experience what it means, for me. In this example subjective experience and meaning are informed by and through the intellect, but the intellect alone is not enough nor is it the only source of meaning. Such academic researches into a piece of music might lead me to believe that I will respond in a particular way, but the only way that I can actually 'know' is to listen to the music and to notice how I respond. Of course, it might turn out that my understanding is purely theoretical and intellectual. I might notice the elegant way in which a musical theme is treated, inverted, recapitulated, harmonized and so forth. But my suggestion is that typically we do not respond in such a detached and analytical manner to what we hear and that instead we react emotionally. Of course, what moves one person can leave another listener quite perplexed and puzzled over the emotional relationship the other person has with the music. This attachment might be the result of personal experience or a particular memory, but music also has the capacity to move us in ways that are quite unpredictable and that consciousness and intellect cannot readily account for.

The same argument holds good for psychological insight. It seems that as humans we have two different propensities regarding psychological awareness. One is to behave as though our psychological understanding of ourselves is correct. For the most part we assume that we have understood the emotional dynamics of a situation correctly and that we know the reasons for our own behaviour and beliefs. Once these patterns of understanding have been formed, they set rock hard and we hold on to them with great tenacity. However, it is also the case that as enquiring and questioning beings we are inclined to analyse ourselves and the way we are in the world. Jung emphasized this latter aspect, while also acknowledging that many individuals choose not to follow this inner call to individuation. Recognizing and accepting the tension to become more aware of ourselves, and how this is matched with an equally strong desire not to change, is one small part of the process of human maturation that Jung identified. So too in the cinema we may choose just to watch a film, or we can opt to reflect on it. Another option is to make the decision to engage with a film and to enter into the cinematic experience in which mind, body, thought and feeling, intuition and sensing, and consciousness and the unconscious, come to manifest themselves in the present moment. Importantly, deciding to engage with a film in this way may not be a decision that we are fully conscious of making, even though it happens. The cinematic has the capacity to 'animate' our psyche and to bring to life those aspects of ourselves which in everyday life remain either hidden or dormant.

An important part of my project in writing this book about the meaning of the cinematic has been to place the individual firmly into film theory and to see how the psychological meaning of images can be highly personal. Such individualized meanings are often felt and embodied and they come from the interplay between our personal unconscious, our collective concerns and the experience of the film. These conditions give rise to the emergence of the 'third image' that is a felt sense which contains the psychological meaning of the cinematic experience for us. As an image, it is akin to the type of image we 'hear' or experience when we listen to a piece of music. In this sense the cinema is something that is embodied, personal and also collective. Film is a material commodity but cinema exists as an experience in which we allow the images and sounds of a film to coexist with the unconscious aspects of ourselves. It is the interweaving of film and the unconscious that creates the cinematic experience.

The term 'cinematic experience' extends beyond the realm of the personal as it also encompasses the physical conditions of cinema and the phenomenology of the cinematic experience. Here the tiny details and rituals that surround going to the cinema are of the utmost importance. Together they create a process in which the result is much greater than any of its parts. The purchase of a ticket, the requirement to attend at a specific time and place, the arrangement of viewers, the darkened auditorium, the huge screen and the qualities of immersive surround-sound all have an important contribution to make in the meaning that we are going to find in the experience. My suggestion has been that the material and ritualistic conditions for viewing films are part of the cinematic experience. Together they combine to provide a psychologically safe space that is contained and defined. This containment is partly physical, but it is also a psychological containment in which we are emotionally held and where we are able to respond emotionally and authentically.

The cinematic experience has one foot in the physical world and another in the imagination. Part nocturnal and part diurnal, it straddles this apparent divide and in so doing it allows our unconscious to come out to play, as it were. This is a serious sort of play in which the cinematic experience becomes part of our psychological life as we engage in the activity of recognizing those hidden aspects of ourselves that we normally keep deeply buried. In this broadly Winnicottian sense, films become a type of transitional object, while the cinematic experience assumes the role of a transitional phenomenon. These are the play spaces of culture in which we experiment and experience what otherness and difference are like. They are also liminal and transitive spaces that allow us to get a glimpse of our own interiority, and in so doing we come to form a new relationship with our inner self. One of the insights that comes out of such experiences is the realization that what we had thought were personal and private concerns are more commonplace and collective than we had realized. Of course, this realization is both welcome and unwelcome. On the one hand, it binds us into the collective as we see that we are not alone in our anxieties and in our sense of how the world functions. On the other hand, the price we pay for this is the loss of ourselves as completely unique individuals, and it can feel as though a very personal and private space has been invaded and violated. The tension between the personal and collective, between the narrative meaning of a film and our personal experience of it, is central to the cinematic experience. It is also at the heart of psychotherapy, the core purpose of which is to help us become the people we are and not just to live the life that society has in mind for us. To achieve this aim we both need to have clear sense of our own understanding of how we are in the world and we also need to see the ways in which we are not so different. The challenge is to hold together these competing tensions in a way that has personal meaning for us.

We have also seen how the idea of the cinematic experience can usefully be extended to include the material conditions of the cinematic apparatus (by this I mean the shot, framing, editing, lighting, mise-en-scène, sound, music and direction along with the other components that are used to tell stories in the cinema). When these are combined with the phenomenology of the cinematic, we have the conditions for the 'cinematic frame'. What I have been arguing for is not any one aspect of the above, for they are all parts of the cinematic, and it is only through their combination that we get the whole picture, so to speak. I have chosen to focus on the role of the individual because that aspect of the cinematic experience has gone relatively under-theorized by film studies. However, that is not to downplay the importance of those other elements and in particular the importance of regarding film as text. Of course it is the case that films have narrative meanings as well as personal ones. We come to understand these through our awareness of the established codes of cinematic meaning and they are enhanced and refined by our aesthetic and intellectual sensitivities and perspicacity. I do not want to suggest otherwise and indeed most of us, most of the time, respond to films in ways that we can understand in terms of images and sounds of films.

However, it seems that it is also the case that cinema is more than just the film. Structurally, we might say it is also an institution, it is the business of production, distribution and exhibition. Cinema is also composed from the texts and intertexts that the films themselves spawn. Interviews with movie stars and directors, fan culture, soundtracks and director's cuts of films are all intertexts (or paratexts or auxiliary texts, to use Genette's (1982) taxonomy) that form part of cinema. I have sought to emphasize the centrality of the personal psychological relationship that we have with films. In doing so, I have underscored the importance of the cinematic experience as an embodiment of the unique psychological meanings that films can engender.

With this stress on the individual, as I mentioned in the Introduction, I can see why it might mistakenly appear that I am advocating an essentialist approach to films, to the unconscious and, indeed, to the cinematic experience itself. However, this is not my intention. Instead, I want to adopt a position that attempts to hold together these competing tensions around the meaning of films in a way that is going to be productive. My contention is that the cinematic experience does not offer an escape from the real world. Rather, it provides a means through which to descend into one's own inner life. The cinema offers a point of transition, a liminal space through which to enter into the interiority of our being. It lets us bypass the defences of consciousness to gain a valuable insight into the core of our psychological being. An essentialist approach would serve to locate meaning in the epistemology of personal empiricism. I hope that it is clear that I do not regard psychological meaning as fixed. Instead, I have suggested that meaning is a matter of negotiation, it is in a state of flux, and it arises and is contained within a field of influences in which the subjectivity of the individual has a central role to play. Yet at the same time I also want to acknowledge that films clearly do have narrative meanings and that their images and sounds have inscribed and intended meanings that the filmmakers expect viewers to understand. How then might we resolve the apparent contradiction between a somewhat fixed narrative meaning with the idea that meanings also are in a state of flux inflected and created by the individual relationship we have with films?

A partial answer is found in the idea of relativism, as the pre-Socratic Greek philosopher Heraclitus advances it. His ideas influenced Jung's thinking about the form that opposites take in the psyche. Instead of regarding opposites as pulling in different directions, Heraclitus suggested that opposites exist in a state of unity. The somewhat puzzling idea of a state of unity is what lies behind Heraclitus' famous dictum that the path ahead and the path back are the same. For him, it follows from this condition that the universe must be in a state of flux and a consequence of this flux is that it becomes impossible for anyone to have the same experience twice. It is for that reason that you cannot step into the same river twice, as the river has changed and moved on. It is no longer the same river, nor are you the same person. Some of these ideas have informed my thinking about the shifting and changing nature of the meanings that we find in films. It is not so much that films are without meaning, or that the author of a text is the reader (as Roland Barthes (1977) argued in 'The Death of the Author'). Rather, each and every time that we watch a film its meaning is constantly remade and remediated through the lens of our personal psychology. So, too, the meaning I find in a film will be different to the meaning anyone else finds. Sometimes this is a question of subtle differences but there are instances when my understanding is personal, unique to me and idiosyncratic.

That films also retain a narrative meaning, and an inscribed narrative, takes us back to the question of relativism. Heraclitus offers the following example, and it is one that will be instructive for us. He gives the example of how the ocean is both life-giving and poisonous. It is life-giving if you are a fish, it is poisonous if you are a human. The sea then has two qualities and its 'meaning' is dependent on the position that is adopted 'relative' to the sea. (Heraclitus has a number of other engaging examples, including rotting food which is dangerous for us to eat but is the basis of a sound meal for a pig.) So too the meaning of cinema is dependent on how we are positioned relative to it. The idea of the third image that I have been developing is a way of trying to encapsulate this philosophical and psychological idea and to locate it as an integral part of the phenomenology of the cinematic experience. The third image, as the subjective experience of meaning, is composited onto the first and second images. To recap briefly, the first image is the signifying surface of the film, both aural and visual, and it involves viewers in the act of interpreting those signs. Such interpretation is partly conscious yet it also takes place at a pre-conscious level. Here it is possible to move between being aware of the film, while also letting it unfold in front of us as we enter a state of semi-hypnagogic reverie. The second image arises from the conscious and intentional act of interpretation. Here our intellect, our experience and our aesthetic sensibilities are of the utmost help and importance. Yet this activity too is engaged with our intuition, our 'gut feelings', and relies upon our individual perspicuity. It follows that it also has a strong unconscious component, which relies upon personal qualities. To varying degrees, these three images overlap, and at different times one can be held in a greater degree of relief than the other. However, the relationship between them is one of shifting emphases as they remain in a state of constant flux. As a result, they position us as viewers via a set of different relationships, all of which are relative to the film.

An echo of this idea can be found in the work of the film theorist Vivian Sobchack whom we looked at in some detail in Chapter 6 above. In the following quotation she draws our attention to the way in which the relationship we have with cinema is one that embodies past, present and future. Consequently, we might say that cinema transcends normal time, as it opens up a psychological space:

> Each film (as each spectator) exists as simultaneously presentational and representational, as viewing subject and visible object, as an embodied 'presence' informed by the transcendent activity of retention and protention that grounds a reflection of time as past, present and future. Each film (as each spectator) exists as a continuous 'becoming'.
>
> (Sobchack, 1992: 299)

Here I want to stress the dynamic and reflexive relationship that, as Sobchack rightly identifies, we have with films and that is central to the cinematic experience. It seems to be a fundamental quality of the cinematic that, almost regardless of the quality of the film or its aesthetic beauty and sophistication, it is possible for us to develop a meaningful psychological relationship with it. As the analytical psychologist James Hillman (1979) reminds us, the psyche does not discriminate on aesthetic grounds. Instead we find and make meaning in the most unlikely of places. The fertile ground of the psychological imagination seems to be stimulated by the conditions of the cinematic experience rather than by aesthetic or intellectual engagement with the film. It is as though something simple, archaic and primitive from deep inside ourselves momentarily takes over the rational and conscious part of our being. The intensity of the experience is such that we can carry this 'infatuation' and its psychological significance for us out of the cinema and into the world. This is what lies at the core of cinephilia, which is a love not so much of film but of the cinematic experience and also of the great pleasure and joy that can be attained from the awakening of the psyche in a meaningful and playful manner. This is not to sidestep the issue of unpleasant emotions that emerge when we view film, as we have dealt with those earlier in the book. Rather, it is to notice that any anxiety we feel about engaging in the process of self-awareness seems to be outweighed by the benefits that are gained. Indeed, we might say that in this regard cinematic pleasure makes the recognition of the darker and more frightening aspects of our psyche a more palatable prospect. The embodied experience in the cinema, which at times can be frightening and disturbing, also brings with it the frisson of self-awareness that accompanies such insights. Just as dreams can disturb us and yet we continue to dream, so too the cinematic experience continues to have an enduring appeal. It seems that no matter how we feel about their content both films and dreams are important parts of our psychological life. Indeed, their significance might lie in their capacity to let us experience those aspects of ourselves that the rational and 'enlightened' part of the psyche knows are unacceptable in our society.

Going to the cinema is a public act, and it is also a furtive one that is carried out in darkened rooms and away from the everyday. To experience the cinematic is also a prurient activity that lets us look into the lives of others, rather like a therapist in the consulting room. But in a unique turn of events, it turns out that the life we are looking into in the cinematic experience is actually our own. What we had thought was a voyeuristic activity is actually in no small part an act of introspection. This is elegantly depicted in the opening shot of *Citizen Kane* (Dir. Welles, 1941) in which the screen is filled with a sign on a wire fence that reads 'No Trespassing'. Ignoring this injunction the camera moves up and over the fence and into the bizarre landscape of Kane's house and the grounds of Xanadu. A series of matched dissolves take us inside the mansion to Kane's deathbed, and via some close-ups and distorted wide-angle views we find ourselves in a real world and a magical world, with a broken snow-globe filling the screen, its disproportionately large synthetic snow falling across the screen. Kane's now immortalized last word 'Rosebud' opens the doorway to the rest of the film which is devoted to solving the enigma of a life that can never be fully understood. This in miniature is the cinematic experience – a liminal space, with one foot in the world of dreams and the other in our waking lives, and its very liminality encourages us to reflect on ourselves and how we understand the way we are in the world.

Certainly the relationship we have with the cinematic experience, which has the capacity to hold and contain what appear to be competing and conflicting views of ourselves, can also help us in our process of continuous 'becoming'. This process is analogous to the one that Jung refers to as individuation. We have also noticed how our own relationship with a film results in different meanings and gives rise to a variety of ways of understanding that film. As such, the film too is in a process of becoming, as it changes and develops in parallel with its viewers. This type of relationship means that the visual and aural aspects of film are not enough if we are to understand its meaning. Instead we need to head in the direction of experience as eye, ear and by extension brain can only give us a partial insight into the meaning of the cinematic experience. As Sobchack puts it:

> Thus we cannot depend upon an analysis of the objectively visible to tell us everything we want and need to know about vision. The visible is never the whole of vision. It is never experienced by us as complete. The content of our sight is never simply all there is for us.
>
> (1992: 293)

The statement that 'the visible is never the whole of vision' points us to the ways in which a solely conscious engagement with the cinematic experience fails to adequately account for the psychological meanings we find, negotiate and to an extent make when we view films. Like film theory, literary theory has sought to understand the appeal of fictional worlds for readers and the relationship they have with them. The literary theorist Keith Oatley in his book *Such Stuff as Dreams: The Psychology of Fiction* suggests that one of the purposes of fictional worlds is to provide readers with the opportunity for the vicarious experience of relationships in a manner that allows them to be transferred to our daily lives. For him, reading is an activity that has a direct relevance for the social world.

> Fiction is principally about the problems of selves navigating in the social world.... Readers of fiction tend to become more expert at making models of others and themselves, and at navigating the social world.... Reading a fictional piece puts people into a frame of mind of thinking about the social world.
>
> (Oatley, 2011: 160)

From this position he advances the idea that there are four beneficial effects that arise from engaging with fictional literary worlds. It is important to note that the types of novels that Oatley has in mind are literary ones and not the type of paperback fiction that we might think of as roughly analogous to 'Hollywood' films. His suggestion is that reading the observations and thoughts of a perceptive author makes us better able to understand the dynamics of our own relationships.

> By reasoning backwards from the effects that have been found of improved social abilities of empathy and theory of mind in readers of fiction it's possible, perhaps, to indicate what it is about fiction that is likely to have beneficial effects. Four themes can be inferred: exploration of the minds of others, investigation of relationships, dynamics of interactions in groups, and grapplings with the problems of selfhood.
>
> (ibid., 167)

Oatley might well be right in suggesting that literature, and indeed films, present us with models of behaviour that allow us to understand our own thoughts and feelings with greater clarity. However, his focus on the text as a literary artefact does little to explain the appeal of more popular fiction. Nor does he account for our ability to transfer only appropriate models of behaviour. The question of how we distinguish between destructive behaviours and insightful ways of behaving in a relationship remains somewhat unresolved. It also suggests a normative view of human relationships that is at odds with the more psychological view of individuation. That said, his comment that fictional worlds help us to 'grappl[e] with the problems of selfhood' is helpful and very much along the right lines. While Oatley retains an intellectual rather than a psychological orientation he nonetheless thinks himself into a psychological insight, albeit through the use of some rather rarefied literary texts.

> The emotions we experience are not primarily those of the characters, they are our own, in the contexts we imagine.... Emotion is that process

> in life by which events become meaningful to us. Often it brings the events to consciousness.... Art is not simply taking a ride on preoccupations or prejudices, using a schema that runs as usual. Art enables us to experience some emotions in contexts that we would not ordinarily encounter, to think of ourselves in ways that we usually do not.
>
> (ibid., 115–18)

Oatley is certain that the fictional worlds of literature have the capacity to help us reframe and understand afresh our deeply embedded schema. My view is that cinema is even better positioned than literature to reveal our inner personal psychologies. We have seen that it is not enough to regard cinema as just an aural or visual or tactile medium. Of course, the cinematic experience is built from those building blocks but it is much more. Tempting though it might be, it is important to resist the desire to consign cinema to either the world of illusion or a material world. It is not merely an apparatus nor is it solely imagination, as the psychological qualities of cinema derive from its liminal position.

In his *Notes on the Cinematographer* the director Robert Bresson observes, 'Your film is not made for a stroll with the eyes, but for going right into, for being totally absorbed in' (1975: 95). His insight is a profoundly psychological one. While not framing it in these terms, Bresson captures an essential aspect of the phenomenology of the cinematic experience. He understands that the cinematic is both intensely personal and also shared. The cinematic needs to be experienced not just through the senses but through the totality of our being as it is cinema itself as a medium that contains the opportunity for a profound tectonic change in the foundations of our being. We have seen how Jung's conception of the image has a metaphorical quality and a life of its own, being partly a response to the unconscious and also an expression of how the conscious part of our self grasps and comprehends our life. We see this clearly in dreams where, without the watchful eye of the conscious mind, our unconscious makes itself known. Dreams provide an insight into the reality of lives, the interiority of being and the meaning of our relationships. They are dynamic and symbolic, and their psychological images are vibrant and full of meaning. To experience these unknown parts of ourselves somatically is to bring them into our waking life and it is also to bring them into the felt sense of our being. This is not just the prerogative of dreams. The cinematic too is a place where, as Bresson puts it, we experience the 'Shudderings of images awakening' (ibid., 125).

NOTES

INTRODUCTION

1 Thanks to Alexandra Fidyk for this distillation.

1 THE CONSCIOUSLY CONSTRUCTED FILM

1 Jung's use of gendered language needs noting and indeed this tendency permeates his writing. The identification of nature with the feminine is also a product of his time, but whereas the initial impulse might be to forgive him for this, we should also note that this is also an impulse of our own cultural production today: the character of Calypso/Tia Dalma in the most recent Pirates of the Caribbean film *At World's End* (2007) is figured as a cruel mistress, an exotic and powerful racial other. Moreover, do not meddle with her, for she is formidable and unforgiving. Jung's identification of nature as female can perhaps be best understood as belonging to a reactionary and deeply conservative part of his psyche. He frequently confuses female sexuality with the part of the male psyche that he thought of as contrasexual and culturally feminine in its construction (he terms this the *anima*).

2 Admittedly from a different standpoint, Christian Metz (1982) elaborates this point from a psychoanalytic perspective in 'The Imaginary Signifier'.

3 www.raindance.org/site/index.php?id=478,6076,0,0,1,0 (8/12/11).

4 I am indebted to Greg Singh for this point (cf. Singh, 2011).

5 The thoughtful and interesting TED talk by Colin Stokes is one such example: www.ted.com/talks/colin_stokes_how_movies_teach_manhood.html (January 2013).

6 There are numerous aggressively anti-Jar Jar Binks websites, for example: www.angelfire.com/nv/jarjarbinksmustdie/frames.html (30 November 2011).

7 www.salon.com/2000/03/22/lucas_2/ (30 November 2011).

2 BEING IN THE CINEMA

1 Cf. Jung's essays 'Psychotherapists or the Clergy' (1932) and 'Psychoanalysis and the Cure of Souls' (1928) both make interesting reading on this point – they are in Volume 11 of the *Collected Works* of C. G. Jung.

2 Some of these ideas are found in a somewhat different context in Miller (1987).

3 Perhaps the lack of this sense of otherness is one of the reasons why on-line therapy via Skype and such like has yet to flourish. When clients travel abroad I sometimes offer them the possibility of Skype sessions. While some are taken by the idea, many feel that it is too associated with work – too much like everyday life.

4 www.lesamisdulouxor.fr (19 October 2012).

5 I am grateful to Greg Singh for this insight.

6 More recently there is of course an ever-growing body of writing from a broadly neurological perspective that explores the relationship between life experiences, the neurological structures of the brain and psychological life. Cf. Damasio (2000, 2006, 2012).
7 Cited in Burgin (2004: 32).
8 Again, thanks are due to Greg Singh for his thoughts on this point.

5 SEEING THE IMAGE

1 Unsurprisingly, there is quite a body of knowledge on this topic. We have already mentioned the approach that has been formulated by cognitive film theory in which a process of 'enaction' serves to drain away inappropriate emotional responses to fictional stimuli in the form of films. Horror films have proved productive territory for these speculations, and in particular for psychoanalytic formulations (cf. Carroll, 1990; Hills, 2005; Schneider, 2004).

6 BEING TOUCHED BY THE IMAGE

1 Thanks are due to Greg Singh for this observation.

7 FEELING THE IMAGE

1 My thanks go to Nadi Fadina for her help and continuous support in all matters Russian.
2 Again, thanks are due to Nadi Fadina for drawing the importance of Koschei to my attention.

BIBLIOGRAPHY

Abram, D. (1996) *The Spell of the Sensuous*. New York: Vintage Books.

Allen, R. (1977) *Projecting Illusion: Film Spectatorship and the Impression of Reality*. Cambridge: Cambridge University Press.

Bach, R. (1977) *Illusions: The Adventures of the Reluctant Messiah*. London: Heinemann.

Barker, J. (2009) *The Tactile Eye: Touch and the Cinematic Experience*. Los Angeles: University of California Press.

Barker, M. (1998) *Knowing Audiences: Judge Dredd – its Friends, Fans and Foes*. Luton: The University of Luton Press.

Barthes, R., trans. Miller, R. (1973) *The Pleasure of the Text*. New York: Hill and Wang.

Barthes, R. (1975) *'En sortant du cinéma'*, *Communications*, 23: 104–7.

Barthes, R., trans. Heath, S. (1977) *Image-Music-Text*. Glasgow: Fontana.

Baudry, J. (1974–5) 'Ideological Effects of the Basic Cinematic Apparatus', *Film Quarterly*, 28(2): 345–55. Reprinted in L. Braudy and M. Cohen (eds) (1999) *Film Theory and Criticism: Introductory Readings*, 5th edn. Oxford: Oxford University Press.

Baudry, J. (1975) 'The Apparatus: Metapsychological Approaches to the Impression of Reality in Cinema', *Communications*, 23: 760–77. Reprinted in L. Braudy and M. Cohen (eds) (1999) *Film Theory and Criticism: Introductory Readings*, 5th edn. Oxford: Oxford University Press.

Bellour, R. (1987) 'The Pensive Spectator', *Wide Angle*, IX(1): 6–10.

Benjamin, W., trans. Eland, H. (2002) *The Arcades Project*, ed. R. Tiedemann. Cambridge, Mass.: Harvard University Press.

Berger, J. (1972) *Ways of Seeing*. Harmondsworth: Penguin.

Beumers, B. (2000) *Burnt by the Sun*. London: I. B. Taurus.

Bordwell, D. (1997) *On the History of Film Style*. Cambridge Mass.: Harvard University Press.

Bordwell, D. and Carroll, N. (eds) (1996) *Post-Theory: Reconstructing Film Studies*. Madison, Wis.: University of Wisconsin Press.

Braudy, L. and Cohen, M. (eds) (1999) *Film Theory and Criticism: Introductory Readings*, 5th edn. Oxford: Oxford University Press.

Bresson, R., trans. Griffin, J. (1975) J. *Notes on the Cinematographer*. Kobenhaven: Green Integer.

Buckingham, D. (2003) *Media Education: Literacy, Learning and Contemporary Culture*. Cambridge: Polity Press.

Burgin, V. (2004) *The Remembered Film*. London: Reaktion Books.

Campbell, J. (1949) *The Hero with a Thousand Faces*. Princeton, NJ: Princeton University Press.

Carel, H. and Tuck, G. (eds) (2011) *New Takes in Film Philosophy*. Baskingstoke: Palgrave Macmillan.

Carroll, N. (1990) *The Philosophy of Horror: or, Paradoxes of the Heart*. London: Routledge.

Caughie, J. (ed.) (1981) *Theories of Authorship*. London: British Film Institute.

Cavell, S. (1971) *The World Viewed: Reflections on the Ontology of Film*. Cambridge, Mass.: Harvard University Press.

Cooper, M. (2008) *Essential Research Findings in Counselling and Psychotherapy*. London: Sage.

Costello, A. S. (2006) *Imagination, Illness and Injury: Jungian Psychology and the Somatic Dimensions of Perception*. Hove: Routledge.

Crary, J. (1992) *Techniques of the Observer: On Vision and Modernity in the 19th Century*. Cambridge, Mass.: MIT Press.

Dawson, T. (1997) 'Jung, Literature, and Literary Criticism', in Young-Eisendrath, P. and Dawson, T. (eds) *The Cambridge Companion to Jung*. Cambridge: Cambridge University Press.

Damasio, A. (2000) *The Feeling of What Happens: Body, Emotion and the Making of Consciousness*. London: Vintage.

Damasio, A. (2006) *Descartes' Error*. London: Vintage.

Damasio, A. (2012) *Self Comes to Mind: Constructing the Conscious Brain*. London: Vintage.

Dyer, G. (2012) *Zona: A Book about a Film about a Journey to a Room*. Edinburgh: Cannongate Books.

Ellis, J. (1982) *Visible Fictions: Cinema: Television: Video*. London: Routledge and Kegan Paul.

Elsaesser, T. and Hagener, M. (2010) *Film Theory: An Introduction Through the Senses*. Abingdon: Routledge.

Frampton, D. (2006) *Filmosophy*. New York: Columbia University Press.

Freud, S., trans. Strackey, J. (1922) 'Beyond the Pleasure Principle', *The Standard Edition of the Complete Psychological Works of Sigmond Freud*, Vol. XVIII. London: The Hogarth Press and the Institute of Psychoanalysis.

Galipeau, S. (2001) *The Journey of Luke Skywalker: An Analysis of Modern Myth and Symbol*. Chicago, Ill.: Open Court.

Gauntlett, D. (2005) *Moving Experiences: Media Effects and Beyond*. London: John Libbey Publishing.

Gendlin, E. (1978) *Focusing*. New York: Bantam Books.

Genette, G. (1982) *Palimpsestes: La littérature au second degré*. Paris: Seuil.

Gerrig, R. and Prentice, D. (1996) 'Audience Response', in Bordwell, D. and Carroll, N. (eds) *Post-Theory: Reconstructing Film Studies*. Madison, Wis: University of Wisconsin Press.

Gigerenzer, G. (2007) *Gut Feelings: The Intelligence of the Unconscious*. Harmondsworth: Penguin Books.

Gordon, S. (2013) *Film, Feminism and Melanie Klein: Weird Lullabies (Transformations)*. Hove: Routledge.

Grodal, T. (1997) *Moving Pictures: A New Theory of Film Genres, Feelings, and Cognition*. Oxford: Clarendon Press.

Hauke, C. (2000) *Jung and the Postmodern: The Interpretation of Realities*. London: Routledge.
Hauke, C. and Hockley, L. (eds) (2011) *Jung and Film II: The Return: Further Post-Jungian Takes on the Moving Image*. Hove: Routledge.
Heath, S. (1981) *Questions of Cinema*. Bloomington: Indiana University Press.
Heath, S. (1993) 'From Narrative Space', in A. Easthope (ed.) *Contemporary Film Theory*. New York: Longman.
Hillman, J. (1960) *Emotion: A Comprehensive Phenomenology of Theories and Their Meanings for Therapy*. Evanston, IU: Northwestern University Press.
Hillman, J. (1979) *The Dream and the Underworld*. New York: Harper and Row.
Hills, M. (2005) *The Pleasures of Horror*. London: Continuum.
Hockley, L. (2007) *Frames of Mind: A Post-Jungian Look at Cinema, Television and Technology*. Bristol: Intellect Books.
Hockley, L. (2010) 'Losing the Plot: A Story of Individuation and the Movies', *Quadrant: The Journal of the C.G. Jung Foundation*, XXXX(1): 9–24.
Iaccino, J. (1998) *Jungian Reflections within the Cinema: A Psychological Analysis of Sci-Fi and Fantasy Archetypes*. Westport, Conn.: Praeger Publishers.
Introna, L. and Ilharco, F. (2006) 'On the Meaning of Screens: Towards a Phenomenological Account of Screeness', *Human Studies*, 29: 57–76.
Jenkins, H. (1992) *Textual Poachers: Television Fans and Participatory Culture*. London: Routledge.
Jones, R. (2011) *Body, Mind and Healing after Jung: A Space of Questions*. Hove: Routledge.
Jung, C. G. (1917/26/43) 'On the Psychology of the Unconscious'. In CW, Vol. 7.
Jung, C. G. (1918) 'The Role of the Unconscious'. In CW, Vol. 10.
Jung, C. G. (1921) 'Definitions'. In CW, Vol. 6.
Jung, C. G. (1922/31) 'On the Relation of Analytical Psychology to Poetry'. In CW, Vol. 15.
Jung, C. G. (1926/31) 'Spirit and Life'. In CW, Vol. 8.
Jung, C. G. (1928/48) 'On Psychic Energy'. In CW, Vol. 8.
Jung, C. G. 1928/31) 'The Structure of the Psyche'. In CW, Vol. 8.
Jung, C. G. (1928) 'Psychoanalysis and the Cure of Souls'. In CW, Vol. 11.
Jung, C. G. (1929/57) 'Commentary on *The Secret of the Golden Flower*'. In CW, Vol. 13.
Jung, C. G. (1929/31) 'The Aims of Psychotherapy'. In CW, Vol. 16.
Jung, C. G. (1930/50) 'Psychology and Literature'. In CW, Vol. 15.
Jung, C. G. (1932) 'Psychotherapists or the Clergy'. In CW, Vol. 11.
Jung, C. G. (1934a) 'The Practical Use of Dream Analysis'. In CW, Vol. 16.
Jung, C. G. (1934) 'The State of Psychotherapy Today'. In CW, Vol. 10.
Jung, C. G. (1935) 'The Tavistock Lectures'. In CW, Vol. 18.
Jung, C. G. (1935/54) 'Archetypes and the Collective Unconscious'. In CW, Vol. 9i.
Jung, C. G. (1936/54) 'Concerning the Archetypes and the Anima Concept'. In CW, Vol. 91.
Jung, C. G. (1939/55) 'Psychological Commentaries on *The Tibetan Book of The Great Liberation*'. In CW, Vol. 11.
Jung, C. G. (1947/55) 'On the Nature of the Psyche'. In CW, Vol. 8.
Jung, C. G. (1951) 'Fundamental Questions of Psychotherapy'. In CW, Vol. 16.
Jung, C. G. (1952) 'Answer to Job'. In CW, Vol. 11.
Jung, C. G. (1953/68) 'Individual Dream Symbolism in Relation to Alchemy'. In CW, Vol. 12.
Jung, C. G., trans. Hull, R. F. C. (1953–79) *The Collected Works* [CW], ed. H. Read, M. Fordham and G. Adler. London: Routledge.

Jung, C. G. (2009) *The Red Book: Liber Novus*, ed. S. Shamdasani. New York: Norton.

Kalsched, D. (1996) *The Inner World of Trauma: Archetypal Defenses of the Personal Spirit*. London: Routledge.

Kittelson, M. L. (ed.) (1987) *The Soul of Popular Culture: Looking at Contemporary Heroes, Myths and Monsters*. Chicago: Ill. Open Court.

Kuhn, A. (2002) *An Everyday Magic: Cinema and Cultural Memory*. London: I. B. Taurus.

Kuhn, A. (2013) *Little Madnesses: Winnicott, Traditional Phenomena, and Culture Experience*. London: I. B. Tauris.

Lacan, J. (1977) *Ecrits: A Selection*. London: Routledge.

Laing, R. D. (1959/65) *The Divided Self*. Harmondsworth: Penguin Books.

Lebeau, V. (1995) *Lost Angels: Psychoanalysis and Cinema*. London: Routledge.

Levi-Strauss, C. (1966) *The Savage Mind*. Chicago, Ill.: University of Chicago Press.

Love, M. C. and Sterling, R. W. (2011) *What's Behind Your Belly Button*? USA: CreateSpace.

Lynch, D. (2006) *Catching the Big Fish: Meditation, Consciousness, and Creativity*. London: Penguin.

McGuinn, C. (2005) *The Power of the Movies: How Screen and Mind Interact*. New York: Vintage.

Maguire, A. (2004) *Skin Disease: A Message from the Soul*. London: Free Association Books.

Marks, L. (2000) *The Skin of the Film: Intercultural Cinema, Embodiment and the Senses*. Durham, NC, and London: Duke University Press.

Merleau-Ponty, M., trans. Smith, C. (1962) *The Phenomenology of Perception*. London: Routledge.

Merleau-Ponty, M., trans. Dreyfus, H. L. and Dreyfus, P. A. (1964) 'The Film and New Psychology', in *Sense and Non-Sense*. Evanston, IU.: Northwestern University Press.

Metz, C. (1992) *Psychoanalysis and the Cinema: The Imaginary Signifier*. Bloomington: Indiana University Press.

Miller, J. (1966) 'Suture (Elements of the Logic of the Signifier)', *Cahier pour l'analyse*. Translated and reprinted as 'Suture' *Screen* 18(4) (Winter): 24–34.

Miller, M. A. (1987) 'The Mist of Lake Wobegon: The Archetypal Function of the American Storyteller', in M. L. Kittelson (ed.) *The Soul of Popular Culture: Looking at Contemporary Heroes, Myths and Monsters*. Chicago, Ill.: Open Court.

Mitry, J. (1963/98) *The Aesthetics and Psychology of the Cinema*. London: Athlone Press.

Mulvey, L. (1975) 'Visual Pleasure and Narrative Cinema', *Screen* 16(3) (Autumn): 6–18.

Mulvey, L. (1981) 'Afterthoughts on "Visual Pleasure and Narrative Cinema" inspired by *Duel in the Sun*', *Framework*, 15–17: 12–15.

Mulvey, L. (2006) *Death 24x a Second: Stillness and the Moving Image*. London: Reaktion Books.

Munsterberg, H. (1916) *The Film: A Psychological Study*. New York: Dover Publications.

Oatley, K. (2011) *Such Stuff as Dreams: The Psychology of Fiction*. Chichester: Wiley-Blackwell.

Oudart, A. (1977–8) 'Cinema and Suture', *Screen* 18(4) (Winter): 35–47.

Padesky, C. (1995) *Mind over Mood*. London: Guilford Press.

Paris, G. (2007) *The Wisdom of the Psyche: Depth Psychology after Neuroscience*. Hove: Routledge.

Penley, C. (1985) 'Feminism, Film Theory, and the Cachelor Machines', *m/f*, 10: 42–52.

Petley, J. and Barker, M. (2001) *Ill Effects: The Media Violence Debate*. London: Routledge.

Pirsiq, R. (1974) *Zen and the Art of Motorcycle Maintenance*. London: Bodley Head.
Plantinga, C. and Smith, M. (eds) (1999) *Passionate Views: Film, Cognition, and Emotion*. Baltimore, Md.: Johns Hopkins University Press.
Ramos, D. G. (2004) *The Psyche of the Body: A Jungian Approach to Psychosomatics*. Hove: Routledge.
Roberts, J. (1973) *The Education of Oversoul Seven*. New York: Pocket Books.
Romanyshyn, R. (2007) *The Wounded Researcher: Research with Soul in Mind*. New Orleans: Spring Publications.
Rowland, S. (2005) *Jung as a Writer*. Hove: Routledge.
Samuels, A. (1985) *Jung and the Post-Jungians*. London: Routledge and Kegan Paul.
Samuels A. (1989) *The Plural Psyche: Personality, Morality and the Father*. London: Routledge.
Samuels, A. *et al.* (1986) *A Critical Dictionary of Jungian Analysis*. London: Routledge and Kegan Paul.
Schneider, S. H. (ed.) (2004) *Horror Film and Psychoanalysis: Freud's Worst Nightmare*. Cambridge: Cambridge University Press.
Schore, A. (2003) *Affect Dysregulation and Disorders of the Self*. New York: Norton.
Shamdasani, S. (2003) *Jung and the Making of Modern Psychology: The Dream of a Science*. Cambridge: Cambridge University Press.
Simon, S. (2002) *The Force is With You: Mystical Movie Messages that Inspire our Lives*. Charlottesville, Va.: Hampton Roads.
Singer, T. and Kimbles, S. (eds) (2004) *The Cultural Complex: Contemporary Jungian Perspectives on Psyche and Society*. London: Routledge.
Singh, G. (2011) 'Cinephilia or, Looking for Meaningfulness in Encounters with Cinema', in Hauke, C. and Hockley, L. (eds) *Jung and Film II: The Return*. Hove: Routledge.
Singh, G. (2009) *Film after Jung: Post-Jungian Approaches to Film Theory*. Hove: Routledge.
Singh, G. (2014) (forthcoming) *Double Takes*. Hove: Routledge.
Smith, G. (1999) 'Local Emotions, Global Moods and Film Structure', in Plantinga, C. and Smith, M. (eds) *Passionate Views: Film, Cognition, and Emotion*. Baltimore, Md.: John Hopkins University Press.
Sobchack, V. (1992) *The Address of the Eye: A Phenomenology of Film Experience*. Princeton, NJ: Princeton University Press.
Sobchack, V. (2004) *Carnal Thoughts: Embodiment and Moving Image Culture*. Los Angeles: University of California Press.
Sobchack, V. (2011) 'Fleshing Out the Image: Phenomenology, Pedagogy, and Derek Jarman's Blue,' in Carel, H. and Tuck, G. (eds) *New Takes in Film Philosophy*. Basingstoke: Palgrave Macmillan.
Spinelli, E. and Marshall, S. (eds) (2001) *Embodied Theories*. London: Continuum.
Sprengnether, M. (2002) *Crying at the Movies: A Film Memoir*. Saint Paul, Minn.: Grey Wolf Press.
Staiger, J. (1992) *Interpreting Films*. Princeton, NJ: Princeton University Press.
Tacey, D. (2001) *Jung and the New Age*. Hove: Brunner-Routledge.
Vogler, C. (1992/1999) *The Writer's Journey: Mythic Structure for Storytellers and Screenwriters*. London: Pan Books.
Vogler, C. and McKenna, D. (2011) *Memo from the Story Department: Secrets of Structure and Character*. Studio City, Calif.: Michael Wise Productions.
Wilkinson, M. (2006) *Coming into Mind: The Mind–Brain Relationship, a Clinical Jungian Perspective*. Hove: Routledge.

Williams, M. *et al.* (2007) *The Mindful Way Through Depression*. New York: Guilford Press.

Winnicott, D. (1953) 'Transitional Objects and Transitional Phenomena: A Study of the First Not-me Possession', *International Journal of Psycho-Analysis*, 53: 89–97.

Winnicott, D. (1965) *The Family and Individual Development*. London: Free Association Books.

Winnicott, D. (1958) The Capacity to be Alone. *International Journal of Psycho-Analysis*, 39: 16–20.

Young-Eisendrath, P. and Dawson, T. (eds) (1997) *The Cambridge Companion to Jung*. Cambridge: Cambridge University Press.

Young-Eisendrath, P. and Muramoto, S. (eds) (2002) *Awakening and Insight: Zen Buddhism and Psychotherapy*. Hove: Brunner-Routledge.

List of films and television programmes

Alien (Dir. Ridley Scott, 1979)
Aliens (Dir. James Cameron, 1986)
Avatar (Dir. James Cameron, 2009)
Blade Runner (Dir. Ridley Scott, 1982)
Blue (Dir. Derek Jarman, 1993)
Burnt by the Sun (Dir. Nikita Mikhalkov, 1994)
Chinatown (Dir. Roman Polanski, 1974)
Citizen Kane (Dir. Orson Welles, 1941)
Dekalog 1 (Dir. Krzysztof Kieslowski, 1989)
Dumbo (Dir. Sam Armstrong *et al.*, 1941)
Eat, Pray, Love (Dir. Ryan Murphy, 2010)
Fight Club (Dir. David Fincher, 1999)
The Fountain (Dir. Darren Aronofsky, 2006)
Harry Potter and the Philosopher's Stone (Dir. Chris Columbus, 2001)
The Lion King (Dir. Roger Allers and Rob Minkoff, 1994)
The Maltese Falcon (Dir. John Huston, 1941)
Mamma Mia! (Dir. Phyllida Lloyd, 2008)
The Piano (Dir. Jane Campion, 1993)
Russian Ark (Dir. Alexander Sokurov, 2002)
Secrets of the Soul (Dir. Georg Pabst, 1926)
Solaris (Dir. Andrei Tarkovsky, 1972)
Stalker (Dir. Andrei Tarkovsky, 1979)
Stargate (Dir. Roland Emmerich, 1994)
Star Wars: Episode IV – A New Hope (Dir. George Lucas, 1977)
Star Wars: Episode V – The Empire Strikes Back (Dir. Irvin Kershner, 1980)
Star Wars: Episode VI – The Return of the Jedi (Dir. Richard Marquand, 1983)
La Strada (Dir. Federico Fellini, 1954)
The Thin Red Line (Dir. Terrence Malick, 1998)
Titanic (Dir. James Cameron, 1997)
Tree of Life (Dir. Terrence Malick, 2011)

INDEX